DUNCAN PHYFE
& THE ENGLISH REGENCY

PLATE 1. GEORGE IV BY SIR THOMAS LAWRENCE, P.R.A.

(From the Jacobs Collection in the Baltimore Museum of Art)

DUNCAN PHYFE

AND

THE ENGLISH REGENCY

1795-1830

BY

NANCY McCLELLAND

FOREWORD BY EDWARD KNOBLOCK

WILLIAM·R·SCOTT·INC·PUBLISHER·NEW YORK

MADE IN U.S.A. AND COPYRIGHT 1939 BY NANCY MC CLELLAND

TABLE OF CONTENTS

LIST OF ILLUSTRATIONS

vii

ix

x

AUTHOR'S ACKNOWLEDGMENTS

For his interest and valuable assistance in collecting exclusive photographs and information about English Regency houses and furniture, I am deeply indebted to John A. Pearson, Esq., of London; and for the foreword of this book to Edward Knoblock, Esq. I wish also to make special acknowledgment to Christie's for giving access to records of the Hope Sale of 1917, and to Sotheby and Company for permission to use the photographs from the sale of Hartwell House.

The many English contributors of privately owned furniture are individually mentioned with the photographs of their possessions.

On this side of the ocean, I feel special obligations to certain members of the Phyfe family, who have given generously of their time and contributed many personal souvenirs about their illustrious ancestor, Duncan Phyfe, and his immediate relatives. This list includes: F. Percy Vail, Mrs. J. Bertram Howell, Miss Mary Whitlock, Charles H. Caldwell, Mrs. Charles Bebee, Mrs. Duncan Phyfe, Mrs. Norman H. Parke, Mrs. W. H. P. Phyfe, Mrs. Edward Spalding.

To Herold Rodney Eaton Phyfe, great-grandson of Duncan Phyfe, who skilfully enlarged old family portraits and took special photographs of the entire collection of Eliza Phyfe Vail's furniture for this book, I inscribe a word of particular appreciation.

Also to Frank J. Donald of Dundee, who conducted exhaustive investigations in Scotland, hoping to uncover new information about our greatest nineteenth-century cabinetmaker during the period of his boyhood, before his emigration to America. Mr. Donald's valiant efforts are not the less esteemed because the results proved unfruitful.

The following museums and historical societies have been most helpful and coöperative:

The Edison Institute, Dearborn, Michigan.
The Essex Institute, Salem, Massachusetts.
The Detroit Institute of Art, Detroit, Michigan.
The Metropolitan Museum of Art, New York.
The Albany Institute of History and Art, Albany, New York.
The Historical Society of Pennsylvania, Philadelphia, Pennsylvania.

The New York Historical Society, New York.
The Boston Museum of Fine Arts, Boston, Massachusetts.
The Philadelphia Museum of Art, Philadelphia, Pennsylvania.
The Baltimore Museum of Fine Arts, Baltimore, Maryland.
The Monmouth County Historical Association, Freehold, New Jersey.
The Museum of the City of New York.
The Gallery of Fine Arts, Yale University, New Haven, Connecticut.
The Taft Museum, Cincinnati, Ohio.
The House of History, Kinderhook, New York.
Homewood, Baltimore, Maryland.
The Board of Directors of City Trusts, Philadelphia, Pennsylvania, for Girard College.
The Frick Art Reference Library, New York.

I am also keenly appreciative of the assistance rendered in various ways by Mrs. Harry Horton Benkard, Mr. Joseph Downs, Mr. Allan B. A. Bradley, Mr. and Mrs. Andrew Varick Stout, Mr. Henry F. du Pont, Mr. R. T. H. Halsey, Mr. Fiske Kimball, Mr. James E. Leath, Mr. Henry McIlhenny, Mrs. Louis Guerineau Myers, the Library of Congress, Girl Scouts, Inc., Mr. Thomas H. Ormsbee, Miss Ethel A. Reeve, Mrs. James Ward Thorne, Miss Garda Olesen, the late Homer Keyes, Miss Florence Weiss, secretary of the First Presbyterian Church of New York, Miss Pauline Fullerton, Mr. Harry McNeill Bland, Mr. Merritt A. Clegg, Mr. Winsor D. White, William E. Katzenbach, and *Country Life,* London.

N. McC.

ACKNOWLEDGMENT OF PHOTOGRAPHERS'
WORK

INSTEAD of printing a credit line under each picture, the names of the photographers are listed here. These men and women have contributed much to this book. Beside each name are the numbers of the plates which have been made from their admirable photographs.

Beals, A. Tennyson; New York. Plates: 124, 271

Berla, Harold Amzi; Orange, New Jersey. Plates: 273, 274

Brayton, George; Arlington, Massachusetts. Plate: 76

Brown & Flewelling; Poughkeepsie. New York. Plate: 246

Commercial Photographer; Philadelphia, Pennsylvania. Plates: 213, 215, 216, 218, 219, 223

Cousins, Frank, and the Essex Institute; Salem, Massachusetts. Plates: 206, 207

Duryea, Drix; New York. Plates: 53, 88

General Photographic; New York. Plates: 87, 94, 119, 120, 197, 271, 272

Gray Studios; New York. Plates: 4, 52, 72, 73, 86, 91, 98, 121, 122, 125, 137, 138, 154, 157, 158, 161, 162, 166, 168, 183, 184, 237, 275, 276, 277, 278, 279, 280, 282, 283

Hagelstein Brothers; New York. Plate: 61

Hancock, James W.; Savannah, Georgia. Plate: 262

Hildyard; London. Plate: 66

Hindemith, Rudolf; New York. Plates: 92, 93, 130, 149, 177, 178, 190, 191, 198, 212

His Majesty's Office of Works; London. Plates: 16, 17

Hubbard, C. V. D.; Philadelphia, Pennsylvania. Plates: 224, 225

Juley & Son, Peter A.; New York. Plate: 115

Keyes, Murray K.; New York. Plate: 266

Law, Elliot; Ontario, Canada. Plates: 238, 239, 240

Millar & Harris; London. Plates: 37, 58, 59

Nyholm; New York. Plates: 247, 248, 249, 250

Old Masters Associates; New York. Plate: 173

Peck; Charleston, South Carolina. Plate: 294

Phyfe, Hal; New York. Plates: 99, 100, 102, 103, 105, 106, 107, 108, 109, 110, 111, 112, 113, 114, 116

Pound, George H.; New Brunswick, New Jersey. Plates: 290, 292, 293

Ralston-Hughes; Chicago, Illinois. Plate: 36

Rowles, S. G.; Hudson, New York. Plates: 96, 141, 153, 167, 194, 263, 264, 265
Savastano; New York. Plate: 64
Schaefer, J. H.; Baltimore, Maryland. Plates: 226, 227
Sims Limited; London. Plates: 27, 29, 31, 38, 39, 40, 41, 45, 46, 48, 49, 50, 51, 55, 56, 57, 67, 70
Spence of Nottingham. Plate: 2
Van Nes, Hans; New York. Plate: 35
Weber, Paul J.; Boston, Massachusetts. Plates: 220, 284, 285, 286, 287, 288
Woolford, Burdett; New York. Plate: 152

THE REGENCY STYLE

FOREWORD BY EDWARD KNOBLOCK

A DEFINITION of the word Regency as denoting a style in decoration or furniture does not occur in the *Oxford Dictionary* of 1933. In the Larousse, the word Empire is not only quoted as a definite style, but is amply illustrated by a page of various kinds of furniture, designed and decorated in that manner. This only shows that the present appreciation of Regency, as a distinct and interesting period, is one of very recent growth. For many years previous to, let us say, 1935, it could boast of only a comparatively few devotees. Now their number has swelled to a very considerable one. But even so the term is often misapplied to furniture and decoration of an earlier or later date, so that a work dealing with the origin and development of this particular style may not come amiss.

The first standard book dealing with this subject appeared, oddly enough, not in France, as one would suppose, but in England. It was published by Thomas Hope in 1807 under the title of *Household Furniture and Interior Decoration*. The first work on its sister movement in France appeared five years later, in 1812, and was published by Percier and Fontaine, the high priests of the Empire style, both in architecture, decoration and furniture. But although the French produced no important book on the subject till such a late date, there is unquestionable proof that they began to evolve the style considerably before it began to appear and find favor in England.

As early as the late period of Louis XVI we find certain motifs introduced in the furniture of that date, which afterwards became the leading ornaments and often the inspiration of entire pieces of Empire furniture. I refer particularly to the use of the sphinx. On a table in Marie Antoinette's boudoir at Fontainebleau, the application of sphinx heads clearly shows that this particular motive was already beginning to find favor with the great designers of that epoch. This clearly proves that the sphinx was not introduced, as is generally supposed, as a reference to General Bonaparte's campaign in Egypt. The use of it became undoubtedly accentuated because of his military triumphs there. But the reason why the sphinx first grew to be what I may term an "active" ornament must originally be traced to its employment in the decorations of the ruins of Pompeii.

The enthusiasm aroused throughout the world by the wonderful discovery of these classic remains inspired the Adam brothers to create a new style which to us nowadays is known as Adam—an appellation usually misquoted as Adam*s*. This fresh departure in art was greatly admired by the French ambassador then accredited to the Court of St. James. On his return to France, he introduced it to his countrymen. From it the great French decorators of the day created a new style of their own, which differed in every detail from the flourishes and flounces of Louis XV, till then in vogue. Thus the neoclassic of the brothers Adam proved the source from which the furniture and decoration known as Louis XVI drew its first inspiration. It was, as it were, a roundabout path back to antiquity and indicated a direction which coming events were to accentuate more and more.

The French, however, were not so faithful to the severity of the classic line as the brothers Adam had been. The frivolity of the court obliged designers to soften the motifs of antiquity. Particularly was this the case in their furniture. Garlands and festoons of drapery in ormolu were introduced; bits of Chinese and Japanese lacquer, plaques of Sèvres porcelain, and even engravings framed in metal often provided the central ornamentation of a scheme for a cabinet or table. And when finally Marie Antoinette's passion for rural ingenuousness set a universal fashion, the furniture began to abound in rustic carvings or inlay representing trophies of gardening—rakes, hoes, watering-cans, and similar emblems of an affectedly simple life.

Fundamentally, of course, the daily round at court was far from simple. The aristocracy was playing a game as complicated and insincere as when the great Augustus of Rome sat once a year on the marble steps of his palace, disguised as a beggar, in order to impress his mighty empire with his carefully studied ceremony of humility.

The *ancien régime* by this final, false attempt to return to nature, had reached its climax of overcivilization. Something had to happen to burst these artificial bonds. And it did happen. The Revolution came. And with that mighty upheaval the pastoral comedies of court were swept away once and for all. Life became real and earnest and tragically direct. The frills of yesterday were stripped from the impatient body of today. Truth, or at least such as the awakened world then thought it to be, stood suddenly revealed before the nation. The cry of "Liberty, Equality, Fraternity," leveled all distinctions. And this leveling at once produced an entirely new interpretation of life, not only in ideals and speech and manners, but also in art, in dress, and the very housing of the people.

The old order had come to an end forever. Quickly the artists of France —those nimble-witted reflectors of the moods of their patrons—set to work to discover the right formula for interpreting the change. But as every genuine expression of art must, of necessity, take time in creating a new formula before breaking completely with the past, even in this violent new order of things, a bridge had to be built to link what had gone before with what was to come. And this link was found in the style we now know as the Directoire.

The Directoire is a simplification of the style of Louis XVI. Gone are the delicate emblems of the flowery days of Marie Antoinette. Only the severest motifs of her reign are now allowed to continue in the decoration of the furniture and rooms. And as history led Bonaparte to Egypt, the sphinx, which had already appeared in a very modified degree during the latter days of the Queen, now had a very definite reason for becoming one of the symbols of the new order of things.

But there were other reasons, too, why French art took such a decided turn toward classic simplicity. The new Republic of France found a certain self-satisfaction in basing itself on the ancient Republic of Rome. The severity of the Roman father, the unbending justice of Roman law, the stern morality of those far-off days, flattered the vanity of these latter-day rulers. They aped its speech. They aped its ideals. They even aped its dress. But as men are always more conservative in clothes than women, the male sex contented itself by wearing toga-like capes in peacetime and helmet-like headgear in war. The women, however, were bolder as always, when it comes to a question of fashion. They stripped their limbs till they reached a nudity which aroused the indignation of the workaday rabble. They sandaled their bare feet and bound their locks with fillets. In time the extremists modified their clothes and settled down again to rational decency. The ultimate result was the charming Empire costume which has not been surpassed in beauty by any other great epoch of woman's dress.

So much then for France, where a combination of Roman and Egyptian inspiration finally gave birth to a complete Empire style, which set a standard for the rest of the world and with certain modifications was followed by all the countries of Europe—Germany, Austria, Holland, Italy, and Spain. But with few exceptions, as in the furnishing of royal palaces, the Empire in those countries is not of the best design or execution. Napoleon's campaigns impoverished the resources of the conquered kingdoms and made it difficult for the average household to spend much on luxuries of any kind. Hence the workmanship is often second rate, the wood of none too fine a quality, and the design, in a desire to be individual, often clumsy and lacking in proportion.

But this is not the case in England between the years of 1810 and 1830. The style then reigning happens to be called Regency because George, Prince of Wales became Prince Regent in 1811. In 1820, nine years later, he was crowned King and reigned till 1830. So that more than half the time of this period he was no longer Regent and, to be quite exact, the actual taste for what is now known as Regency had begun several years before he was made Regent.

The great protagonist of Regency in England undoubtedly was Thomas Hope. There are some other men who advocated and applied the style. But to him belongs the honor (and personally I should like to call it the glory) of having first pointed out the beauties of this particular type of architecture, decoration, and furniture. Moreover, he not only preached it, but he practiced it, for he was in the very fortunate position of being a man of unlimited wealth—one of the richest men of his time, in fact. It is easy to support one's theories if one is able to do so out of one's own pocket. Most of us find that our fancies, when put into practice, evaporate on the wrong side of the ledger. Only Kings like Louis Quatorze could afford to build a Versailles and damn the consequences. And, of course, one must not forget that to the same category belong the great American millionaires of yesteryear who have done so much to encourage art in the United States.

Now Thomas Hope happened to be such another millionaire. His father was a Dutch banker, John Hope; his mother a Van der Hoeven. Thomas was born in Amsterdam in about 1770 and very early in life evinced a taste for architecture. Being of a Continental family, these talents were fostered and developed. Had he been an Englishman he would probably have been destined to embrace the only careers then open to a gentleman—

PLATE 2. PORTRAIT OF THOMAS HOPE BY SIR WILLIAM BEECHEY, R.A.

(By permission of the City of Nottingham Art Gallery)

the army, the clergy, the law, or politics. But, luckily for him and the subject of this book, he was sent off on his grand tour fully equipped as a draftsman. He wandered for eight years about Egypt, Greece, Sicily, Turkey, Syria, and Spain, soaking himself in the spirit of classic architectural monuments and remains. He did not settle till sometime about 1796 in England, where other members of his family had gone on account of the occupation of Holland by the French.

During the next five years he added to the collection he had begun on his travels. Greek vases, Italian pictures, contemporary sculpture, and ancient marbles were his predilection. In 1801 he bought for 4,500 guineas sixteen cases from Sir William Hamilton's second vase collection; but his taste and judgment had by then become so acute that he disposed of 180 of them in the next few years as not satisfying his standards. To display these treasures in an appropriate setting, he purchased two houses—one in Duchess Street, Cavendish Square—the other at Deepdene near Dorking, Surrey, a property that had once belonged to the Howard family. The London house has long since changed its skin, outside and in. But Deepdene until 1917 remained practically untouched, when the dwindled fortunes of the Hopes obliged them at last to put the collections and house up to auction.

It was my good fortune to be able to attend these sales—both at Christie's in London, where the vases and marbles were dispersed—as well as the sale at Deepdene, where during two long days hundreds of examples of the very finest Regency furniture were knocked down for lamentable prices. Lamentable for the shades of Thomas Hope—but not for the modern collector. I was lucky enough to acquire such pieces as I felt would be useful to me. Thomas Hope's genius has presided over me ever since and I can assure the reader that twenty years of association with these perfect specimens of his craft has only increased my profound admiration for him. The daily sight of fine furniture, living with it, using it, and learning to understand all its qualities, gives one a knowledge that no study of it in museums or in other people's houses can possibly provide. One becomes on terms of intimacy with it and from that intimacy one develops an instinct which makes one tell at a glance whether other pieces of the period are genuine or not. There is something about the real article that is as unmistakable as the face of an honest man. Not that extremely clever copies and forgeries have not been produced (just as there are rogues with "angel" smiles); but luckily

Regency furniture, up to the present, has not been in the fashion long enough to call for a demand above the supply of the "unfaked" specimen.

But I am digressing. You must set it down to the enthusiasm of a successful collector. Let me return to Thomas Hope. In 1807 he published an illustrated folio called *Household Furniture and Interior Decoration*. In this beautifully printed book, he describes with accuracy not only the possessions of his own two houses, but shows how he arranged his vast collection of vases and statues in appropriate settings. An introduction of eighteen pages explains his theories and his reasons for presenting a "totally new style of decoration" to the British public. The article is, of course, far too long to quote. I shall just pick out a few illuminating phrases. He defines his work as an "association of all the elegancies of antique forms and ornaments with the requisites of modern customs and habits . . . capable of ennobling, through means of their shape and their accessories, things so humble in their chief purpose and destination as a table and a chair, a footstool and a screen." Like all innovators he decries the taste of the time as "borrowed from the worst models of the degraded French School of the middle of the last century." Chippendale, Adam, and Sheraton he completely ignores. He is, in fact, a thoroughgoing revolutionary—a prophet crying in a pantechnicon.

Needless to say, his message received considerable derision. He was dubbed "the man of chairs and tables, the gentleman of sofas," by the sharp tongue of Sydney Smith. The *Edinburgh Review* dismissed his effort as frivolous. Nevertheless, it was not very long before his ideas began to have a marked influence on public taste. Only a year later, a well-known designer of furniture, George Smith, "Upholsterer extraordinary to his Royal Highness the Prince of Wales," published a quarto book entitled *A Collection of Designs for Household Furniture and Interior Decoration, in the most approved and elegant taste.* The prophet had found a disciple. Smith was a man of practical bent and a tradesman of standing. He would certainly not have risked his business by advocating a style which might have turned away customers. The innovation had caught on. The cause had won—and that in less than a twelvemonth.

No doubt, of course, the Empire style in France must have already exerted a certain influence in England. But one must remember that political reasons—the two countries being at war during many years of the Napoleonic domination—made it difficult for French furniture and decoration

xxi

PLATE 3. BOOKCASE DESIGNED BY THOMAS HOPE, 1807
Built entirely of mahogany, the classic heads and griffins are painted to simulate bronze.
(Courtesy of Edward Knoblock, Esq., London)

to find its way to English shores as readily as it might have under normal conditions. Besides, Thomas Hope evolved his style from his own vast personal experience gained on his long travels in classic countries. How much he may have been indebted to France is difficult to say. Every epoch in the history of art has shown the different nations of Europe to be imbued simultaneously with a similar spirit—with all the resemblances and variations typical of the various members of a large family.

From the Preface of Hope's book it would appear that he had thought and worked for a long time to produce his particular ideas of decoration. Many of his details are undoubtedly at variance with the French idea of the neoclassic. But as both draw their inspiration from the same source—the art of antiquity—there are bound to be certain similarities in both. Another reason why the general effect of the French and English designs of the period appear to run on parallel lines is that in France the great creators of the style were Percier and Fontaine, both distinguished architects of the day, while Hope as well had studied architecture from earliest childhood.

There is then something very architectural, massive, monumental in all furniture of the opening of the last century, as the outlines of it are based on the temples, the monuments, and all the indestructible materials of antiquity. And yet how closely Hope arrived at the reconstruction of the actual furniture in wood may be seen by a pair of large mahogany chairs in the Egyptian style that I happen to possess. When the tomb of Tutankhamen gave up its treasures not twenty years since, some of Hope's chairs followed so nearly the designs of three thousand years ago, that they might actually have been made in the days of the Pharaohs.

What distinguishes the English from the French work of the period is that the English is on the whole either far heavier or far lighter in design than the French. This sounds like a paradox, so let me explain myself. The large, important English pieces are very much more massive. I am referring to the huge bookcases in large town and country houses, the ample sideboards, the vast library tables. They are, as a rule, of superb mahogany and show little or no ornamentation in bronze, depending almost wholly on nicely calculated proportions. The motif of the sphinx is not as usual in England as is the griffin, the panther, or the lion. The applied bronzes, when not of the finest, as they are with all of Hope's furniture, are poor in quality compared to the ones of French casting. But in every other way the English

PLATE 5. CABINET BY GEORGE SMITH

This rosewood cabinet with a white marble top and gilded bronzes was designed for the Regent.

(Courtesy of Edward Knoblock, Esq., London)

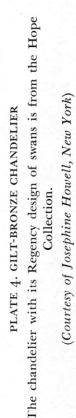

PLATE 4. GILT-BRONZE CHANDELIER

The chandelier with its Regency design of swans is from the Hope Collection.

(Courtesy of Josephine Howell, New York)

workmanship is superior, as the work, even to the smallest details of the interior of an English piece, shows an attention to finish unknown in any but the best pieces of French manufacture.

In the case of Hope's personal furniture, the wood itself is of such a superb quality that one can always tell at a glance any piece which belonged to him. He evidently insisted on perfection of every material used in the carrying out of his designs. He employed not only ebony to inlay some of his tables, but ivory, as well, and even silver. The result is very fine indeed—and not in the least vulgar or garish, as it might sound. All his embellishments are of the utmost discretion and simplicity. His bronzes are often "antiqued" —that is, not brilliantly gilded as is general in French Empire, but of the dull, dark-green tone which one finds on some of the bronzes dug up at Herculaneum. That he took an infinite amount of trouble over his metal ornamentations is proved by a reference to them in the Preface to his book, in which he speaks with high praise of two artists he managed to discover in London. By an irony of fate they both happened to be foreigners—Decaix, a French "bronzist," and Bogaert, a carver, born in the "Low Countries." Who Hope's cabinetmakers were he does not mention. All honor to them, whoever they may have been. They were good gentlemen and true, from first to last.

I have ventured to assert that the French domestic Empire provided the furniture of medium weight and size, in contradistinction to the English pieces of ponderous dimensions as well as those of a very light design. The everyday English household cabinets, chairs, tables, and bedroom furniture of the day, inspired by Hope's influence, which was carried on by men like George Smith and others, are of a singularly graceful and attractive character. They are therefore all the more sought nowadays, when people have a tendency to live in small rooms and cannot crowd their limited space with pieces of importance. The shapes of these little intimate pieces are completely English—in no way related to any of such furniture of Continental origin. The leg of the chair is almost universally what is known as the Trafalgar leg—a leg curved inwards, the shape resembling that of a scimitar. The backs are often decorated with a carved shell or a lion's head. These chairs are sometimes painted black, with a discreet touch here and there of gilding. This scheme of black and gold is also found among some of Hope's larger pieces. The idea of treating furniture in this way was quite a com-

xxv

PLATE 6. REGENCY ARMCHAIR BY GEORGE SMITH

Black and gold, the design is somewhat ponderous. The pole screens are similar to a drawing in
Plate 18 of Hope's book.

(Courtesy of John A. Pearson, Ltd., London)

mon one, even in the later chairs and little cabinets and tables designed by Hepplewhite, so that one can call it a national characteristic. The French were more given to painting their furniture in shades of beige or white, relieved with either gold or blue or brown. Their earlier Empire, on the whole, was of a tendency to squareness, which only gave way to curves after Napoleon's marriage to Marie Louise. After that blissful event, the bronzes, till then classic designs of trophies of arms and helmets, turned to wreaths of flowers, marguerites and butterflies, Cupid's bows and darts.

Such fancies were not indulged in by English Regency. The designs always remained strictly classical; the ornamentation always of a severer, more conservative character. There is, however, one exception—the Chinese Regency, which is perhaps one of the oddest mixtures ever invented by man, and is, in a great measure, due to the Oriental and flamboyant taste of no less a person than George IV himself.

To call him George the Fourth is, of course, a misnomer. For he already evinced this passion for glamor and glitter in the days when he was still the Prince of Wales—long before the sobering influence of Thomas Hope had made itself felt. The Pavilion at Brighton is perhaps the most fantastic place ever built for a monarch, if one excepts the castles of the demented Louis of Bavaria, which are creations of a delirious mind. The Pavilion, on the other hand, is an airy, witty paraphrase of the East, like the daydream of some traveler returned from the Orient whose memory plays him tricks. For here are welded into one the decorative motifs of China and Burma and India interpreted by the well-balanced mind of the foremost Regency architect, John Nash.

The original building was an old manor house, enlarged in the classic style, the central motif of which was a dome supported by a pillared portico. It was built from 1784 to 1787. In 1800 the house and grounds were acquired for the Prince of Wales and in ensuing years the entire building was reconstructed and, according to an old guidebook, became "strictly Oriental, resembling in a great degree the Kremlin at Moscow." Another stranger's guide remarks "that an idea has been not sparingly disseminated of the Pavilion's being characterized by frivolity or gaudiness"—but, it adds pompously, "The King of England is almost *de facto* King of India; and therefore, may we not say without fanciful exaggeration, that an eastern palace, placed on the shores of that element by the ancient and continual sovereignty of which England wields such a powerful sceptre, presents an idea to the mind, full, interesting, and effective."

After this loyal outburst let us just have a glimpse of the interior. We quote again from our friend. "The Chinese gallery (162 feet long, and 17 wide) is throughout of a dark pink, termed peach-blossom. At both ends are double staircases of iron, the railings of which are painted in imitation of bamboo. The Banqueting Room boasts of walls of mother-o'-pearl with historic groups in rich enamel, varied by candelabra, like blue lapis lazuli, sur-

xxvii

mounted by white glass lilies and immense chandeliers, of numerous flowers, in silvery glass. . . . It is a palace for Diana, or some lovely and beneficent fairy, who is favourable to virtue."

Here, I must admit, the author stretched a point. For virtue was not exactly the outstanding quality of its principal inhabitant! Space does not allow me to enlarge on the qualities of the place—for although the description of it sounds somewhat bewildering, the general effect is so continuously fantastic that somehow it achieves a curious unity. Let me add that I have seen a letter written by one of the Regent's much beloved ladies who describes his taste as "effeminate."

What this lady undoubtedly meant by using that particular word was that the Regent's taste was not of a kind which appreciates simplicity and soberness of design. The severity and dignity of line which characterize Hope's scheme of decoration never appealed to him. Even in his London residence at Carlton House, we can gather from the old prints that his furniture, although of the period, was flamboyant and overladen. A great many of the pieces are now housed in Buckingham Palace. They are of superb workmanship, but generally heavily gilt and based on the elaboration of the acanthus motif. This motif was ultimately to become the basis of early Victorian, where it flourished to excess, till during the great Exhibition of '51, it was finally replaced by a return to a modified Louis XV.

I shall only mention the Gothic movement in passing. It found its fullest expression during the romantic movement of the Forties, but it had already been foreshadowed as early as the middle of the eighteenth century by Horace Walpole with his Gothic castle at Strawberry Hill. Hope ignores Gothic altogether. But George Smith in his book in 1808 produces a considerable number of plates of most elaborate beds, bookcases, and chairs which must have appealed to the piety of many an archbishop of the day. Later on Smith, in a new book, *The Cabinet Maker's Guide,* published by him in 1826, displays further examples in the Gothic manner. In this work he also shows countless designs for elaborate acanthus-scrolled furniture, which nowadays we would without hesitation assign to the Victorian period. In a word, eleven years before the Queen came to the throne, the style which was to be identified with her reign had already been created. This only proves how any art is always a question of inception and development, till it grows to the full, flourishes, and finally fades away, to be in its turn re-placed by some new expression of human ideals.

And so the Regency style was born and grew and spread till at last it was choked off by the elaborate vegetation of Victorianism. It is odd to think that the Regent, who now lends his name to a distinguished period of decora-tion, should have been one of the few people of his day who failed to appre-ciate its beauty. By rights the style should be called the Hope period, for its purest and noblest expression is due to Thomas Hope and him alone. He was the creator of it, the producer of its finest examples, the first to introduce it to the English public and to set a standard which his followers attained in only a very minor degree.

In the United States the Regency style found a keen advocate in the person of Duncan Phyfe. He spent nearly sixty years of his life—from the age of seventeen—in America, and consequently may be justly looked upon as the American "opposite" to Thomas Hope. Some of his earlier pieces show a distinct influence of Hepplewhite and Sheraton. But his finest work un-doubtedly belongs to the period from 1810 onwards, by which time he was one of the leading cabinetmakers in the United States. His work is distin-guished by great elegance of line. Comparatively little bronze ornamenta-tion was employed by him, and he preferred delicately carved motifs to accentuate his design. This habit of his was probably due to the impossi-bility of finding good metal casters in America at that date. But Phyfe made a virtue of this difficulty by relying almost exclusively on his admirable sense of balance and proportion. There is a feeling of beauty in his work which justifies the Americans in according him the position they have. Undoubt-edly he is the leading artist among early makers of furniture in the United States.

PART ONE

THE ENGLISH REGENCY

I

THE REGENT AND THE TIMES

THERE was never a period when the tone of English society was more polished, more animated, or more corrupt than during the days of the Regency. The history of the time is a strange and fascinating story of manners and pleasures, with a brilliant kaleidoscope of famous people—Wellington, Thackeray, Macaulay, Keats, Byron, Charles Lamb, Sir Walter Scott, Sheridan, Thomas Lawrence, Sydney Smith, Jane Austen, Shelley, Mrs. Siddons, William Pitt, Charles James Fox, Henry Holland, John Nash, Thomas Hope, Beau Brummel—and a great company of gamesters, tipsters, dandies, and parasites revolving ceaselessly around the central figure of the Prince Regent, the *arbiter elegantiarum,* who ruled with "a golden thread of fantastic eccentricity."

It is difficult justly to estimate this central figure, so different are the opinions expressed by his contemporaries. His tutor, Bishop Richard Hurd, said of him at the age of fifteen that he would be "either the most polished gentleman or the most accomplished blackguard in Europe—possibly both."

Some excuse for him was made thirty years after his death by Thackeray: "The dreadful dulness of Papa's court, its stupid amusements, its dreary occupations, the maddening humdrum and stifling sobriety of its routine would have made a scapegrace of a much less lively prince."

But then, again, Thackeray did not spare him: "This George, what was he? I look through all his life and recognize but a bow and a grin. I try and take him to pieces and find silk stockings, padding, stays, a coat with frogs and a fur collar, a star, a blue ribbon, a pockethandkerchief prodigiously scented, one of Truefitt's best nutty-brown wigs reeking with oil, a set of teeth and a huge black stock, underwaistcoats, more underwaistcoats, and then nothing.

"There may be something behind, but what? We cannot get at the character; no doubt never shall."

On the other hand, Wellington, who perhaps knew him best and spoke in the frankest manner, appraised the Regent quite differently. "He was indeed," he said, "the most extraordinary compound of talent, wit, buffoonery, obstinacy and good feeling—in short, a medley of the most opposite qualities with a great preponderance of good, that I ever saw in any character in my life."

There are certainly many important things to be entered in his favor, on the right side of the ledger. The most notable contributions made by the Prince to his generation have been summed up in the following manner:

George was the first English ruler since Charles the First who was entertaining and gay, and who preferred the company of wits to that of half-wits. . . . He formed an interesting collection of Old Masters, helped to found the National Gallery and built Carlton House and the Royal Pavilion. He rebuilt, with the greatest taste and tact, too, Windsor Castle. Further, he was responsible for a thousand pillared houses and intricately planned, gracefully curving streets by Nash, the loveliness of which we are only beginning, with their destruction, to appreciate. And, just as much, we must bless the memory of the Regent for nearly all its former beauty which London yet retains; for Carlton House Terrace and Regent's Park, for the Serpentine and the charming bridge which crosses it, for its planting, for Decimus Burton's elegant screen at Hyde Park Corner, and for many other such delights.*

George, Prince of Wales, was declared of age January 1, 1781, when he was only a little more than eighteen years old. His father gave him a small separate establishment of his own, arranging a suite of rooms for him in Windsor Castle and some apartments in Buckingham House in London before installing him in Carlton House.

On June 23, 1783, the Lords and Commons voted him £50,000 for income and £100,000 for outfitting his household. With this well-filled purse, his varied and checkered career immediately began.

In less than four years the Prince was more than £150,000 in debt. His creditors began to press for payment. The King was appealed to but refused to interfere. *The Four Georges* recounts the record of these days: "Three applications to Parliament; debts to the amount of £160,000, of £650,000. . . . What did he do for all this money? If he had been a manufacturing town or a populous rural district or an army of five thousand men, he could not have cost more."

The Prince had no difficulty in squandering a vast fortune in so short a time. His tastes were more than luxurious; his interests well diversified. Architecture was one of the polite amusements which he permitted himself.

* See *Brighton* by Osbert Sitwell and Margaret Barton.

Carlton House, his London residence, was outfitted as a royal palace. This, in fact, was the beginning of his building mania. The newly decorated and refurnished residence was opened with a magnificent ball on March 10, 1784, followed by a breakfast for six hundred people on the eighteenth of April, and from then on London society reveled in the sumptuous entertainments given there.

Soon the Prince began to feel the need of a country residence. More to exasperate his father than for any other reason, on coming of age he announced his intention of going to Brighton to visit his uncle, the Duke of Cumberland, who was on very bad terms with the King. The young Prince thoroughly enjoyed this visit—so much so that he was "ordered" by his physician to return there the following year for a course of salt-water baths. This treatment, most fortunately for him, coincided with the Race meetings at Lewes and Brighton. "A respectable farmhouse" with a view of the sea was engaged for him. The next summer, the Prince's architect, Henry Holland, was commissioned to enlarge this building and every year after that, for twenty years to come, the house received alterations and additions from different hands until it became the curious and exotic building which we know today as the Brighton Pavilion. There is no way of estimating what immense sums were spent on it.

Up to this time, Bath had been the watering place favored by the conservative fashionables of London and presided over by Beau Nash. This famous Master of Ceremonies, to show his importance, always wore an immense white hat and rich embroidery on his clothes. He drove in a chariot drawn by six gray horses and heralded by laced lackeys and French horns. Such was Beau Nash who directed the pleasures of the kingdom for more than fifty years. Oliver Goldsmith records that it was he who "diffused a desire of society and an easiness of address among a whole people who were formerly censured by foreigners for a reservedness of behavior and an awkward timidity in their first approaches. He first taught a familiar intercourse among strangers at Bath and Tunbridge, which still subsists among them."

The important thing at Bath was, of course, the amusement of bathing. Between six and nine o'clock every morning, "the lady is brought in 'a close chair,' dressed in her bathing clothes, to the bath; and being in the water, the woman who attends her presents her with a little floating dish like a basin, into which the lady puts a handkerchief, a snuff-box and a nosegay.

5

She then traverses the bath . . . and, having amused herself thus while she thinks proper, calls for her chair and returns to her lodgings."

The bathing was followed by a general assembly at the Pump-house. Some went for pleasure, some to drink the hot waters. The intervals were enlivened by music and conversation. From time to time the ladies withdrew to a Female Coffee House and the gentlemen to theirs, to read their papers. Men and women bathed together, which Doctor Johnson called "an instance of barbarity that could not be paralleled in any part of the world." After dinner the company met again at the Pump-house to conclude the evening with balls or plays or visits to the gaming tables.

Compare with this moderate simplicity the gay and roistering days at the new watering place which the Prince was now making fashionable. The "Carlton House Gang" went with him to Brighton, and behaved in Brighton exactly as they behaved in London. When he set out in his "randem"—a three-horse team with the lead horse ridden by a postilion and two others driven by the Prince in tandem formation—his aim was to cover the distance from London to the little seashore town in the shortest possible time. One famous day he made the hundred and eight miles there and back in ten hours. "Morning rides, champagne, dissipation and nonsense," said the *Morning Post* for July 6, 1785; "jumble these phrases together and you have a complete account of all that's passing at Brighthelmstone."

Among the boon companions who accompanied the Prince was Beau Brummel, who directed the fashions of the day at Brighton as Beau Nash had done at Bath in preceding years. The Prince often visited Brummel at his dressing hour in an ardent desire to learn the newest way of tying a neckcloth or of arranging the hair. Beau Brummel is said to have had three hairdressers at this time—one responsible for the hair on his temples, the second for the front part of his head and the third for the back of it. When asked what blacking he used to give such brilliance to his shoes, he replied, *"Blacking?* I never use anything but the froth of champagne!"

Like Beau Brummel, the Prince indulged himself in a wardrobe whose magnificence and extravagance amazed all Europe. When he took his seat in the House of Lords, his coat was black velvet richly embroidered with gold and pink spangles and lined with pink satin. His shoes had pink heels. At the Brighton ball he appeared in a beautiful cut-velvet "gala suit of a dark color with green stripes, superbly embroidered down the front and

6

seams with a broad embroidery of silver flowers intermixed with foil stones; the waistcoat, of white and silver tissue, embroidered like the coat; the Garter fastened with a shoulder knot of brilliants."

Edward Rymer, bootmaker of Cockspur Street, when his bills were protested, explained the high prices on the Prince's boots and shoes as being due to the waste of leather occasioned by the fact that "His Royal Highness had his shoes made to fit the different feet and never wore a shoe made for his right foot on his left foot."

When George's wardrobe was sold after his death, it realized the sum of £15,000. In the sale were all the coats he had worn during the past fifty years, for he never gave any of them away. There were splendid furs. The Earl of Chesterfield gave two hundred guineas for a sable pelisse that was a present from Emperor Alexander of Russia. Over five hundred pocketbooks were discovered among his possessions and in every one there was money, amounting to more than £10,000. His "cellar" of snuff contained no less than sixteen hundredweight and brought £400.

Wine and women were also among the Prince's extravagances. It was the day of four-bottle men. Dining-rooms had to be planned to accommodate their guests, not only around the table but *underneath* as well, and the man with the greatest number of mistresses excited a certain envy and renown. In the summer of 1784, the Prince, who had enjoyed many passing amours, fell headlong in love with a twice-widowed lady of fashion, a Mrs. Fitzherbert. Mrs. Fitzherbert "resisted, with the utmost anxiety and firmness, the flattering assiduities of the most accomplished Prince of his age." She loved him deeply but, being wiser and less headstrong than the Prince, she clearly recognized the barriers that separated them. The King insisted on royal birth for any consort of the royal family and without his consent no marriage was valid. Besides, Mrs. Fitzherbert was a Papist. By marrying her, the Prince would automatically forfeit his right to the throne. His mistress she would never become, being too devout a Catholic to consider the idea. The Prince finally overcame her scruples and they were secretly married in December, 1785, in her own drawing-room. Suspected, gossiped about throughout the kingdom, denied in Parliament by Fox, screened in a conciliatory speech by Sheridan, this marriage was a mystery unsolved until after the death of George IV, when King William IV, in the attempt to make all possible reparation to Mrs. Fitzherbert, called on her in Brighton, saw the wedding certificate, and requested her to put on widow's weeds and to dress her servants in the royal livery for the rest of her life.

Because of all his extravagances, the Prince's debts piled up. Huge sums of money were spent on jewels, on improvements to Carlton House, on clothes. An allowance of £10,000 a year was promised to Mrs. Fitzherbert. Annuities and bonds were freely offered to other ladies in whom the Prince was interested. He could find no way of raising the money to settle these obligations.

It was his favorite of the moment, Lady Jersey, who finally persuaded the Prince that there was only one solution to his problem—he must marry according to his father's wishes. How he arranged to ignore the already existing marriage is incomprehensible, but the fact remains that eight years after having been united in holy wedlock to Mrs. Fitzherbert he agreed to wed his cousin Princess Caroline of Brunswick. It was a most unhappy union. The Prince himself was at heart deeply distressed over his treatment of Mrs. Fitzherbert, for whom he cared more than for any other woman in the world. Caroline was unattractive and wretched. But Lady Jersey was right, for, upon the Prince's official marriage, Parliament increased his annual grant to £125,000, and he thus obtained the means to free himself from his debts.

Caroline bore him a daughter, the Princess Charlotte. Soon afterwards the royal couple separated and the Prince brought disgraceful charges against his miserable wife, accusing her of guilty intercourse with Sir Thomas Lawrence, Sydney Smith, Captain Manby, and others. She was exonerated in a public inquiry. The Prince and his mother, Queen Charlotte, were hissed and booed in London by a public which disapproved of this humiliation of the Princess of Wales and the Prince himself narrowly escaped being stoned when he drove out alone.

King George III had suffered several attacks of dementia from which he subsequently recovered, but in 1811 he became hopelessly insane and the Prince was appointed Regent. The great ceremony of the installation and the levee took place at Carlton House, on the King's birthday, with a supper to two thousand people. Extravagant and fantastic decorations filled the place. At the head table, in front of the Regent, was a circular basin with a small temple, and from it to the bottom of the table flowed a green-banked stream, stocked with gold and silver fish and crossed by three or four extraordinary bridges. On the following day the public was admitted to see the decorations. Some thirty thousand people assembled outside of Carlton House; the crush was so great that there were many accidents and the attendants were obliged to close the doors, to the bitter disappointment of thousands who had waited long and patiently to see the marvels of which they had heard rumors. As a matter of fact, there had been a great outlay for furniture in the latest fashion for this event and the rooms were done over in the newest manner, according to the Regent's desires. Lady Beaumont is reported to have reproached the splendor of Carlton House as being so overpowering that, no matter how fine the dresses of the company, they were never seen, for all eyes were drawn to the gorgeous attire of the great apartments.

On the death of George III in 1820, the Regent became King. Caroline, in a belated attempt to regain her place as Royal Consort, returned to England and attempted to force her way into Westminster Abbey for the Coronation, but was refused admittance. She crept away, humiliated, and died a month later of a broken heart. Sir Walter Scott wrote on this subject: "You must have a full account of the only disagreeable event of the day—I mean the attempt of the misguided lady who has lately furnished so many topics of discussion to intrude herself upon a ceremonial where, not being in her proper place, to be in any other must have been a voluntary degradation."

George IV reigned as king for ten years. His affection for Brighton—the fishing port transformed into a king's playground by royal favor—long remained constant. But suddenly, for no apparent reason, he deserted Brighton for Windsor. It is believed that, swollen by dropsy and crippled by attacks of gout, he preferred Windsor, where he could be driven about in the seclusion of the grounds.

Apparently the King had entirely forgotten Mrs. Fitzherbert, but upon his death a miniature of her was found on his breast, which was buried with him by his express request.

II

ARCHITECTURAL BACKGROUND OF
THE ENGLISH REGENCY

Historically, the period of the Regency began in 1811 when George III was declared mentally incompetent and his eldest son was named Regent. As it affected the decorative arts, however, the movement was actually born ten years earlier, in protest against the detail and overdecoration of Adam style. It developed with the participation of men like Sir John Soane, who built the Bank of England; William Wilkins, who built the National Gallery; Sir Robert Smirke, who built the façade of the British Museum; Decimus Burton, who designed and built some of the houses in Regent's Park; Henry Holland, architect to the Prince of Wales until 1806, who remade Carlton House and began the alterations on the Brighton Pavilion; Thomas Sheraton, Thomas Hope, and George Smith, designers of furniture; John Nash, the architect, who, after Holland's death, took over the work at Carlton House and Brighton, created Trafalgar Square, proposed the site of the National Gallery, and added to the beauty of London by laying out Regent's Park, Park Crescent, and Regent Street, finally building the last of the great Regency buildings, Buckingham Palace.

Through the work of these men, Regency became a restrained expression of Classicism sometimes Roman, sometimes Greek in its elements but forming a transition between the Adam style and the Greek Revival. We may place its approximate beginning and its fullest flowering between 1795 and 1830. Interior and exterior architecture and all sorts of furnishings were affected by this movement. Archibault Allison wrote in 1817:

> In the succession of fashions which have taken place in the article of ornamental furniture within these few years, everyone must have observed how much their beauty has been determined by accidental association . . . and how little the real and permanent beauty of such forms has been regarded. Some years ago, every article of this kind was made in what was called the Chinese taste, and, however fantastic and uncouth the forms in reality were, they were yet universally admired because they brought to mind those images of Eastern magnificence and splendour of which we have heard so much and which we are always willing to believe because they are distant.
> To this succeeded the Gothic taste. Everything was now made in imitation, not

indeed of Gothic furniture, but in imitation of the Forms and Ornaments of Gothic Halls and Cathedrals. This slight association however was sufficient to give Beauty to such Forms, because it led to ideas of Gothic manners and adventure, which had become fashionable in the world from many beautiful Compositions, both in prose and verse.

The taste which now reigns is that of the Antique. Everything we now use is made in imitation of those models which have been lately discovered in Italy; and they serve in the same manner to occupy our imagination by leading to those recollections of Grecian or Roman taste which have so much the possession of our minds, from the studies and amusements of our youth.

The earliest classical building in England was Soane's Bank of England. Through Soane's activities, Classicism became established as a definite architectural creed. Impetus to this movement was given also by Piranesi's work, by the publication of Stuart and Revett's *Antiquities of Athens,* and by the bringing of the Elgin Marbles to London.

Soane had been in Rome for three years' study. On his return he began what was to be his lifework. The Bank of England was started in 1788; he worked on it continuously for forty-five years. Many startling innovations were evolved during the course of its construction. Soane felt that the classical orders were not suitable for interior use. In their place he designed wall treatments from which all projections were banished. In place of pilasters, he used flat antae; in place of the florid ornament of the Adam brothers, he used simple incised ornament based on the Greek fret and similar devices. This ornament he wove with great dexterity from classical motifs. He was most successful in his handling of vaults and ceilings, using flat saucer domes with decorations of thin, reedlike, radiating lines, shallow moldings, and flush paneling. The façade of his own house at Lincoln's Inn Fields is a typical example of his incised wall decoration, and his book of garden buildings and seats published in 1778 shows a vivid imagination used in creating variations on classic themes.

The Classic Revival carried all before it on a wave of intoxication. Women tried to acquire Greek simplicity in their dress and adopted fillets and classic styles of hairdressing. The beaux and dandies of the day were given the name of "Corinthians." Moses, an artist of the time, published a series of sketches showing the fashionable world, busied with tea drinking and various occupations. These carefully drawn sketches are valuable docu-

11

ments, as they interpret the dress, interior decoration, and social life of their epoch (Plates 7, 8, 9).

Soane at the beginning of his career had been articled to George Dance and afterwards to Henry Holland, both architects of note. Holland was to become one of the most important influences on style in the early years of the Regency. When Holland was appointed architect to the Prince of Wales, he sent a young assistant, Charles Heathcote Tatham, to Rome to make drawings of details that were afterwards used in Carlton House. He stressed

PLATE 7. REGENCY COSTUMES AND INTERIORS
Drawn by Henry Moses in 1823, this shows the classic robes and classic furniture of the day.
(*Courtesy of the Metropolitan Museum of Art*)

the simplicity and the beauty of classic forms, both in architecture and furniture. The furniture made under his direction for the Prince of Wales was among the first designed by English craftsmen in the Greco-Roman style. The same spirit is found in the furniture made for Samuel Whitbread of Southill in 1795–1800 (Plates 19 and 20), and in that made for a friend of Whitbread's, the owner of Hartwell House. The contents of this house were sold at auction in April, 1938 (Plates 21, 45, and 46). It may easily be seen

PLATES 8 AND 9. REGENCY DRAWINGS BY HENRY MOSES
(*Courtesy of the Metropolitan Museum of Art*)

that the aim of Regency designers was to translate the iron and bronze furniture of ancient Rome and Greece into wood.

Holland's principal work, the alteration and enlargement of Carlton House, started in 1788, when the building was assigned as Residence to the Prince of Wales. Under his hands the place underwent complete restoration and rebuilding for the royal occupation. Pyne, however, wrote in 1818: "Notwithstanding the extensive alterations and improvements which this structure has experienced under the direction of its present Royal possessor, which have changed its character from that of a plain mansion to the magnitude and splendour of a palace, it yet assumes no other than its original title, 'Carlton House.'"

In front of the Residence, Holland added a fine Corinthian portico (Plate 10) and an Ionic screen, whose shadow may be seen in the print. The great row of pillars forming the screen was the subject of much discussion at the time. A popular verse about them chanted ironically,

> Dear little columns all in a row,
> What do you there? Indeed we don't know.

When Carlton House was torn down in 1827, this row of pillars was fortunately preserved and now forms part of the portico of the National Gallery.

Holland worked on Carlton House until his death in 1806; he was followed by Thomas Hopper and by James Wyatt who were in charge until 1813. After the death of Wyatt, John Nash, by command of the Prince Regent, stepped into his place and was appointed to continue work on "the Palaces which are the Personal Residences of the Prince Regent."

An excellent idea of Carlton House at the height of its renown may be obtained from the descriptions in Ackerman's *Microcosm of London* and in Pyne's *History of the Royal Residences*. Ackerman says of the Great Hall that "it was conceived with a classic elegance that does honor to the genius of the late Mr. Holland." The columns (Plate 11) were of yellow porphyry with bronze bases and capitals; the walls of granite green; the pavement of veined marble in large octagons, separated by diamonds of black marble and bordered with the same material. In the four niches were casts from the antique. The circular dining-room was considered one of the most splendid apartments in Europe. Its walls were entirely covered with silver, on which

PLATES 10 AND 11. FAÇADE AND GREAT HALL, CARLTON HOUSE

Above is the north front with its Corinthian portico. The shadow of Holland's Ionic screen may be seen at the right. Below is one of the fine architectural interiors designed by Holland.

Etruscan ornaments were painted in relief. Eight fine Ionic columns in relief had bases and capitals of silver.

The main floor of Carlton House was given over to the state apartments, including the great crimson drawing-room, the circular room, the throne room, and the rooms of private audience. In all of these rooms there was a profusion of great mirrors, fine furniture, candelabra, tripods, and splendid draperies. The cut-glass chandeliers were one of the notable decorations. There was one with fifty-six lights, designed to represent a fountain which cascaded into a large reservoir. Another formed a pagoda of drops. One looked like a vase of shining spangles and still another had the form of a tent. Others are described as being built up of ormolu hoops enriched with honeysuckle ornament, hung with icicle glass pendants and festoons of faceted drops, and fitted with ormolu arms similarly adorned.* All of these magnificent lusters are now in the state rooms of Buckingham Palace.

The inventory of the furniture for Carlton House includes many "large, indulgent sofas and chairs." Much mahogany and rosewood was used as a foil to brass and ormolu moldings. Ornament was reduced to the simplest terms and played a minor role. A large part of the furniture designed under Holland's direction is preserved in Buckingham Palace, including the pair of gilt pier tables with marble tops (Plate 12) made for the Chinese drawing-room, and illustrated in the *Cabinetmakers' and Upholsterers' Drawing Book* that was published by Thomas Sheraton in 1802. Holland stressed the Greek rather than the Roman classic and his designs for domestic furniture were perhaps lighter and more graceful in spirit than some of the Regency developments that followed.

A year after Holland's death, a book on household furniture by Thomas Hope appeared, giving new impetus to the Classic Revival. Hope belonged to a rich family of Amsterdam merchants and since an early age had studied architecture. His hobby, which his circumstances permitted him to indulge to the full, was the collecting of ancient sculpture and vases, and the building of proper backgrounds for them. Mr. Knoblock, in his foreword, has mentioned the fact that Hope purchased a large part of Sir William Hamilton's second vase collection and that it took two houses to hold his various treasures, the London house in Duchess Street and a country house

* See H. Clifford Smith, *Buckingham Palace.*

at Deepdene in Surrey. In the London house the rooms were decorated after classic and Oriental models by Hope himself. Farington speaks in his Diary of a visit to Thomas Hope's house and says that it was not so bad as he thought it would be, that he can even imagine that it might do some good by getting the designers of England out of their rut of devotion to certain styles.

Deepdene remained untouched until 1917, when some of the furniture was sold at Christie's in London, the remainder being disposed of a few weeks later in the house itself. The portrait of Thomas Hope (Plate 2) in

PLATE 12. THE CHINESE DRAWING-ROOM, CARLTON HOUSE
The consoles and Chinese figures by Holland are now in Buckingham Palace.
(*From* Cabinet Maker's and Upholsterer's Drawing Book *by Thomas Sheraton 1793*)

Turkish costume by Beechey was sold at that time. This was the costume worn by Hope in the Levant. A small enamel copy of the portrait was painted by Sir Henry Bone and was included in the sale. Hope felt that he had raised only a feeble voice in favor of the Fine Arts, "but still," he said, "the most general flame may begin in a single spark; and should I succeed in kindling for the arts a purer, a more intense, a more universal love; should I thus be

17

instrumental in promoting in the country a new source of health, wealth, strength, vigor and patriotism and nobleness of mind and feeling. . . . I shall think myself the humble instrument of the greatest good that can be conferred upon humanity."

When John Nash succeeded Holland in the position of Architect to the Prince Regent in 1813, he introduced the greatest richness into all the rooms of Carlton House. The moldings and all the ornaments gleamed with gold. Nash's name became the symbol of the spendthrift builder and he was harshly criticized by those who did not like the "Carlton House Gang," which was associated with vice and extravagance. An epigram of Peter Pindar rebuked him bitterly:

> Master Nash, Master Nash,
> You merit the lash
> For debauching the taste of our Heir to the throne.
> Then cross not the seas
> To rob the Chinese,
> But learn to be wise from Vitruvius and Soane.

The stucco which Nash used for many buildings in the course of the reconstruction of Regent Street and other thoroughfares was considered a flimsy and fake substitute for the honest and substantial red brick of the days of George III. Hence the adaptation of a famous saying:

> . . . Nash, a very great master,
> Who found us all brick and left us all plaster.

But Nash, it is now generally admitted, did much that was excellent for the plan and the appearance of London during his lifetime.

It is often said that he could not have accomplished his "Metropolitan Improvements" if a certain John Fordyce had not preceded him. Fordyce was Surveyor General of His Majesty's Land Revenue in 1793. He proposed first that an accurate survey of the Crown's holdings in London and Westminster should be made and second that all future changes should be considered in relation to a general scheme of improvement. He also proposed that an architect of eminence should be asked to report on every change, "not only in relation to the property itself but to the street or district in which it is situated and to the improvements which are practicable."

Fordyce's first proposition concerned the great tract of land lying north

18

of London then known as Marylebone Park, but which was renamed Regent's Park after the Prince Regent. A competition for architects was authorized by the Treasury. Fordyce, however, died before anything had come of it. After his death, the commissioners decided to act without further loss of time. Four architects were instructed to prepare plans and make immediate reports. Of the four, Nash's designs were the most pleasing. He described them as "having a definite pattern of trees and houses." After much discussion, all was settled to everyone's satisfaction and Nash was instructed to proceed with the work.

His final plan included a main approach to Regent's Park from Portland Place through a large circus, another circus in the middle of the Park, an artificial lake around the center, a pleasure pavilion for the Prince, and a driveway running around the entire Park. The villas were to be so arranged on sites of twenty to forty acres and so planted with trees that "no villa should see any other, but each should appear to possess the whole of the Park." The canal which enters on the east side and leaves the Park on the north was named the Regent's Canal.

Regent Street was the natural outcome of this new plan for Regent's Park. It led from Portland Place to the low façade of Carlton House. More than seven hundred houses were demolished to make this street and for years it was a disfiguring scar across the face of London. The novel feature of the street was the long curving colonnade that stretched from Oxford Street to Pall Mall. Over the colonnade were balustrades to form balconies. Lodgings were arranged above the shops that occupied the ground floor.

In 1821 Nash was seventy-seven years old and ready to retire. He had done, in addition to his work on Carlton House and Regent's Park, a prodigious amount of work on the Brighton Pavilion. But he was still at George's beck and call. The Prince Regent had by then become King; he ordered Nash to design Buckingham Palace as a residence for him. As the building progressed, the King was so pleased with it that he decided to hold his courts there, and to pull down Carlton House. Nash attempted to dissuade him, but in vain. Buckingham House became Buckingham Palace.

The expense of the Palace developed into a scandal. Nash was exonerated, but in 1830, after the death of the King, his commission was suspended; he retired to the Isle of Wight and died there five years later in the Gothic villa which he had constructed for himself.

PLATE 13. BRIGHTON PAVILION IN 1788
The "respectable farmhouse" transformed by Holland for the Regent's use.
(*From an aquatint by Charles Middleton*)

THE BRIGHTON PAVILION

No picture of the Regency would be complete without more than a passing reference to that fantastic building known as the Brighton Pavilion, which stands today, as it did then, an example of the Regent's folly, of sumptuous Oriental magnificence, of glamour and dreamlike imagination, a "pleasure dome" and setting for the court unequaled by any other palace in the western hemisphere. From 1784, when the Prince of Wales decided that he needed a residence at Brighton, a long procession of architects were employed in constructing and reconstructing the Pavilion. It was in the beginning a simple sort of edifice described by a visitor as a "respectable farmhouse." Weltje, the famous cook and factotum of the Prince, when dispatched to find a suitable property, selected this house with a fine view of the sea. With great perspicuity he purchased it from Mr. Thomas Kemp for the sum of £3,000 and leased it to his master in 1786. For a number of years the Prince was the tenant of his own cook, but when Weltje died suddenly,

George bought the property from the widow for the sum of £17,300 and also arranged an annuity for her.

This Weltje was altogether a most extraordinary character. It is common knowledge that the nucleus of the collection of Dutch paintings now in Buckingham Palace was formed by him at the request of the Prince, for the faithful servitor was actually a far better connoisseur of art than his master!

In the summer of 1801 plans were made to enlarge the Pavilion and the commission was given to the Prince's architect, Henry Holland, who, absorbed in the reconstruction of Carlton House, handed the work on the Pavilion to a pupil of his, Robinson. Changes and alterations continued without ceasing. In 1805 the Prince summoned Humphrey Repton to Brighton to give his advice on new improvements. Repton was directly responsible for the Indian influence that is to be found in the Pavilion. He had just been employed by an Indian nabob to build into an English home memories of the Hindu gardens and mosques with which he had lived in the East. Working with the architect Cockerell, Repton had created an ex-

PLATE 14. THE PAVILION IN 1820

The "respectable farm house" after reconstruction with Oriental domes and minarets by Nash and Repton.

21

otic building, which, on the exterior at least, succeeded in giving the impression of an Oriental fantasy. For the Prince of Wales, Repton prepared a similar plan for the house and gardens at Brighton, which would have transformed them completely into Indian style. Unfortunately lack of funds made it impossible to carry out the scheme. Both the Prince and Repton were deeply disappointed. Repton died in 1818 and it was Nash who finally capped the building with the great Indian dome, weighing sixty tons, and began the Oriental skyline. Nash was in charge of the work from 1814 to 1822. From time to time he added smaller domes. Tall minarets grew up. Year by year the Pavilion became more nearly what it is today. Nash in his enthusiasm exceeded the estimates by about £11,000 and fell into disfavor with the Prince.

The new and extraordinary style excited all sorts of comments and witticisms. Sir Walter Scott wrote to a friend, "Set fire to the Chinese stables, and if it embraces the whole of the Pavilion it will rid me of a great eyesore." Byron in *Don Juan* declared:

> Shut-up—not the King, but the Pavilion,
> Or else 'twill cost another million.

The Pavilion was dubbed "a pot-bellied palace, a minaret mushroom, a gilded dirt-pie, a congeries of bulbous excrescences." Hazlitt, as he looked at it, was reminded of a collection of stone pumpkins and pepperboxes. "It seems," he wrote, "as if the genius of architecture had at once the dropsy and the megrims." A writer in the *Gentleman's Magazine* said that the "whole congestion is a sort of professional frolic running a short-lived antic around the chaste and modest elevation of the Pavilion." Sydney Smith's comment was perhaps the shrewdest. "It looks as if the Dome of St. Paul's came to Brighton and pupped!"

In spite of its extraordinary style, the Pavilion had dignity and a certain curious beauty. It was indeed an amazing building to find in a simple little fishing town which still held to its old customs. When the court was in Brighton, for example, a deputation of fishermen arrived regularly to present to their sovereign the first mackerel caught in the new year. What must these simple folk have thought of the strange magnificence that surrounded them when they were received with their fish in the regal Chinese rooms of the Pavilion?

PLATE 15. BANQUETING HALL, BRIGHTON PAVILION
The Chinese idea of decoration was characteristic of the Regent's taste. Architect Nash is seated
at the end of the table at the right.

The interior of the building had been done largely in Chinese fashion even before the exterior was transformed into its present style. The principal architectural decorators were Frederick Crace and Robert Jones, who also designed much of the furniture. To quote here what Sitwell and Barton say in their delightful book on Brighton:

The Chinese decoration of the Pavilion is different from all previous attempts. . . . The novelty of the Chinoiserie style, as presented to us in the Pavilion, resides in its exuberance, its massive effects of colour, as opposed to the almost Pompeian delicacy which had attended it in the earlier epoch. Porcelain, furniture and fittings of every description completed the effect which, though lovely, sailed perilously near to a pantomime transformation scene.

The most singular feature of the Pavilion, however, is that its rooms do actually bear resemblance to Oriental rooms of the same period; especially, perhaps, to those in the palaces at Hué. . . .

23

Many of the red lacquer rooms, with their tented ceilings, down the four sides of which crawl gilded dragons; with their silvered ceilings and hanging chandeliers, recall the famous interiors of Brighton rather than of the immense halls of Pekin. And then, too, lying as it does between India and China, a certain Indian influence manifests itself in Hué as also in the Pavilion.

Just a glimpse of the Pavilion will be interesting to those who want to follow the development of decoration during Regency days. The gallery was in Chinese style, with panels of painted paper, Chinese statues in niches, and hanging lanterns with tassels. Chinese porcelains and Chippendale Gothic furniture were used there. The music room had a Chinese pagoda at the side of each window and by the mantel. The wall decorations were gold on a red ground. The banqueting room was again Chinese, with painted wall panels, lotus chandeliers, and dragons. A fretwork dado and frames around the panels suggested bamboo.

Much of the original furniture was removed from the Pavilion by Queen Victoria, who disliked the Pavilion and wished to have its furnishings in London. The many van loads transported by her order were taken to Buckingham Palace but they were not included in any special manner in the furnishing of the rooms there until Queen Mary became interested in them and assembled the Regency Room and other apartments.

In 1849 the Pavilion was sold to the town of Brighton and since then it has been used for all sorts of public affairs—balls, conferences, and meetings.

During the World War, it served as a hospital for convalescent Indian soldiers, in the hope, perhaps, that they would feel more at home in this strange land if they were lodged under domes and minarets that recalled their own temple buildings.

Recently a movement has been started to restore the Pavilion to its former grandeur, and bit by bit many of the pieces which formed part of its original furnishings are coming back to it. Things that were sold in Brighton have been collected and put back again in their places. Queen Mary aided greatly in this movement by returning many of the things taken away by Queen Victoria.

III

THE CHARACTER OF THE ENGLISH REGENCY STYLE

THE word Regency as applied to furniture styles and decoration has long been a rather vague and obscure term in the mind of the general public. It is indeed time to clarify and define it, so that there will be no further misunderstanding.

Regency styles developed in England at the beginning of the nineteenth century as a revolt against overelaborate and florid Adam decoration. They

PLATE 16. DRAWING-ROOM, ADMIRALTY HOUSE

All the early Regency furniture in this room is carved with dolphins.

(*Reproduced by permission of the Lords Commissioners of the Admiralty*)

PLATE 17. DRAWING-ROOM, ADMIRALTY HOUSE

Admiralty House is the official residence of the First Lord of the Admiralty.

(*Reproduced by permission of the Lords Commissioners of the Admiralty*)

were a return to the classic manner, for the aim of the neoclassicists was to introduce cool and calm restraint in the form of a Greco-Roman revival. To this end they began by eliminating all unnecessary ornament. In this respect, their ideas of simplification and their use of metals and other materials of decoration closely resemble the work of modern designers of today.

Henry Holland and John Soane attracted much attention by their work in the new manner and soon they had hundreds of followers. They stripped from the walls the wood paneling that had been the pride of the Georgian period and used a flat, linear treatment whose detail was rigidly classic. Wood carving disappeared almost completely. The doorway of the eighteenth century with its architectural overdoor and broken pediment gave place to the

26

six-panel mahogany door in a plain frame. Walls became flat plaster surfaces, either painted in color or covered with wallpapers and Pompeian wall decorations. Occasionally the dado and chair rail were retained, but for the most part Regency rooms had unbroken plaster from floor to ceiling.

At the beginning of the Regency, popular wall colors were pale and rather subtle in tones inherited from Adam. A favorite combination was maroon and yellow. Fawn color, lilac, pea-green, light blue, cream, pale terra cotta, Chinese pink, buff, and rose were often used. Toward the end of the period, colors became stronger and bolder, both in walls and in upholstery and curtains. Scenic papers appeared on the walls and also relief in gold.

Mirrors of large size were much used as wall decorations. There was a great demand for light and air, so windows increased in size, panes of glass were larger, and many bays were made. Marble mantels took the place of the Georgian mantels of carved wood. In the finest houses, they were usually black with gold veining, though occasionally white, gray, or rose marble was

PLATE 18. FINE REGENCY HALL TABLE
This table of green and gold lacquer came from Brighton Pavilion.
(*Courtesy of Messrs. Lenygon & Morant*)

used. These mantels were classic in design, without much ornamentation, and often had free-standing columns with Doric or Ionic capitals, considered suitable for drawing-rooms. In less important rooms mantels had plain or molded pilasters. Every fireplace had its hob-grate and cast-iron or steel facings.

Against such unpretentious, almost severe, backgrounds, definite and arresting furniture was needed and this was created by the furniture designers in Greek and Roman style. Chairs were made like the bronze models discovered in Pompeii. Sofas were designed like old Roman beds and couches. Bookcases followed the lines of temple façades, with columns and entablatures. The Roman tripod furnished the model for candlestands. Though this furniture had a certain simplicity, it had at the same time a

PLATE 19. DRAWING-ROOM AT SOUTHILL
This room was designed by Henry Holland in 1795 for Samuel Whitbread.
(*By permission of* Country Life, *London*)

PLATE 20. LIBRARY AT SOUTHILL
(*By permission of* Country Life, *London*)

sophistication that won the admiration of all the advanced spirits of the time. It suited its background and was designed to meet the new requirements of the machines that had just been invented to take the place of hand labor. It was masculine in feeling, but still did not lose the grace and beauty of the classic forms.

As early as 1791, an English engineer, Sir Samuel Bentham, attempted to employ the accuracy of machines in manufacturing certain articles of wood. Sir Samuel had an original mind that excelled in unusual and strange ideas. In Russia, where he had been stationed in a remote part of the country, he designed what he called an "amphibious carriage, specially adapted for traveling in a country intersected by rivers at every hand." For voyages on land, it was suspended on wheels; for water trips, the wheels lifted off and were stowed in the bottom of the carriage, which then became a boat.

29

During the construction of this vehicle, Bentham noted the slowness of the workers and their inaccuracy. It was then that he dreamed of substituting machinery for manual labor.

A tour through the manufacturing districts of England in 1791 confirmed this intention. With Jeremy, his brother, he introduced steam as a driving force, made rotary saws, arranged to give curvature by bending, cut moldings and bored holes by machinery, made mortises and tenons and

PLATE 21. OCTAGONAL LIBRARY TABLE FROM HARTWELL HOUSE
This table is similar to one made by Henry Holland for Southill.
(*Courtesy of W. B. Henderson, Esq., Bath*)

turned wood in various forms in a lathe. Cabinetmakers took advantage of many of these inventions in early nineteenth-century furniture making.

A good idea of the woods used in these operations may be gained from George Smith's practical observations in 1804–1806. He says:

Mahogany, when used in houses of consequence, should be confined to the Parlour and Bedchamber floors; in furniture for these apartments, the less inlay of other woods, the more chaste will be the style of work; if the wood be of a fine, compact, and bright quality, the ornaments may be carved clean in the mahogany; where it may be requisite to make out panelling by an inlay of lines, let those lines be of brass or ebony.

In Drawing-Rooms, Boudoirs, Ante-Rooms or other dressed apartments, East and West India satinwoods, rosewood, tulipwood and the other varieties of woods brought from the East may be used; with satin and light-coloured woods, the decorations may be of ebony or rosewood; with rosewood, let the decorations be ormolu and the inlay of brass; bronzed metal, though sometimes used with satinwood, has a cold and poor effect; it suits better on gilt work and will answer well enough on mahogany.

Regency furniture of the early years of the century—that is to say, 1800 to 1810—bore a great similarity to the French Directoire style. This similarity remained typical of much Regency design throughout its duration. But the ensuing twenty years of war against Napoleon cut off to a great extent communication between England and the Continent, so that English styles developed their own characteristics, distinct and different from the

PLATE 22. COMBINATION WRITING TABLE AND BOOKCASE
A fine piece of Regency furniture, this combination table has concave doors with brass grilles and carved lions' heads and paws.
(*Courtesy of J. B. Botibol, Esq., London*)

31

French. For the most part, English Regency furniture was more varied in shape than French; it was also more gracious and less severe.

Henry Holland, the Regent's first architect, may be called the most important influence at the beginning of the new style. His young assistant, Charles Tatham, sent to collect ideas at Pompeii for use in Carlton House,

PLATE 23. REGENCY FIRESIDE TABLES AND POLE SCREEN

The supports of the tables are carved to simulate palm trees. The pole screen has a bouquet of flowers and leaves done in paper work.

(Courtesy of Lady Violet Henderson, Cirenchester, and of Lord Ivor Charles Spencer Churchill, London)

32

PLATE 24. MAHOGANY SIDEBOARD OF THE HOPE SCHOOL

This handsome piece of furniture is finished with contemporary lion's head-and-ring handles. The pedestal cupboards have scroll tops typical of the classic Greek Regency design.

(*Courtesy of Messrs. Lenygon & Morant*)

published a book of etchings in 1843, representing the best examples of Grecian and Roman architectural ornament drawn from the originals. In the book he pays warm tribute to Piranesi and also to his own countrymen, Stuart and Revett, for aiding to establish the true principles of Grecian simplicity and perfection, which were carried out by Holland.

Holland introduced into Carlton House the fashion of marbleizing, adopted from the French. Regency painters took delight in seeing how

33

cleverly they could imitate the graining of wood, of marble, and of bronze with a brush and colors. And the makers of wallpapers also aided in carrying out these ideas. Paper borders and friezes were fashionable at this time and paper pilasters or flat patterns in strong colors were introduced.

Thomas Hope, who followed Holland, criticized English furniture for

PLATE 25. REGENCY SIDEBOARD, EGYPTIAN INFLUENCE
Carved Egyptian figures are here combined with lions' heads and ring pulls.
(*Courtesy of John A. Pearson, Ltd., London*)

the lack of many qualities. He declared that it had no breadth or repose of surface, no distinctness and contrast of outline, no harmony and significance of accessories, no accord between details and the main object.

In his book on household furniture and interior decoration, he describes his attempts to make it possible for the lover of fine furniture to get superior objects in England which formerly he could only obtain from abroad and he tells of all his difficulties. He was unable to find any profes-

34

sional man possessed of sufficient intimacy with literature to suggest ideas or with sufficient practice in drawing to execute designs that would "ennoble simple objects like tables and chairs, footstools and screens." Therefore he had to depend largely on his own drawings.

Some of Hope's designs are doubtless carried to an extreme, but through his influence many of the objectionable peculiarities of Sheraton's late styles were eliminated and furniture returned to a closer adaptation of Roman traditions. In furniture thus inspired, the monopodium with a lion's head or a griffin's head was often used. It has been said that this leg is to the Regency what the cabriole leg is to Chippendale styles.

Metal was used in various ways as a decoration for furniture of this epoch. One of the favorite methods was to set an inlay of plain brass into table tops or other plane surfaces, done in simple scrolls or floral forms and

PLATE 26. REGENCY SOFA TABLE
This sofa table is also a gaming table, for its sliding top conceals a backgammon board.
(*Courtesy of James Pendleton, New York*)

PLATE 27. REGENCY WRITING TABLE
Rosewood is here inlaid with brass.
(Courtesy of Mrs. Claire Marion-Cox, Datchet-on-Thames)

classic patterns. These inlays were not engraved. Brass galleries were used around the tops of sideboards, secretaries, writing tables, and pedestals. Lion's paws and dog's paws in brass were used for the feet of many articles of furniture, and rings and lion's masks for pulls.

It is interesting to glance over the kinds of furniture produced in this period, and to see how they reflect the social manners and customs of the times. Among the small tables that were enormously popular were teapoys and quartetto tables. George Smith says of them that they were used in drawing-rooms "to prevent the company rising from their seats when taking

36

refreshments." Quartetto tables came in nests of four which, sliding one under another, could be arranged in a small space when not in use. They were made of mahogany, rosewood, bronze, and gilt to suit the room. Sometimes they are found in Gothic or Chinese designs. Teapoys had pedestals and were used either for tea or coffee.

"Déjeuné tables" were designed for ladies' boudoirs or morning breakfast rooms. They were generally expected to be of the richest decoration, for they were destined to hold breakfast sets of superb china, but "in only slightly decorated rooms" they merely imitated bamboo or else were japanned black and gold.

Some extremely complicated pieces of furniture were produced at this time, such as the sideboard designed by George Smith (Plate 92 in his *Collection of Designs for Household Furniture*). This consists of a long table in the center, with bronze legs and lion's-paw feet. It contains three drawers for serviettes. At the two ends are separate pedestals with Egyptian figures in

PLATE 28. REGENCY WRITING TABLE
Made of satinwood and mahogany, the mounts and brass gallery are original.
(*Courtesy of Daniel H. Farr Co., New York*)

37

bronze on the corners, surmounted by full-sized Egyptian slaves holding lights. One of the pedestals is for bottles; the other is lined with tin racks to hold plates, which are kept hot by an iron heater. There is also a drawer below containing water to wash glasses during dinner. Thus, in this one piece of furniture, the owner is provided with a cellar, a pantry, a stove, candelabra, and a linen closet!

Wall brackets, footstools, fire screens, and jardinières are among the small pieces of furniture to which Regency designers devoted much attention. The sofa table, ordinarily placed in front of the sofa instead of behind it as at the present time, figures importantly in furniture inventories of the period, while commodes and chiffoniers, writing desks and escritoires, small worktables, sofas, and couches of all sorts were also made in quantity.

But perhaps the most important contribution of the Regency is to dining-room furniture, which before this time had not been designed to give the greatest amount of comfort and ease. Following Sheraton's idea, pedestal

PLATE 29. ROSEWOOD WRITING TABLE

This table is inlaid with brass and has three drawers with a lift-up reading rack in the center of the top.

(*Courtesy of Edward H. Benjamin, Esq., London*)

38

dining tables were made, but for the first time they consisted of several sections which could be used separately if desired or could be clipped together at the edges to accommodate a large company. The fact that each section had its own pedestal, which did not interfere in any way with the feet of the guests, added greatly to the popularity of this design. One of the most curi-

PLATE 30. ROUND HALL TABLE
Made of beech painted black, this table has a dark-green marble top
with carved and burnished gilt decoration.
(Courtesy of Mrs. Claire Marion-Cox, Datchet-on-Thames)

ous and interesting examples of sectional dining tables is the table from Hartwell House (Plate 32), formed of four sofa tables fastened together. This indeed is innovation. Chairs were made for use at the long table, adequate in size and conforming to the lines of the human body so that the occupant was comfortable and at ease. The good French food introduced into society by the Prince Regent had resulted in longer hours at table and a greater appreciation of the fine art of dining.

No new style ever develops without resulting in some exaggerations and absurdities, and this is true of Regency as well as of all its predecessors. One of its most ridiculous expressions consisted of the so-called zoological furniture, where crocodiles and sphinxes and winged lions and griffins were rampant (Plates 35, 65, and 66). Many of these particular manifestations appeared after Napoleon's campaign in Egypt. "Think!" exclaimed Miss Mitford in the book called *Our Village*, "Think of a crocodile couch and a sphinx sofa! The room was *swarming* with crocodiles and sphinxes!"

In addition to the Egyptian styles popularized by the Regency, there

PLATE 31. A REGENCY TORCHÈRE AND WINDOW SEAT

The torchère is one of a pair in black and gold, with brass lions'-head handles and brass feet. The window seat is beech wood, painted black and gold.

(*Courtesy of Mrs. Claire Marion-Cox, Datchet-on-Thames*)

was the revival of Chinese styles in furniture and decoration due largely to the personal taste of George IV. This phase accounts for the prevalence of Chinese wallpapers, of pagoda designs, and of lacquered furniture. Also attempted was a revival of Gothic styles which had had a vogue toward the end of the eighteenth century, but did not attain popularity again until the reign of Queen Victoria.

Some ridiculous rules were published for the guidance of the furniture designer in the Regency epoch. Richard Brown, in his *Rudiments of Drawing Cabinet and Upholstery Furniture,* published in 1822, discussed at length the symbolism of motifs used on furniture. He cautions his readers never to use fig leaves on a dressing table or dolphins on a grate, where they are most decidedly out of place. He warns solemnly against using foliage for the tails of griffins and insists that shields and battle-axes shall be used only in military apartments. He also states as an axiom that brass stars should be reserved for beds and chandeliers, but does not go into detail to explain why.

The Regency was a great day for the upholsterers. Window draperies of the period assumed such importance that the curtain men prided themselves on "associating an imperishable grandeur with all their performances." Undercurtains of the finest muslin were used, or of superfine cassimere, with fringe in contrast to the drapery. For overcurtains, the materials

PLATE 32. SET OF FOUR SOFA TABLES FROM HARTWELL HOUSE, CIRCA 1810
These four mahogany tables were made to fit together and form a most unusual long dining table.
(*Courtesy of Capt. C. G. Lancaster, London*)

41

differed according to the rooms. In elegant drawing-rooms there was plain satin or damask, lustring, and tabarets. Calico was a third choice, with small chintz patterns. All of these to be used in "the continuation of festoons." The cornices were gilt. For rooms in Chinese style it was proper to have them japanned or lacquered. Eating rooms and libraries called for materials of more substance than these finer rooms. For them, cassimere or undressed moreen in scarlet and crimson were found to fill the need. All of these curtains were continued across the pier glasses placed between the windows, so that a great portion of the room seemed furnished with drapery.

PLATE 33. PAINTED REGENCY TABLE, CIRCA 1800

The carved details are colored green to resemble bronze. The capitals of the crossed legs are gilt.
(*Courtesy of Mr. and Mrs. Henry W. Bagley, Greenwich, Connecticut*)

42

PLATE 34. PAINTED ARMCHAIRS
They are black and gold, with cane seats.
(*Courtesy of John A. Pearson, Ltd., London*)

Beds were draped in the same elaborate manner as windows, often with two or three different kinds of materials. For libraries or dining-rooms, "military window-curtains" were considered appropriate, and supporting spears of mahogany and bronze or of gilt and bronze were made as curtain poles. Many directions for such draperies are given in George Smith's drawing book. Mr. Stafford of Bath seems to have had ideas slightly less stuffy, for he declared at the same epoch that drawing-room curtains might be of light-green silk, lined with pink taffeta, the festoons supported with the eagle of Jupiter embracing a thunderbolt.

Small appreciation of Regency's possibilities was shown until after the Great War when Messrs. Lenygon and Morant inaugurated a series of exhibitions in London to stimulate interest in the decorative arts. Having progressed through all the great epochs of the eighteenth century, they decided finally to show a wealth of Regency material which they had discovered, and to call this exhibit "the last of the great English periods." A year was spent in preparing a background and collecting furniture. Cautioned that their collection of earlier furniture, ending with Chippendale, would be contaminated through association with a collection of this later date, a separate entrance was provided to the gallery when it was opened.

The exhibition created quite a sensation. Royalty came to see it, as well as connoisseurs who had an interest in decoration. For six months the exhibit was kept open and the attendance steadily increased. A great revival of a fascinating period was on its way.

PLATE 35. SHELL-SHAPED COUCH WITH CROCODILE LEGS
This is a good example of Regency zoölogical furniture.
(*Courtesy of Decor, E. S. Boteler, Ltd., New York*)

IV

ENGLISH REGENCY
A PICTORIAL SUPPLEMENT

PLATE 36. MINIATURE REGENCY ROOM

This small-scale model was made by Mrs. James Ward Thorne, with absolute accuracy of detail. The round room has walls of pale-gray marble with darker gray pilasters; the enrichment of frieze, capitals, and mantel are gold. Through the wide doorway is a glimpse of a Regency library with a fine needlepoint rug.

(*Courtesy of Mrs. James Ward Thorne, Chicago*)

PLATE 37. FOYER OF A HOUSE IN BELGRAVE SQUARE

Against the mirror stands a Regency console with Egyptian caryatids and inlaid marble top.

(Courtesy of Mr. Henry and Lady Honor Channon)

PLATE 38. DINING-ROOM IN HOLME HOUSE, REGENT'S PARK

Two serving consoles with Egyptian figures stand against a corrugated wall covered with silk fabric bordered with wide *galon*. The mirror panels are latticed.

(*Courtesy of Honorable Mrs. Pleydell Bouverie*)

PLATE 39. ENTRANCE HALL, HOLME HOUSE, REGENT'S PARK

The curving staircase and chandelier are unusually fine. Negroid figures hold lights and form the base of consoles.

(Courtesy of Honorable Mrs. Pleydell Bouverie, London)

PLATE 40. LIBRARY OF EDWARD KNOBLOCK

Bookcase, sofa, and large Egyptian chairs are from the Hope Collection. The writing table and desk chair are by George Smith.

(Courtesy of Edward Knoblock, Esq., London)

PLATE 41. REGENCY DRAWING-ROOM AT SATIS HOUSE

Charmingly arranged with Regency couches, chairs, and painted bookcase, in the center is a round table-bookcase.

(*Courtesy of Mrs. Claire Marion-Cox, Datchet-on-Thames*)

PLATE 42. REGENCY ROOM IN BUCKINGHAM PALACE

From *Buckingham Palace; Its Furniture, Decoration and History*, by H. Clifford Smith.

(By special permission of the Lord Chamberlain)

PLATE 43. A FINE REGENCY SECRETAIRE

Faded satinwood, cross-banded with amboyna, is inlaid with delicate brass work and ebony.

(*Courtesy of Miss Susan Lowndes, London*)

PLATE 44. CANTED BREAK-FRONT SECRETARY FROM HARTWELL HOUSE
This piece is fitted with drawers and pigeonholes, panel doors, gilt pilasters, beading and scroll
supports.
(*Courtesy of Colin S. Anderson, Esq., London*)

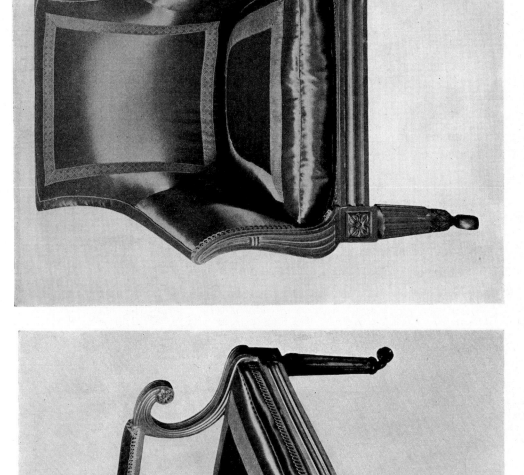

PLATE 46. ARMCHAIR FROM HARTWELL HOUSE

Attributed to Henry Holland, this chair has a reeded and gilded scroll frame and carved flower paterae.

(Courtesy of Felix Harboard, Esq., London)

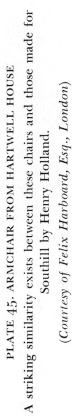

PLATE 45. ARMCHAIR FROM HARTWELL HOUSE

A striking similarity exists between these chairs and those made for Southill by Henry Holland.

(Courtesy of Felix Harboard, Esq., London)

PLATE 47. MODEL OF A REGENCY ROOM

Made in miniature by McMillen, Inc., New York. The miniature portrait was painted by Boutet de Monvel.

(*Courtesy of McMillen, Inc.*)

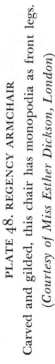

PLATE 49. ROSEWOOD CHAIR

This is one of a pair inlaid with brass which shows the Regency use
of metal and wood.

(Courtesy of P. S. Ralli, Esq., London)

PLATE 48. REGENCY ARMCHAIR

Carved and gilded, this chair has monopodia as front legs.

(Courtesy of Miss Esther Dickson, London)

PLATE 50. A REGENCY DINING-ROOM

The mahogany table is inlaid with brass. The sideboard and chairs are also fine examples of the period.

(Courtesy of the Lord Gerald Wellesley, London)

PLATE 51. AN UNUSUAL REGENCY SIDEBOARD

Standing in the dining-room of 35 Wimpole Street, this sideboard is made of light-colored mahogany with ebony stringing, on a marbleized wood platform supported by carved paw feet. A lead-lined wine cooler forms part of the sideboard's design.

(*Courtesy of Edward F. W. James, Esq., London*)

PLATE 52. A DECORATED REGENCY CUPBOARD

Cameo relief decorates the drawers of this mahogany two-door cupboard.

(Courtesy of Elinor Merrell, New York)

PLATE 53. A REGENCY CABINET OF 1810

This is one of a pair in rosewood and gilt with fine metal grilles.

(Courtesy of Decor, E. S. Boteler, Ltd., New York)

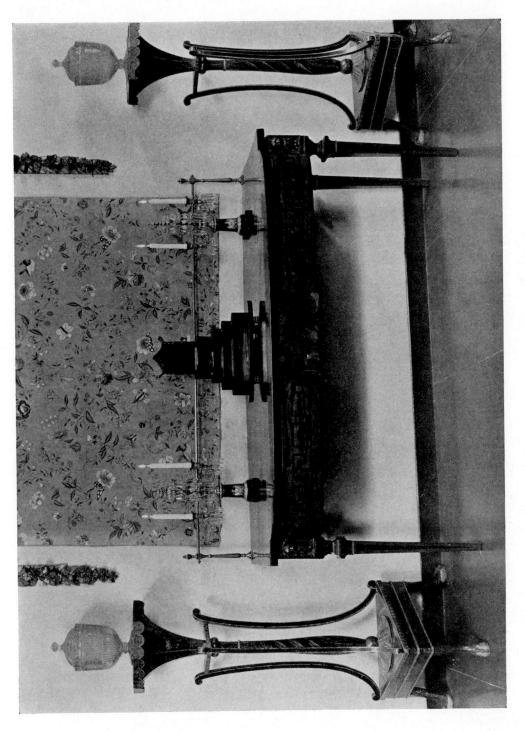

PLATE 54. REGENCY SIDEBOARD AND TORCHÈRES

The mahogany sideboard is inlaid with the wall-of-Troy design. The torchères are painted black and gold.

(Courtesy of Josephine Howell, New York)

PLATE 55. SMALL DINING-ROOM, REGENCY STYLE
The center table and consoles are from the Hope Collection.
(*Courtesy of Edward Knoblock, Esq., London*)

PLATE 56. MAJOR-GENERAL NEIL CAMPBELL BY CARBONNIER, 1818

Major Campbell was the official escort of Napoleon when the Emperor was exiled to Elba. Note the swan chairs, the winged sphinxes on the table, the Greek anthemions at the top of the columns—characteristic motifs both of the French Empire and the English Regency.

(Courtesy of Mrs. Claire Marion-Cox, Datchet-on-Thames)

PLATE 57. THE CORRIDOR AT SATIS HOUSE

Leading to the Regency drawing-room is this formal corridor with a niche, presided over by a bust of Byron.

(Courtesy of Mrs. Claire Marion-Cox, Datchet-on-Thames)

PLATE 58. REGENCY LYRE FURNITURE

These decorative pieces form part of the furnishings of Lady Diana Cooper's drawing-room.

(*Courtesy of Sibyl Colefax, London*)

PLATE 59. THE REGENCY DRAWING-ROOM OF LADY DIANA COOPER

(Courtesy of Sibyl Colefax, London)

PLATE 60. REGENCY ROOM AT THE HOVE MUSEUM

Reconstructed to represent a period room of 1810–1825. The walls are painted green; the curtains are green and ecru striped silk. A writing desk, a harp, a couch, and some fine Regency portraits are used in the decoration.

(*Courtesy of the Hove Museum, Sussex*)

PLATE 61. REGENCY SIDE TABLE

Mahogany with brass bands, the tassels are carved and gilt.

(Courtesy of W. & J. Sloane, New York)

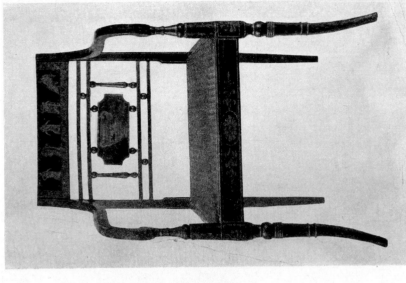

PLATE 63. ARMCHAIR BY RICHARD
SMIRKE (1778–1815)
Classic designs are painted in terra cotta on
a brown-black ground.

*(Courtesy of Mrs. Johnson, Bowden Hall,
Alsager, Cheshire)*

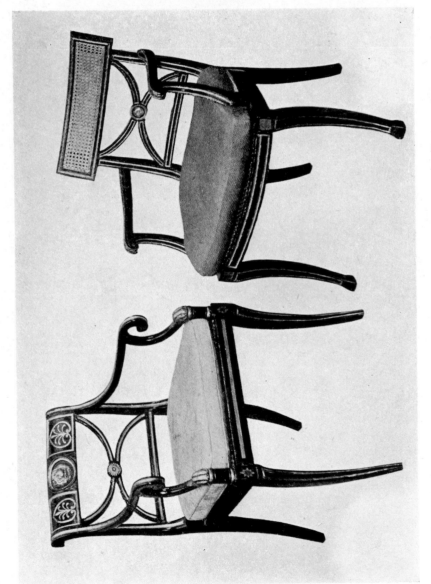

PLATE 62. CANE-SEATED ARMCHAIRS
These Regency armchairs are decorated in black and gold.
(Courtesy of John A. Pearson, Esq., London)

PLATE 64. REGENCY CABINET AND CHAIR

The cabinet has carved Egyptian figures as supports. The chair is inlaid maple.

(Courtesy of Daniel H. Farr Co., New York)

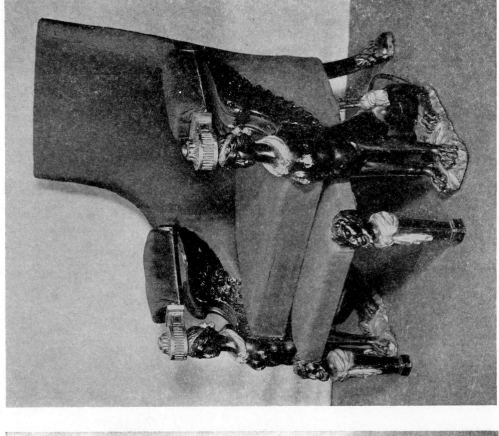

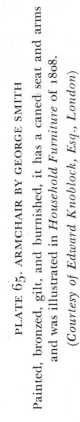

PLATE 66. MAYORAL CHAIR OF RAMSGATE

This chair was made for a state visit of George IV.

(*Courtesy of Montague Marcussen, Esq., London*)

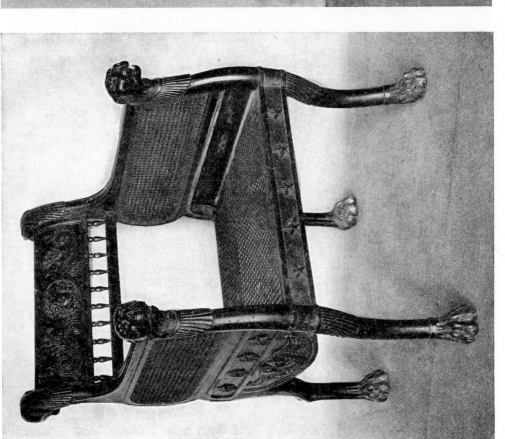

PLATE 65. ARMCHAIR BY GEORGE SMITH

Painted, bronzed, gilt, and burnished, it has a caned seat and arms
and was illustrated in *Household Furniture* of 1808.

(*Courtesy of Edward Knoblock, Esq., London*)

PLATES 68 AND 69. REGENCY GRATES

Above is a sarcophagus-grate of steel and polished brass; below a hob-grate of steel with chased-brass mounts.

(Courtesy of the Brothers Brothers, New York)

PLATE 67. LIBRARY GRATE OF HOLME HOUSE

The basket-grate with recessed overmantel adds much to the charm of this room.

(Courtesy of Honorable Mrs. Pleydell Bouverie, London)

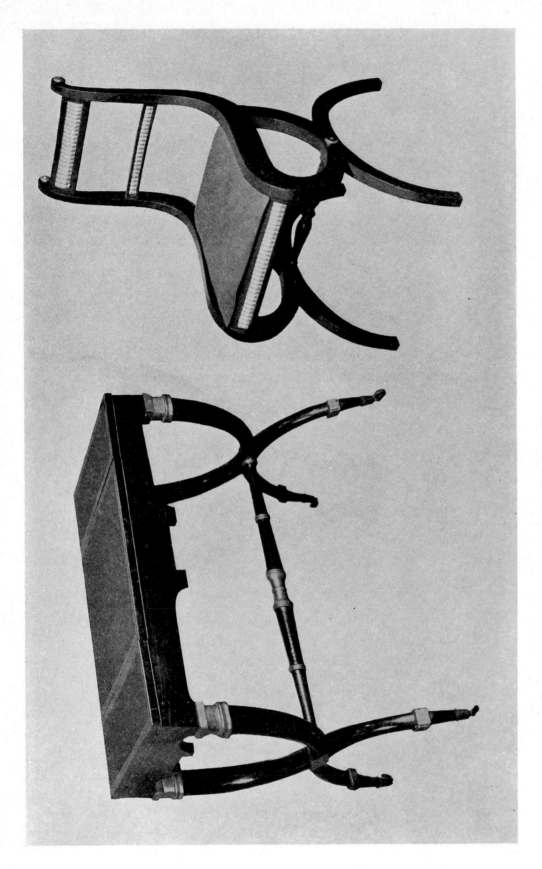

PLATE 70. PAINTED WRITING TABLE AND CHAIR

The writing table, of beech painted black with gilt ornaments, has its top cross-banded with rosewood and inlaid with a stringing of box. The chair is one of a set of eight side chairs painted black and gold with cane seats and loose cushions.

(Courtesy of John A. Pearson, Ltd., London, and of the Hon. Katherine Norton, London)

PLATES 71 AND 72. PAINTED REGENCY COUCH AND TOLE URNS

The black-and-gold couch above has saber legs and a rolled head; the urns are also painted black and gold.

(Courtesy of Decor, E. S. Boteler, Ltd., New York, and of James Pendleton, New York)

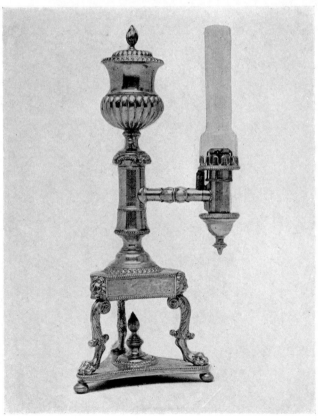

PLATE 73. SMALL DRESSING
MIRROR

This mirror, painted black and gold,
was made to stand on a chest of
drawers.

*(Courtesy of James Pendleton,
New York)*

PLATE 74. A FINE SILVER-PLATED
ARGAND BURNER

*(Courtesy of Robert Ensko, Inc.,
New York)*

PART TWO

DUNCAN PHYFE

V

THE CLASSIC REVIVAL IN AMERICA

In America at the outset of the nineteenth century there were no trained architects like Holland, Soane, and Nash. Thomas Jefferson and George Washington were the first leaders in American styles. Jefferson, who became President of the United States in 1801, was desirous of forming the taste of his countrymen by familiarizing them with classic models. He wrote to Major l'Enfant: "When it is proposed to prepare plans for the Capitol, I should prefer the adoption of some one of the models of antiquity, which have had the approbation of thousands of years."

Jefferson's plan for the Richmond capitol is often cited as the first use in America of the temple as a model for a public building. This antedates the building of the Madeleine in Paris by twenty-two years. Due to his study of French architecture during his term as French Minister in 1794, and due also to his interest in the work of the French architects who were making their homes in America, the classic style favored by Jefferson was largely that of Rome as seen by the French.

The same revolution in architecture that took place in England developed in America at the beginning of the nineteenth century and there was a general adoption of classic styles throughout the country. At the time of Jefferson's administration, the most important public building under consideration was the Capitol at Washington. It is difficult to say whether the President spent more time on questions of State or on the erection of this building. He was, to be sure, the founder of the Democratic party, but he was also the designer of Monticello and of the University of Virginia, and architecture played a large part in his life.

The building of the Capitol had been the subject of a competition in 1792. Dr. William Thornton, an architect living in the West Indies, wrote asking permission to compete. His plans were judged the best of all those submitted. They were approved by President Washington in 1793. The second-best designs were those of the Frenchman Stephen Hallet, who was placed as Thornton's assistant, in charge of construction.

After Thornton's death, Jefferson appointed as Surveyor of Public Buildings Benjamin Henry Latrobe, recently arrived from England. Latrobe was a trained architect who had passed his "seven long years" in the office of Mr. Cockerell, then considered the best of his profession in England. On his American début he distinguished himself by building the Bank of Pennsylvania in Philadelphia and by designing an elaborate plan for the city water supply. He brought with him from abroad the newly awakened enthusiasm for classical architecture, introducing Greek as well as Roman forms into his work. Latrobe was followed as architect of the Capitol by a young Bostonian, an enthusiast of classic style named Charles Bulfinch, a graduate of Harvard, who had been sent to travel in France while Jefferson was Minister there.

Bulfinch was a self-taught architect. Starting as an amateur, he developed into a professional of wide practice. While Jefferson's designs were monumental, Bulfinch preferred slender and refined types with much delicate detail that was reminiscent of Adam. He had, however, a splendid sense of monumental composition, as he proved in his design for the Boston State House, enthroned on Beacon Hill, which in 1800 was the most conspicuous building in the United States.

He is better known today for his public than for his private work, but he designed many simple dwelling houses that introduced important reforms in architecture. He is reputed, for example, to have built the first curved staircases used in New England. He introduced circular and oval rooms that bowed out the fronts of houses in a swelling line. He designed the circular portico afterwards used in the White House. Among the homes known to be his work are the Joseph Barrell house in Charlestown, Massachusetts, a house for Joseph Coolidge in Bowdoin Street, Boston, one for Elias Hasket Derby in Salem, which was later modified by McIntire, two Harrison Gray Otis houses, one on Mount Vernon Street and the other at 45 Beacon Street. The lovely house at Orford, New Hampshire, built for General John Wheeler in 1820 is attributed to Bulfinch, and also the Phelps house at Andover, Massachusetts, built between 1809 and 1812.

Bulfinch has been called our first practising architect. He did not, like earlier builders, use model plans from the handbooks of the time. He was not a craftsman of the building trade, but created designs in his own mind and made sketches and working plans for builders to follow.

Samuel McIntire of Salem was his immediate and most successful disciple. This famous member of a famous family was born in 1757 in a simple

PLATE 75. A STAIRCASE OF 1810

These graceful "flying stairs" are in the House of History, Kinderhook.

(*Courtesy of James E. Leath*)

CHARLES BULFINCH
1763 — 1844
BY MATHER BROWN
DEPOSITED BY MISS ELLEN S. BULFINCH

PLATE 76. CHARLES BULFINCH, ARCHITECT

This portrait by Mather Brown was described by Bulfinch as "very rough . . . in the modish style introduced by Sir Joshua Reynolds."

(*Courtesy of the Massachusetts Historical Society*)

dwelling built by his father who was a housewright. He learned his father's trade in his father's shop. Beginning modestly as an unpretentious carver and designer, he developed his genius along architectural lines and ended by practically rebuilding the city of Salem. Although he was self-educated, he had "the blood and the traditions of the craftsman to build on." His

PLATE 77. ORIGINAL DESIGN BY BULFINCH
(*Courtesy of R. T. Haines Halsey, Esq.*)

houses are notable for their fine proportions and beautiful workmanship, for their entrances with slender columns, and for their gracefully carved friezes, mantels, and door casings. McIntire was the first architect to use square fence posts with delicate pilasters, surmounted by urns. Records and bills that still exist in the Essex Institute prove that McIntire often carved bed-posts, sofas, and chairs for the various cabinetmakers of Salem. There is, however, no actual proof that he made furniture himself, although many of the pieces carved by him are known as "McIntire furniture."

In the fine houses designed and built by McIntire, much of the best carving, especially that of mantels, was done by his own hand. Overdoors and large panel decorations he frequently made in French putty, molded in his own designs and applied. Certain motifs are so characteristic of his work that they are looked for almost as hallmarks. One of these is the basket of fruit or flowers which is found on the top rails of settees as well as on mantels and overdoors.

Another important person in the architectural world at this time was Asher Benjamin, who also lived in Salem. His contribution to the life of the day was considerable for, in addition to being a practising architect, he

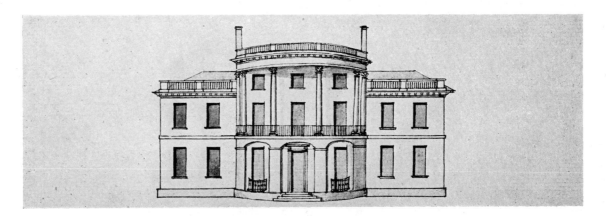

PLATE 78. ORIGINAL DESIGN BY BULFINCH
(*Courtesy of R. T. Haines Halsey, Esq.*)

modified and adapted the elements of the classic styles and made them available to builders throughout the country by his publication of five architectural books. His most popular book was perhaps the *Builder's Companion, or a System of Architecture Particularly Adapted to the Present Day of Building,* published in 1806. Another was *The Builder's Guide, or Complete System of Architecture.* Still a third was called *The Architect or Practical House Carpenter.* These books are certainly the best records of the architecture of the time by a man of the period. They were eagerly read and used by small builders throughout the country.

These three men, Bulfinch, McIntire, and Asher Benjamin, built into American tradition the same architectural ideas that prevailed abroad—emphasizing the adoption of classic forms to the uses and needs of modern life.

James Hoban, an Irish architect who settled in Charleston before the Revolution, was noted for his work on the White House in Washington. He went there in 1792 and was employed on the public buildings for more than twenty-five years. When the White House was burned by the British in 1812, he rebuilt it; he also assisted in superintending the construction of the Capitol from Thornton's plans.

It is worth while reviewing the list of some of the fine and charming houses built at this time in different parts of this country. There was the Wilson Glover house, built in 1800, in Charleston; the Sweat house, Portland, Maine, built in 1800 by Alexander Parris, architect for Hugh Mc-Lennan; the Burd house, built in Philadelphia in 1801; Homewood, Baltimore, 1801; the Samuel Cook Oliver house, built in Salem in 1804 by Mc-

PLATE 79. ORIGINAL DESIGN BY BULFINCH
(*Courtesy of R. T. Haines Halsey, Esq.*)

Intire; the John Gardner house, Salem, by McIntire, 1805; the House of History, Kinderhook, 1806; the Waln house, Philadelphia, by Benjamin Latrobe, 1807; the Markoe house, Philadelphia, by Latrobe, 1808; Hyde Hall, built in 1811, on the shores of Otsego Lake, by Philip Hooker of Cooperstown, New York; Ampthill, Virginia, by Jefferson, 1815; Bremo, Virginia, designed by Jefferson in 1815 for John Hartwell Cock and begun in 1818; the Marshall house, Rodman's Neck, New York, built about 1820; the Martin Baum house, Cincinnati, 1820.

In Savannah, Georgia, are some extremely interesting houses of the Regency period, designed by an English architect, William Jay, who was brought up in Bath. His grandfather had worked as a stone-mason on the famous Fonthill Abbey, William Beckford's Gothic home. His father was a clergyman, but young William preferred architecture to archangels, so he apprenticed to an architect in London. Before his three-year apprenticeship had terminated, however, when he was but twenty-three years old, he left London to pay a visit to his sister who had married Robert Bolton, a cotton merchant of Savannah. Arriving in this city in 1817, he found the opportunity to build several important houses which show great imagination and versatility in design. The Thomas house (Plate 81) is one of the delightful examples of his work. Others are Scarborough House, the Savannah Theatre, the Bullock house, the Telfair house, and the United States Bank.

James S. Buckingham, an English traveler and lecturer who came to Savannah in 1840, said: "There are many handsome and commodious buildings occupied as private residences and a few mansions built by an English architect, Mr. Jay, which are of beautiful architecture, with sumptuous interiors, and combine as much of elegance and luxury as are to be found in any dwellings in the country."

Charleston, in South Carolina, also has many fine dwellings dating from this period. So many of its eighteenth-century buildings had been destroyed by fire, flood, tropical storms, and earthquakes that the city was of necessity almost entirely rebuilt in the early nineteenth century. The most gifted architect of this day was Gabriel Manigault, who in 1790 built the Joseph Manigault house. In 1801 he designed the building now used as the Charleston City Hall, in 1802 the Charleston Orphan House Chapel, and in 1804 the South Carolina Society Hall. When a new era of prosperity began after the War of 1812, many fine churches were erected in Charleston and dwelling houses were built on classic models, reflecting the ideas both of France and England.

The Regency or Greco-Roman phase that inspired these buildings was of short duration, for about 1815 the so-called "Greek Revival" movement came into force and swept the country. Nicholas Biddle is said to have made the profound remark, "There are but two great truths in the world—the Bible and Greek architecture." Every state of the Union broke out into Greek temples: the infection spread as if it were the smallpox. All types of buildings, whether private or public, church or dwelling house, were erected on the same model. Still standing in the South, in the Middle West, in the North, and in New England are many examples of this style.

86

PLATE 80. THE TAFT MUSEUM, 1820

The house was built in 1820 for Martin Baum and is an interesting example of the architecture
of the period.

(Presented to the City of Cincinnati by Mr. and Mrs. Charles P. Taft)

PLATE 81. THE THOMAS HOUSE, SAVANNAH, GEORGIA

Built in Regency style by William Jay, an English architect.

*(Courtesy of Miss Margaret Thomas, Mr. John Mead Howells, and the Magazine of
Interior Design)*

With the Greek Revival came an influx of marble mantels, which up to this time had been somewhat of a rarity in America. There is a record that Samuel Vaughan of England sent a fine Adam mantel of marble as a present to George Washington, who declared: "I greatly fear it is too elegant and costly for my room and my Republican style of living." This mantel, however, is in the banquet hall at Mount Vernon, where it doubtless took the place of a wooden mantel.

Because furniture and architecture always keep step, it was natural for the furnishings of the day to reflect the ideas exemplified in the buildings which were to contain them, so our cabinetmakers became neoclassicists as well as the architects. The styles they evolved in the nineteenth century were nothing more nor less than American Regency. They have been variously called Post-Colonial, Federal, and Styles of the Early Republic. After all, names are of little moment. The important thing is that the Regency ideas which swayed England had also a full and complete development in this country. Mr. Charles Messer Stowe, commenting on Margaret Jourdain's book on Regency furniture in the New York *Sun* on March 2, 1935, remarked: "It is strange that so little attention has been paid to Regency styles in this country. Generally speaking, in making attributions, students skip from Sheraton to Victorian, not remembering that a period of great importance came in between." In the same article Mr. Stowe noted: "One of the best workers in the Regency style was our own Duncan Phyfe, who may be credited with developing in this country the equivalent of the current mode in England."

Edgar G. Miller, Jr., refers to this paragraph in his book, *American Antique Furniture,* and adds:

In some of our Grecian sofas illustrated in this section, certain features of the French Directory style are noticed, and in the English book referred to are illustrations of several Grecian sofas with the same distinctive features; these sofas . . . are apparently regarded in England as being in the English Regency style. It thus appears that the American cabinet-makers who made furniture with these features must have invented the features or followed either the French Directory designs or the English Regency designs. The similarity could not have been accidental.

Mr. Stowe and Mr. Miller are almost the only American writers on historical styles who have recognized the existence of a Regency period in American furniture. A slight reference to it is made in the third series of

89

Colonial Interiors, dealing with the Federal period and the Greek Revival. The authors, Harold Eberlein and Cortlandt Hubbard, "invite attention, now more generally favorable than heretofore, to the many excellencies of the Regency or Federal manner that commend it to contemporary regard."

Walter Storey says:

The similarity between English Regency and French Directoire furniture, which were practically contemporary, is due mainly to the fact that they had a common source and were directed by a similar trend—the interest of the civilized world in Greek and Roman design. . . . But into the Regency style came other motifs, not always used with success. The simple, direct concept of classic art to which Robert Adam limited himself in designing houses, furniture and room decoration was replaced by a confused experimentation with Gothic, Moorish, Egyptian, and Oriental fashions. In the American furniture of the Federal period, which was less fanciful, more simply ornamented and which followed mainly the Roman-Grecian inspiration, the real charm of the Regency style is often discerned.

VI

HIMSELF

With great pride the *New York Directory* in 1805–1806 announced that the city "is upwards of two miles in length and from half a mile to two miles in breadth," housing a population of "at least 70,000 souls."

This year there was an innovation in the *Directory*—the various trades were classified and listed in groups. "This improvement," says the editor,

PLATE 82. MAHOGANY WINDOW SEAT

Caned seat, cabriole legs, brass paw feet. Exquisite care is shown in the details of carving and reeding.

(Courtesy of the Metropolitan Museum of Art)

91

"was in contemplation last year but . . . could not be completed in season for the publication."

So for the first time the cabinetmakers of New York appear in a body. By way of introduction, the remark is made: "This curious and useful mechanical art is brought to a very great perfection in this city. The furniture daily offered for sale equals in point of elegance any ever imported from Europe and is scarce equalled in any other city in America."

Little information is to be gleaned about any of the individual firms, except the testimony furnished by the work of their hands. Often it is more than difficult to identify this work and make correct attributions, due to the fact that all cabinetmakers of the day used similar patterns, "borrowed" unhesitatingly any ideas that were fashionable, and seldom troubled to put their names on furniture made by them. It is therefore of greatest interest to find a piece that is accurately labeled, or a bill that verifies an article so completely as to leave no room for doubt.

Outstanding among the furniture makers of this period is Duncan Phyfe, the Scotchman, who dwelt and worked in New York for more than sixty years. Since he had one of the largest establishments and made much of the finest furniture for the wealthy families of New York, Philadelphia, New Jersey, and the South, it is not surprising that we have more facts about him than about many of his contemporaries, yet, on the whole, the information is singularly sterile when we consider that he lived to be eighty-six years old and spent all but twenty of those years not only in the same city but in the same house.

Family records tell us that Duncan *Fife,* as the name was spelled in the old country, was born in Loch Fannich, Scotland, about thirty miles from Inverness in the year 1768. It is a bleak, dour country, where the sheep that Duncan's father tended must have had difficulty in finding enough nourishment to live, and it is so remote from any great houses or from any center of manufacture that Duncan himself must have had difficulty in finding inspiration there for what was to be his lifework.

From data furnished by a member of the family, I have learned that the parish church in the district where Duncan's family lived was completely destroyed by fire, with all its records, but, in the attempt to uncover facts that might contribute something additional to the meager information that we now possess about our most illustrious nineteenth-century cabinetmaker,

PLATE 83. SATINWOOD CARD TABLE

This rare example of Phyfe's work is an albino among his mahogany masterpieces. It has a clover-leaf top, brass edge, carved vase support, and tripod stand with brass paw feet.

(*Courtesy of Ginsburg and Levy*)

PLATES 84 AND 85. PIANOFORTE
DATED 1815 AND STOOL

The action was made by John Geib, Jr.;
the carved mahogany case, trestle, and
stool by Duncan Phyfe.

*(Courtesy of the Mabel Brady Garvan
Collection, Gallery of Fine Arts,
Yale University)*

my friend Mr. Frank Donald of Dundee offered to undertake an expedition into the Fife country. On May 31, 1938, he wrote me the following lively account of his investigations:

On Friday afternoon we left in my car for Inverness and the North, where we stayed till Monday morning. Today, Tuesday, I have been in Edinburgh, visiting the Register House, and making all sorts of inquiries, and the upshot of it all is, I can find no trace or record of the family from which Duncan Fife sprung.

You see, it is all so long ago. The Records at Register House only go back to 1778, some ten or eleven years after Duncan Fife was born, according to the information in your letter, and, as you can very well understand, these records to begin with, would be of a very incomplete order. Mr Paton at the Register House was most anxious to be helpful and tried to trace if Fife was a well-known name in Ross-shire, in which county Loch Fannich lies, but a reference to old wills and titles shed no light on that, either. From many enquiries made in the neighbourhood of Loch Fannich and in Inverness, the name Fife is practically unknown, although an old residenter in Inverness told me he thought he remembered the name in his early days. This I may confirm at a later date.

Loch Fannich is, as you say, about thirty miles from Inverness, but the last nine miles of the way are on a private road leading only to Loch Fannich Lodge, which, incidentally, requires very careful driving.

Our first call was on the minister at Loch Luichart. He was a young man, with only eight years of the ministry behind him—a Highlander, but from the Island of Lewis. He sent us on to the gamekeeper at Loch Fannich Lodge, one Angus, by name. We soon told him of our quest, and, to make it quite clear, read part of your letter and then he was all interest and excitement. Angus proved a most interested and intelligent man, with quite a sense of humor. But he had never heard of a Fife living near Loch Fannich. He told us, however, to call on another gamekeeper, again near Loch Luichart, on another estate—one Sandy McLennan, who perhaps knew more than anyone of the old residents around these parts. Sandy was away. Our next call was on a Miss MacKenzie, the registrar for the district, at Garve. We were of course told by her that her records did not go back anything like so far; no records went back so far, but her mother (and Miss MacKenzie was quite an aged woman), and her grandmother and her great-grandmother had all lived in the neighbourhood, and she had never heard anyone speak of a family called Fife.

Some records were held by a minister in Strathpeffer we were told and so we went to him. He was an old man, and, I imagine, was busy preparing his sermon for the next day, but he took us down to the church and showed us his oldest books, very quaint, but none dating back in the eighteenth century.

We meant to return home on Sunday, but were not satisfied. We both felt we would like to have a talk with Sandy McLennan, and so decided to have another day

95

PLATE 86. PIANOFORTE BY GIBSON AND DAVIS

Their stamp reads "New York from London." The mahogany case and acanthus-carved trestle were
made by Duncan Phyfe.

(From the collection of Mrs. John W. Castles, Jr.)

up the Glen, our first objective being an old graveyard at Achanalt, the nearest graveyard to Loch Fannich. It was an old and very neglected place and many of the stones, *"recumbent tombs of the dead in desert places,"* had no inscriptions on them at all. We searched about and took a picture, but we learned nothing, at least, that shed any light on the family of Fife.

The name *Fife* is not a Highland name. That in itself is puzzling. Men from Fife—"Fife Adventurers," they were called—made history in the Island of Lewis, and one of the families may have drifted down to Loch Fannich, but then the name of Fife would be only a patronymic. It is all very puzzling and all very intriguing and I am by no means finished yet. I have ever so many friends helping me and "feelers" out in quite a number of directions and have still the press to tap, also Dr Watson, professor of Celtic at Edinburgh University.

We may in the end discover that our man was actually *Duncan of Fife*.

Sent by Mr. Donald for my files is a letter from the Public Record Office in Chancery Lane, London, saying that their returns from the Scottish ports were discontinued in 1776, when emigration had practically ceased.

Mr. G. W. O'Keefe, Assistant Collector of the Port of New York, informs me that our earliest American record of vessel arrivals is dated October 5, 1789, and the earliest passenger lists are for the year 1820.

The Registrar of Births at Strathpeffer, Scotland, writes that he has no records prior to 1855.

Dr. Watson, Professor of Celtic at Edinburgh University, states that the name Fife is quite unknown to him in the North, either as a surname or as a patronymic. He says:

One might conjecture that it might have been given as a by-name to a man who had been in Fife for harvest work—the north country folk often went south for the harvest. My own grand-aunts used to go to Lothian for that purpose, and Gaelic poetry refers to the custom. The Old Statistical Account of the parish of Fodderty notes "the want of employment here forces those who are industriously inclined to go and find labour in the southern districts of Scotland; so that great numbers of both sexes leave their homes in the months of May and June, and return again in November." Fodderty is next to Contin, in which Fannich is situated (vol. vii, published in 1793).

Mr. Paton of the Register Office in Edinburgh, with every desire to be of assistance, is unable to contribute information other than the fact that no register was kept in the Highlands prior to 1778.

However disappointing the result of these inquiries may be, they have a certain negative value in eliminating the possibilities of certain sources of information.

PLATE 87. SMALL SECRETARY-DESK

This satinwood desk, *circa* 1805–1810, has characteristic turned feet and reeded legs, ivory knobs, inlays, and borders of rosewood.

(Courtesy of Mr. and Mrs. Andrew Varick Stout)

I had hoped, through these investigations, to find something that would indicate that Duncan as a lad was apprenticed in Edinburgh, or in one of the other large cities, to learn the trade of cabinetmaker, before leaving Scotland. But his boyhood history is completely unknown and we must depend on family tradition for the beginning of his life in America.

He and his numerous brothers and sisters, together with his widowed mother, left their native land in 1784, when he was sixteen, to come on a sailing vessel to America. The long and tedious voyage was not without sad results. One of the children, perhaps unable to support the rigors of travel as a "deck-passenger," died and was buried at sea. She was Duncan's favorite sister, Isabella, for whom he later named his youngest daughter. On their arrival in this country, the Fifes went directly to Albany, New York, which was one of the important cities of the Hudson River, rich, prosperous, and flourishing. To account for their choice of a dwelling place, Mr. Thomas Ormsbee advances the supposition that they may have had relatives in that city—possibly survivors from the Scotch regiments that served under Burgoyne during the war of the Revolution. It would be interesting if proof could be found to support this theory. In Albany, at any rate, young Duncan was apprenticed to work at the cabinetmaker's trade, and after a time went into business for himself, in a small shop in State Street. After six years' training and experience, he screwed his courage to the sticking point and moved to New York.

When Duncan decided to come down the river, he had his choice of four different means of transportation. He could have done the hundred and fifty miles on foot. He could have made the trip on horseback. He could have come by packet boat, sailing when there was wind, drifting along when there was none, stopping at countless small docks and yards on both sides of the river to unload or to take on cargo. But I feel certain that such methods were far too slow and tedious for him on this particular occasion. Surely he would have preferred to travel by fast stagecoach. Was he not on his way to the capital of the United States to open a business there?

So it is most likely that for three days he bumped along over rough roads, faring forth at five o'clock each morning and traveling until ten o'clock at night. For this he paid fourpence a mile. The stage carried fourteen pounds of baggage for him free. It could not be called luxurious traveling. The discomfort, the dust, the flies were almost unbearable. Duncan must

99

PLATE 88. DRAWING-ROOM OF THE LATE CHARLES OVER CORNELIUS

The two Phyfe armchairs harmonize well with the background of classic architectural motifs. The Regency window draperies hang from poles surmounted by eagles.

have been thoroughly delighted when his lumbering conveyance finally rattled into the streets of the city and drew up at the door of Fraunces Tavern. I can imagine him stretching his stiff limbs as he descended from his seat, with a pitying glance at the voyagers gathered there to set out the next morning for Boston or Philadelphia. They little knew what was in store for them!

Duncan's first task was to discover a suitable shop for himself, and in looking about he got his initial glimpses of New York. He soon found that most of the cabinetmakers were clustered together in one part of the city. Their warehouses and places of business were in Beekman Street, Pearl Street, Chambers, Mott, Broad, Cortlandt, Roosevelt, William, John, and Cherry Streets. Naturally, then, he concentrated his search in this district for a place to carry on his trade. He finally engaged a small workshop on Broad Street, sent for his brother to join him, and felt that he had at last become a part of the busy capital of the nation.

One could not go far in this city without realizing what opportunities it offered for businesses associated with culture and gracious living. Since the inauguration of Washington the previous year and the establishment of the seat of government there, great changes had taken place. Fine homes were building; the city was rapidly expanding. Even so young a man as Duncan (he was only twenty-two) could not fail to appreciate what this meant in a commercial sense.

New York was intensely interesting. It was much more of a city than Albany. The streets were wider. Some of them had footways, paved, with a curb to separate them from the road. They were not broad enough, however, to protect pedestrians from being splashed with mud when an occasional horse-drawn vehicle drove by, and it was the custom for ladies to take precipitant refuge on the steps of the nearest dwelling, their skirts held tightly, until the danger was past.

The finest homes were of brick or stone, with roofs of slate or tile. Duncan learned that south of Broome Street this construction was required by law for any edifice over two stories high, in the attempt to prevent destructive fires from which the city had already suffered greatly and from which other severe ravages were still to occur. Many low structures of wood still existed in the less prosperous districts, where no footwalks had yet been made and where it seemed the custom to deposit all refuse from the houses openly in the streets, leaving disposal of it to the pigs that ran loose. Duncan heard that it had even been necessary to drive some of these animals out of the way of the inaugural procession so that President Washington's yellow coach might pass without running over them!

In the harbor swarmed a great multitude of sailing vessels of all sorts, arriving at the docks or leaving the roadstead. Yawls, brigs, sloops, schooners, Atlantic packets, merchantmen, East Indiamen, smacks, hoys, coastwise boats, and barkentines crowded the busy port, "the reason why so much business could be done without noise and without wagons."*

Federal Hall, on the northeast corner of Wall and Nassau Streets was the most pretentious building in the city. It had just been altered by Major l'Enfant, a Frenchman, to permit its use by the Federal Government—indeed it was not entirely completed when Duncan saw it for the first time. And before long he heard that the moneys raised by taxation for alterations had already been expended, and that £13,000 more were required to finish the construction. A vast sum, indeed! The city was unable to provide it. Two lotteries were organized to carry on the work with tickets at forty shillings apiece. Such a sum was undoubtedly prohibitive to a canny Scot starting in business though he may have wished he had risked it when the grand prize was awarded in the first lottery, for a sum equivalent to $3,000 was won by two young girls who held a ticket purchased with savings from their laboriously earned pittances.

It was somewhat surprising to hear that Major l'Enfant, in payment for his work on this important building, received merely the freedom of the city, the thanks of the Corporation, and, lastly, ten acres of Provost's land on the Post Road, occupying a situation which is now Third Avenue between Sixty-eighth and Sixty-ninth Streets. L'Enfant did not particularly appreciate the gift of land; he petitioned for a sum of money, instead, and was then offered $750, which he politely declined.

Duncan's Scotch sense of economy was severely shocked to find that, in spite of all the money it had cost, Federal Hall was grossly neglected and gradually allowed to fall into decay. Twenty-two years later he saw it razed to the ground. Partial explanation for this lay in the change of plans of the Government. Preparations had begun to make New York the permanent capital. A magnificent Government House was in course of erection at the

* St. John de Crèvecoeur, *Letters from an American Farmer* (1787).

102

PLATE 89. SERVING TABLE

This Sheraton-style table has a bow front with three drawers, and stands on turned legs which end in carved wooden paws.

(*Courtesy of Ginsburg and Levy*)

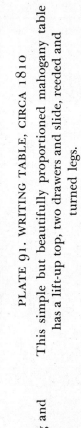
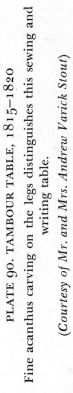

PLATE 91. WRITING TABLE, CIRCA 1810

This simple but beautifully proportioned mahogany table
has a lift-up top, two drawers and slide, reeded and
turned legs.

(Courtesy of Allan B. A. Bradley)

PLATE 90. TAMBOUR TABLE, 1815–1820

Fine acanthus carving on the legs distinguishes this sewing and
writing table.

(Courtesy of Mr. and Mrs. Andrew Varick Stout)

foot of Broadway, on the site of old Fort George, destined to be the residence of all future Presidents. But the city hesitated to deed the ten square acres demanded by Congress, and stoutly refused to give up its port taxes for the support of a resident government. Suddenly Congress announced that it had selected Philadelphia as the capital of the nation, and all the government officials left New York, bag and baggage.

Duncan saw them go with dire misgivings. Had he made a mistake in settling here? The business that he hoped for had not yet come to his doors. It was one thing to be at the heart of a nation; but what would it mean to continue working in a city which the Government had disdained? Perhaps he might better return to Albany.*

The outlook was not as dark as it seemed, however, for here was a city of more than fifty thousand souls situated with every advantage for the development of commerce. Already it had some luxurious dwellings like the Franklin house, where Washington had lived during the inauguration ceremonies. The Walton house, at 324 Pearl Street, was still finer. Five windows wide, built of yellow Holland brick, it was an example of the best type of English construction of the day. Behind it were beautiful gardens, stretching down to the river. Though he had been so short a time in the city, Duncan doubtless had heard talk of the richness of the furniture in this house, of its massive gold plate, and the splendid entertainments given there. Everyone knew that Admiral Howe had reported to Parliament on his return to England that America could well afford to pay taxes if all the dwellings were like this.

What the city needed most, both for business and for pleasure, was a link with the rest of the country by some easy and practical means of transportation—something better and faster than the stagecoach. Given this, nothing could stop its expansion. Whether capital of the nation or not was a matter of small moment.

At any rate Duncan cast in his lot with the fortunes of New York. For sixty-two years he held fast to this resolution and never regretted it. He grew up with the city. He saw all sorts of wonders come true. The "transportation link" became an actual fact when Robert Fulton and Chancellor Livingston organized the building of the *Clermont,* the first steam-driven vessel to make a successful trip on the Hudson River.

* See Addenda, Hagen's memorandum and my note.

A crowd of curious skeptical sightseers had watched John Fitch try out a small yawl on the Collect Pond in 1797. It was fitted with a new invention —a propeller and paddle wheels—but it did not have much more success than his earlier experiments. Poor fellow! he committed suicide the following year, when he could not find anyone to believe in him.

Fulton was luckier, although like Fitch he made some unsuccessful experiments. It was rumored that in Paris he had hoped to enlist the sympathy of Emperor Napoleon in putting steamboats on the Seine. Like Fitch he had bad luck. His first model broke in two and sank since its construction was too light for the weight of the heavy engine. Unlike Fitch, Fulton did not

PLATE 92. ONE END OF A DINING TABLE

This splendid table came from the Van Loo sale. It is in three sections, the center being plain with straight legs, while the two ends have the four carved colonnettes and pineapples supported by four acanthus-carved feet.

(*Courtesy of Ginsburg and Levy*)

PLATE 93. MAHOGANY DINING TABLE

This fine two-part New York table comes from the estate of Dr. Reginald H. Sayre. The supports
are open, with four colonnettes on bases with four reeded and shaped legs.

(Courtesy of Ginsburg and Levy)

commit suicide—he merely came back to America. From Livingston he obtained money for another experiment and ordered an engine from Boulton and Watts in England which he used in the *Clermont*. This craft was built in the shipyard of Charles Brown on the East River and was launched in the spring of 1807. As she went up the Hudson, with flames and smoke belching from her pine-fed boiler, her paddle wheels churning and her machinery clanking, a farmer was so overcome by the strange sight that he ran to tell his wife that he had seen the Devil on his way to Albany in a sawmill!

Fulton himself said of the trip:

The morning I left New York there were not thirty persons in the city who believed that the boat would ever make one mile per hour or be of the least utility. My steamboat voyage to Albany and back has turned out rather more favorably than I had calculated. The distance between the two cities is one hundred and fifty miles. I ran it up in thirty-two hours and down in thirty. I had a light breeze against me both coming and going, and the voyage has been performed wholly by the power of the steam-

PLATE 94. CHAIRS AND CONSOLE TABLE

Photographed in the apartment of the late Louis Guerineau Myers. The upholstered chair came from the estate of Miss Grace Wilkes, of Washington Square, and is a type unusual in Phyfe's work.

(Courtesy of Mrs. Louis Guerineau Myers)

engine. I overtook many sloops and schooners beating to windward and parted with them as if they had been at anchor. The power of propelling boats by steam is now fully proved.

Wild applause greeted this achievement. Seven years later Paul Svinin, Russian visitor, wrote:

Conceive of a vessel having the appearance of a flat-bottomed frigate; imagine it to be unafraid of storms, independent of wind, careless of foul weather, to move at amazing speed and security and to run on schedule time; within are peace, comfort and the very whims of luxurious living; such is the picture of an American steamboat. If we consider that this marvellous invention of the human mind came into being no more than seven years ago, if we note the improvements that have been made in it since then, and if we anticipate that they will continue at the same rate, we have good cause to suppose that in the near future we shall see such craft crossing the ocean, bringing us treasures from the remotest parts of the world.

Livingston obtained from the New York Legislature a state monopoly of steamboat operation; but this was an unwise check to the development of the new method of transportation and was annulled by the Supreme Court. Within a short period of years the establishment of ferry companies and river and transatlantic steamboats offered facilities previously deemed impossible.

There was one cloud in the sky. The outbreak of yellow fever in New York had never been completely conquered. Every year the scourge returned. Finally in 1822 a fearful epidemic swept the city. At that time the yellow-fever quarantine barrier was put up at Duane Street, and the frightened population fled north to Greenwich Village and to Chelsea. The evil and suffering were not without good results, however, for the city decided to take drastic sanitary measures to wipe out the plague. A pure water supply was one of the first questions dealt with. The streets were properly cleaned. Pigs no longer roamed as scavengers. The rats that came into the lower part of the city from the boats in the harbor were vigilantly exterminated. Every citizen had a large rattrap as part of the equipment of his house. (The inventory of Duncan Phyfe's house in 1854 shows that he still kept and used his.) In addition to these measures, all stagnant pools were done away with. Even the Collect or Fresh Water Pond, the city's chief pleasure rendezvous in winter and summer, was filled up and obliterated. A Board of Health was established. Strenuous measures were necessary, for business was at a standstill. Shops and theaters were closed. Scarcely anyone ventured into the streets for fear of catching the malady.

Gradually the panic subsided, hospitals emptied, the number of deaths decreased, and the city returned to its usual daily occupations. But many of those who had gone uptown to live remained there permanently. Thus the boundaries of the city were carried farther north.

One fine day in 1824 the Marquis de Lafayette and his son, George Washington Lafayette, landed at Castle Clinton (now known as Castle Garden). The old Frenchman was fêted wherever he went, by a people that remembered how he had served as Washington's aide during the war. The presentation table made by John Banks (Plate 190) was but one of many tokens of their esteem. Enthusiasm for everything French was fanned into flames. Having known the misery of the Valley Forge days, Lafayette was much impressed by the prosperity of the country as he now found it—impressed and a little puzzled, too. As one after another of the well-to-do citizens was presented to him, he inquired, "But where are the *people?*"

Still further prosperity came to New York in this decade through the opening of the Erie Canal. "Clinton's Big Ditch," as it was popularly called, was completed in 1825. It established communication by waterway with all the country west of the Appalachian Mountains, and by that time about one third of the nation was located there. It cut down the time of travel between New York and Buffalo from twenty days to six, and gave New York a great advantage over the other principal cities of the Atlantic Coast.

This gigantic project cost something over eight million dollars, but through transportation of freight paid for itself in a surprisingly short time. Canal-boat travel became a popular pastime. Duncan's nephew, James, with a party of friends, made the trip through the Canal in 1831, and kept a diary describing it in detail, even to the accident that occurred when two of the party neglected to heed the warning of "Low Bridge" and were knocked down by the structure under which the boat was passing. Travel on the canal boat was democratic. Everybody was singing Parrington's jingle,

> Low bridge, everybody down!
> Low bridge, we're going through a town.
> You'll always know your neighbor,
> You'll always know your pal
> If you've ever navigated
> On the Erie Canal.

PLATE 95. DRUM TABLE AND EAGLE CHAIRS

The small round table has typical Phyfe dovetailing, carving on the pedestal, etc. The drawers
are lined with American soft white pine and whitewood.

(Courtesy of Mrs. Giles Whiting)

PLATE 96. DINING-ROOM IN THE HOUSE OF HISTORY
The Phyfe chairs and pedestal table were shown here in an exhibition of outstanding New York
furniture.
(Courtesy of James E. Leath)

We know that Duncan played a small part in the celebration of the opening of the Canal in 1825. Colonel William L. Stone, in the official narrative of the occasion, writes that: "Some of the water was placed in an American-made glass bottle to be sent to France as a gift to General Lafayette. The bottle was enclosed in a wooden box or casket, made from a cedar log brought down from Lake Erie in the first canal-boat, the 'Seneca Chief,' and Duncan Phyfe was the man who constructed the casket." He also made the boxes for the medals presented to the President of the United States and other distinguished guests.

The great parade through the New York streets on this occasion included all the city societies. Along with the tailors and the coopers, the butchers, the curriers, pilots, tanners, skinners, boatbuilders, and printers, there was a division of cabinetmakers "who exhibited many beautiful miniature specimens of their art, decorated with flowers and borne by members of the Society. The banners were elegant and appropriate." It would be interesting to know whether Duncan Phyfe contributed to this fête and how he was represented, but there is no record. At all events, the clumsy and heavy craft making its slow voyage along the new waterway suggested a name for Phyfe's later work. He is said by Hagen to have baptized the heavy furniture of his third period, "Canal-boat Styles," and even less lyrically, "Butcher Furniture."

Duncan saw the new City Hall erected by John McComb and Joseph Mangin, with its marble façade and its brownstone back. He saw, too, the first blossoming of art and literature in New York City, and watched the port that was the center of finance and commerce become the center of the Fine Arts, as well.

This was due in large measure to the efforts of Robert Livingston, who, when he was Minister to France in 1801, wrote to his friends in New York suggesting that they should open a subscription to raise a fund for the purchase of statues and paintings. The idea found favor and the American Academy of Fine Arts was formed with Edward Livingston as president. George Prince of Wales (not yet Regent) and the Emperor Napoleon were honorary members, as well as Napoleon's brothers Lucien and Joseph.

Livingston's first act was to procure copies in plaster of some of the best examples of ancient sculpture. This novel idea was the topic of all the dinner tables. The famous Theodosia Burr wrote to her husband:

> I dined with Mrs. Montgomery. The Chancellor has sent her out a list of statues which are to be so exactly imitated in plaster as to leave the difference of material only. The statues are the Apollo Belvedere, Venus de Medici, Laocoön, Antinous and some others. The patriotic citizens are now subscribing to the importation of a set here for the good of the public. If they are really perfect imitations, they will be a great acquisition to the city.

The Academy was opened in Government House near the Battery in 1801, with a collection of twenty-four large volumes of Italian pictures and drawings presented by Napoleon. In 1816 it moved to the New York Institute where it had a gallery for the exhibition of pictures and one for statuary. Some fine portraits were ordered. Sir Thomas Lawrence was commissioned to paint Benjamin West, Vanderlyn did a good likeness of Robert Livingston, and there was also a portrait by Raeburn.

A group of New York portrait painters who developed at this time and created reputations that are as brilliant today as they were a century ago includes John Vanderlyn, who worked with Gilbert Stuart and afterwards studied in Paris for seven years; Gilbert Stuart, who spent twenty years with Benjamin West; and John Trumbull, whose historical paintings in the Capitol at Washington rival his portraits in interest. In addition there is the famous family of Peales, the miniaturist Charles Fraser, and our two inventors, Robert Fulton and Samuel F. B. Morse, who distinguished themselves as painters besides creating the steamboat and the telegraph. Morse in 1826 founded the National Academy of Arts and Design.

Although art and literature scarcely existed in New York prior to 1807, their rise was rapid after this time. Our first man of letters was Washington Irving, who belonged to the Knickerbocker Group that included James Fenimore Cooper and William Cullen Bryant. Edgar Allan Poe is another genius of the early nineteenth century, and surely Noah Webster, whose dictionary appeared in 1825, merits a place in the roster of prominent literary New Yorkers.

Partition Street, near the Common, was the location where Duncan finally decided to settle soon after 1800. This narrow street running east and west between Broadway and the Hudson River got its name because it was then the dividing line between the city and the open country that lay north of it. Here Duncan spent the rest of his life, seeing the city grow away from him, flowing steadily northward in the attempt to find breathing space. Once established, he continued to be the fashionable furniture maker, and clients came from long distances to his shop.

The *New York Directory* shows that, for one reason or another, Duncan altered the spelling of his name. When he arrived in Albany and when he first came to New York, he used the form of the name that was general abroad—*Fife*—and was known as a "joiner." In 1794 he is "Duncan *Phyfe,* cabinet-maker." The new and more unusual spelling apparently did not appeal to his brother John, who was in the grocery business at 30 Barclay Street. With true Scotch stubbornness, this member of the family remained a

PLATE 97. PHYFE'S SALESROOMS AND WORKSHOP

This photograph was taken from an aquarelle made by one of his apprentices. The original
remained in the family until the sale of his grandson's effects in 1921.

(*Courtesy of the Metropolitan Museum of Art*)

Fife until 1800, when his name is found in the *Directory* with the same spelling as Duncan's.

Various facts go to prove that part of the Phyfe family remained in Albany after Duncan and his older brothers came to New York. The 1790
Census records as residents of the first ward of Albany, "Issabella Fife as the
head of a family, with two males under sixteen years of age." The mother
died in 1794. A letter of administration in the office of the County Clerk,
dated August 9 of that year, is granted to "Duncan Phyfe of the City of New

115

York, Cabinet-maker, in the estate of Issabella Fife, lately of the city and county of Albany," who died intestate.

On February 17, 1793, Duncan Phyfe and Rachel Lowzada were married by Dr. John Rodgers in the First Presbyterian Church of the City of New York at 14 to 20 Wall Street.* They had seven children—four sons and three daughters. Tragedy awaited one of the children. Isabella, the youngest daughter, disappeared from a night boat on the Hudson River when she was about sixteen years old; no trace of her was ever found. The other members of the family seem to have led happy and normal lives. Their baptismal records exist in the old files of the First Presbyterian Church.*

PLATE 98. DUNCAN PHYFE: HIS SIGNATURE
The deed from which this photograph was taken is
dated 1853, a year before his death.
(*Courtesy of F. Percy Vail*)

Mary, the oldest daughter, married Capt. Sidney B. Whitlock, who owned clipper ships plying between New York and China. As a widow, Mary went to live in a fine old house in Southbury, Connecticut, with her family. Duncan Phyfe bought the house in 1843, as the old deed attests.* Ten years later he deeded the homestead and the "hundred and ten acres of land more or less" to "Mary Whitlock, widow of Sidney B. Whitlock of Southbury." (Deed recorded, June 29, 1853.)

The Southbury mansion (Plate 101) was originally known as the "Mitchell Mansion." Built by Mitchell S. Mitchell, it is listed in the old

* See Addenda.

116

PLATE 99. EDWARD DUNCAN PHYFE

Edward was the eldest son of Duncan Phyfe. He married Mary F. Westlake and was the grandfather of Herold Rodney Eaton Phyfe.

(Courtesy of F. Percy Vail)

books as "a place of amusement." At one time it had an enormous ballroom on one side, which was later moved away to form a separate mansion. Unfortunately it was destroyed by fire.

Governor English is known to have spent a year in the house and with

PLATES 100 AND 101. MARY PHYFE WHITLOCK AND HER HOUSE
Mary, eldest daughter of Duncan Phyfe, married Capt. Sidney B. Whitlock
and brought up ten children in this house at Southbury,
Connecticut, given her by her father.
(*Courtesy of F. Percy Vail and of Mrs. Alexander Thomson*)

his own hand carved the mantelpieces, the overdoors, and the console brackets of the "flying staircase." Curiously enough, an architect who once visited the Mitchell house after having made measured drawings of a house in Mississippi, discovered that the two houses were absolutely identical. This perhaps would indicate that their plans and details may be found in one of the builders' books of the Greek Revival period.

Now owned by Mr. and Mrs. Alexander Thomson, the Mitchell Mansion has been rebaptized by them "The Pillar House." It is easily identified by the tall columns on the façade. In this house the wedding of Mary's son, Duncan Phyfe Whitlock, and Margaret Ronaldson took place. Two of their

Phyfe cousins, Elizabeth Lane and Jane Forbes Phyfe, were bridesmaids. A charming picture of the wedding party may be seen in Plate 102, with Mary looking like Queen Victoria in a lace cap and flowing black silk gown, seated in state, with her eyes fixed on the wedding cake, which stands on a small Phyfe lyre-end table. Families were sizable in those days. Mary's children numbered ten in all. Some of the old residents of Southbury tell how their illustrious grandfather, Duncan, used to come there to visit and play with them, occasionally staying a week or two at a time.

Duncan also spent much time with another daughter, Eliza, who married William Vail, and settled down in a house in New Market, New Jersey.

PLATE 102. A PHYFE WEDDING

Mary's son, Duncan Phyfe Whitlock, was married in the Southbury house to Margaret Donaldson.
(*Courtesy of Mrs. Norman H. Parke*)

Some of the furniture from Fulton Street went there and afterwards became the property of Eliza's grandson, Mr. F. Percy Vail. This house (Plate 104), like the Southbury mansion, is interesting as an example of the popular Greek Revival style of its day. It is now owned and lived in by Major Van Winkle. During the World War it was headquarters for the Red Cross; the large drawing-room was used for making surgical dressings. A small building on the grounds of this New Market property is popularly regarded as having been the workshop of Duncan Phyfe when he came to visit his family. But I fear that, like many other tales about Duncan, this story is only a myth,

PLATE 103. ELIZA PHYFE VAIL

Duncan's second daughter became the wife of William Vail. Born in 1801, she died in 1890.

(*Courtesy of F. Percy Vail*)

for during Eliza's lifetime the little house was used and lived in by the farmer who had charge of the place. After Eliza's death, when her grandson and his family inherited the estate, Mr. Vail, who also inherited his grandfather's tastes for fine furniture and a measure of his craft, used the farmer's house as a workshop, where he could do over old furniture purchased by him from time to time.

PLATE 104. ELIZA'S HOUSE AT NEW MARKET, NEW JERSEY
Duncan furnished this Greek Revival house for his daughter.
(*Courtesy of F. Percy Vail*)

Leaving New Market, let us go back to New York where young Duncan was busy making his fortune. The Scotch have a saying, "It takes seven years to lay down a business." As a matter of fact, it took this son of Loch Fannich almost twice seven years, but by 1803 he was becoming a man of property. The first real estate purchased by him consisted of two adjoining parcels of land on the southern side of Partition Street, one costing $1,625 and the other, $2,500. These two lots together must have comprised the property known as 35 Partition Street. In 1804, for the sum of $3,500, he bought another lot from Peter De Reimer and in 1807 another dwelling house and lot adjoining for $4,500. All of this indicates his increasing prosperity. By these purchases he became the owner of numbers 33, 34, and 35 Partition Street, used for his warehouses and salesrooms.

He then in 1815 purchased a house across the way to be used as his own

PLATE 106. ELIZA'S MAGAZINE STAND

This small rack for magazines and papers was made by Phyfe for his daughter, Eliza.

(Courtesy of F. Percy Vail)

PLATE 105. PERSONAL POSSESSIONS

The gold spectacles Duncan wore for best, the shell rims for every day. His snuffbox may also be seen on the title page.

(Courtesy of Mrs. J. Bartram Howell)

residence. It was the custom of the day for a merchant or professional man to live above his office, or so close by that he could easily walk home to dinner and return to his occupation without loss of time. Business started about nine-thirty in the morning; the dinner hour was two or three o'clock in the afternoon; by six all business was over for the day. Duncan had only to cross Partition Street to join his family at the dinner hour or at the close of work.

In 1816, when Beekman Slip, Fair Street, and Partition Street were rechristened in honor of Robert Fulton, Phyfe, according to the system of numbering then in vogue, owned the three adjoining houses, 168, 170, and 172 (on the corner of Church Street) and his own residence opposite, number 169. A year later these numbers were changed again—168, 170, 172 became 192, 194, 196, and his own house, 193. A charming aquarelle (Plate 97), made by one of his apprentices, is in the Metropolitan Museum. It shows his salesrooms and his workshop, with their decorative Regency façades.

Phyfe also owned a farm, so one of his great-grandsons tells me, far up town, at 39th Street and Fifth Avenue, and a country place in Brooklyn, consisting of twenty-four lots on Turnpike Road leading from Brooklyn to Flatbush.* To these peaceful rural retreats he retired when in need of rest and country air.

From careful search in the Hall of Records in Brooklyn and in New York and from study of the deeds, it is evident that by 1844 Phyfe was the owner of more than $100,000 worth of property in New York and Brooklyn. In making land investments he followed the example of his famous client John Jacob Astor. Mr. Astor's own house, at the time when Phyfe moved to Partition Street, was at the corner of Broadway and Vesey Street, a small brick mansion filled with furs. The office was on the Vesey Street side, where either Mr. Astor or his wife was always ready to receive customers.

In his successful years, more than a hundred men were employed in the Phyfe workshops on Fulton Street. The business was first conducted under the name of "Duncan Phyfe." By 1837 he had taken his two sons, Michael and James Duncan, into business with him and the fast-growing establishment was known as "Duncan Phyfe and Sons."

With him at this time was also his brother Lauchlin Phyfe who is said to have been the best carver and cabinetmaker in the shop. He apparently

* See Addenda.

123

PLATE 107. MAHOGANY SIDEBOARD AND CELLARETTE

These two pieces of furniture, made by Phyfe, were in his house on Fulton Street at the time of
his death and were appraised together at $20.

(*Courtesy of F. Percy Vail*)

had worked with Robert Fisher of Baltimore from 1807 to 1809, and had become expert in his craft. In Duncan's will there is a curious bequest to this brother of the sum of $420 yearly, "to be paid in half-yearly payments."* It suggests that Lauchlin did not have the usual Scotch ability to hold fast

PLATE 108. MINIATURE SHAVING STAND
Duncan Phyfe himself made this stand for his
grandchildren after retiring from business.
(*Courtesy of F. Percy Vail*)

to money, and that Duncan took all possible precautions against extravagance. Nevertheless Lauchlin worked for the firm for several years and made a number of trips abroad to select brasses for furniture, so his brother must have had more confidence in his taste than in his thrift.

After the death of Michael, in 1840, the name of the business became "Duncan Phyfe and Son." Edward Duncan, the son who married Mary Francis Westlake, does not seem to have taken any active interest in his father's work.

The Phyfe name in the *New York Directory & Register* was becoming increasingly important.

* See Addenda.

125

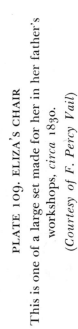

PLATE 110. ELIZA'S BEDROOM TABLE

This useful mahogany stand has three drawers and
a bottom shelf.

(*Courtesy of F. Percy Vail*)

PLATE 109. ELIZA'S CHAIR

This is one of a large set made for her in her father's
workshops, *circa* 1830.

(*Courtesy of F. Percy Vail*)

In 1822–1823 are listed Duncan, Michael, Isaac M. Phyfe (pianoforte maker at 100 Chapel Street), James Phyfe (carver), and John, Junior (ivory turner).

In the edition of 1824–1825, the Phyfe group is as follows:

Phyfe, Duncan, cabinetmaker, at 168, house 169 Fulton Street.
Phyfe, John, Senior, grocer, 30 Barclay Street.
Phyfe, John, Junior, ivory turner, 30 Barclay Street, house 71 Murray.
Phyfe, Michael, cabinetmaker, 31 Harrison.
Phyfe, Martha, widow of William (shipmaster), 173 Chatham.
Phyfe, J. & W. F., upholsterers, 34 Maiden Lane.

Mr. Barrett, in *Old Merchants of New York,* wrote:

John Phyfe Jr. kept shop at No. 19 Murray Street many years under the sign of an immense golden elephant, a wonder in its day. He had served his time with James Ruthven & Son, who were the great ivory and wood turners of their day (1801). John was originally in some business in Barclay Street, No. 30. Old John Phyfe kept a grocery store in the same place. Young John moved afterwards to 19 Murray Street.

The two nephews in Maiden Lane, engaged as upholsterers, may possibly have arranged some family combination to permit them to complete the Phyfe chairs and sofas that needed upholstering and covering, for, remember, Duncan was Scotch and missed no opportunity that might bring gain to the family—an attitude of mind that led him into all sorts of activities. Mr. Cornelius records the fact that he made ironing boards as well as mahogany drawing-rooms! On his labels of the year 1820 he was even advertising "curled hair matrasses, chair and sofa cushions."

There is evidence that he also made piano cases. In 1815 there was an advertisement in the *New York Evening Post* by John Geib, Jr., maker of piano actions, announcing that he could be found at Duncan Phyfe's shop. This was naturally a profitable arrangement, for when Geib sold a piano Phyfe designed and made the case. The piano (Plate 84) from the Garvan collection is one example of this collaboration, and the Gibson and Davis piano (Plate 86) from the collection of Mr. and Mrs. John W. Castles, Jr., is another example somewhat earlier.

The Gibson and Davis piano purchased by Mr. Ford from the Louis Guerineau Myers collection has a case almost identical with that of the Castles piano. It rests on similar end pedestals of carved vases, each pedestal supported by two reeded legs carved with acanthus leaves and terminating in brass paw feet. The stretcher connecting these pedestals is carved with alternating sections of reeding and leaf ornament. Both cases have rounded

PLATE 111. ELIZA'S DINING-ROOM CONSOLE
Though most of Eliza's furniture originally bore her father's labels,
they have all been pulled off or destroyed with the exception of the
one on this piece.
(*Courtesy of F. Percy Vail*)

front corners, but the piano from the Myers collection is ornamented with a border of ebonized and gilt decoration, while the Castles piano has a simple band of beautifully figured veneer.

A bill of Phyfe's to A. Heming in 1827 records the sale of "a piano-table for A. King," whose price was $140 (bill in the possession of Emil Hurja, Washington). Still another maker of piano actions, John Paff, announced in 1816 that he had some pianofortes from London, costing $200 to $300 and added, "For grand upright pianos the purchaser could inquire at Phyfe's Cabinet Warehouse, Fulton Street."

Some of Duncan's profits from these pieces went into silverware. The family tell of a promise made to his wife that, if the War of 1812 resulted favorably for America, he would give her a silver tea set. One morning late in 1814, while in a barber shop, he overheard the casual remark that the war was finished. He inquired of the barber whether it had been settled in our favor and, on receiving an affirmative answer, went immediately to procure

PLATE 112. LABEL ON ELIZA'S CONSOLE, PLATE 111

a quantity of Mexican coin silver and commissioned W. B. Heyer, the silver-smith, to make a tea set for his wife. This tea set is now in the possession of his great-grandson, Mr. F. Percy Vail. Mr. Hal Phyfe photographed it on Duncan's sideboard (Plate 107).

One of Duncan's nephews, William D. Phyfe, was a silversmith. We have a record of him in 1836 working in Boston at 18 Merrimac Street. Later he is at 43 Bank Street, New York, and in 1844 is to be found at 5 Dey Street in partnership with Garratt Eoff. The Vails own a large silver repoussé pitcher stamped "EOFF-PHYFE" and Miss Mary Whitlock has other pieces with the same mark.

Mrs. J. Bertram Howell, a great-great-granddaughter, owns the greater part of the Phyfe table silver. The forks and spoons are initialed in intertwined script "D.R.P." for Duncan and Rachel Phyfe, and are greatly prized for their beautiful, simple lines.

129

PLATE 113. ELIZA'S DRESSING TABLE
In turning and reeding, it matches the bedroom table in Plate 110.
(*Courtesy of F. Percy Vail*)

The great cabinetmaker retired from business in 1847, seven years before his death. On August 19, 1854, the *New York Times* contained merely a brief obituary notice, "In this city, on Wednesday August 16th, Duncan Phyfe, in the 86th year of his life." He died in the same house where he had lived for so many years, across the street from his warehouse. He is buried in Greenwood Cemetery, in the family vault.

An inventory of household goods made after Duncan's death, lists the contents of 193 Fulton Street in detail* and this record, impersonal as it is, affords some interesting glimpses of the manner in which the great man lived. His surroundings were simple. Little furniture was found in the house and that little was unpretentious, if we except the imposing cellarette-sideboard now owned by Mr. Vail and the "best parlor" furniture, which included eight mahogany French chairs, two window seats, a pier table, and secretary.

The entrance hall of the house, like all the lesser rooms, had oilcloth on the floor. Here on New Year's Day, so one of his descendants tells us, was placed the big punch bowl used for such festivities. Only the parlor, dining room, upper halls, and the front rooms of the second story were equipped with carpets or druggets.

Probably for tax purposes the inventory valuations are low. Several field beds and one mahogany high-post bed are listed at $1 to $3.50 apiece, but five feather beds with their bolsters and pillows are considered worth $30.

The usual homely things were found in the kitchen and cellar and storeroom, among them a rattrap and a parrot cage and "one lot spittoons." The two items of the greatest value are the Garratt Eoff silver pitcher and a set of satin damask curtains for three windows; each of these lots was esteemed at $100.

Table silver and china were plentiful and by their quantity indicate the size of the family. Phyfe's gold watch, chain, and seal are valued at $75, but his personal wardrobe is worth only $30. Nearly $500 in cash was found in a strongbox.

To judge from the number of lamps on the inventory, the entire house was lighted by oil. There is a lamp in the front office, and in the front parlor two bronze lamps and a plated solar lamp, constructed on the general prin-

* See Addenda.

131

ciple of an Argand burner, as well as two large gilt lamps with glass drops. The dining room has an astral lamp and marble stand. Upstairs in the bedrooms are candlestands, and in the storeroom is another astral lamp and a solar lamp valued at the enormous price of ten cents apiece.

The lower part of the house was heated by stoves, but the garret bedrooms must have been icy in wintertime and whoever slept there must have had Spartan training.

One bathroom appears in the list of rooms; bathing facilities are indicated chiefly by mahogany washstands in the various bedrooms.

The checkerboard, now owned by Mrs. W. H. P. Phyfe, and the parrot cage suggest two of Duncan's harmless diversions. We cannot go much further than this in reconstructing his daily life with the help of the lists from the Hall of Records.

The record of *The Wealth and Pedigree of the Wealthy Citizens of New York City,* published at the *Sun* office, rated Duncan Phyfe's fortune in 1842 at $300,000. At the time of his death, he was worth nearly half a million dollars. This was a considerable sum for those days, and a proud achievement for a man who landed in America with nothing but his bare hands to help him earn his way.

No portrait of Duncan exists—he never consented to have a daguerreotype made. We can only create for ourselves an imaginary picture of the man from what we know of his life and work and his associates. Perhaps, too, the likenesses of four of his children which are shown here will give some idea of what their father was like, if there is anything in heredity. From all reports, we get the impression of a person who was plain, sober, and industrious. He thought of little else but his work. Hagen says that "he was very strict in his habits, and all the members of the family had to be in bed by nine o'clock."

He was a Calvinist, although not a member of any church. He appeared little in public and took small interest in politics or in societies. He was not a member of St. Andrew's Society, to which most good Scotchmen belonged, but in 1792 he did join the General Society of Mechanics and Tradesmen of the City of New York. There are no records of his doing any public work, or making furniture for any of the public buildings, like some of his famous contemporaries.

The oft-quoted story of his receiving Lord John Hays with his pipe in

PLATE 114. ELIZA'S FOUR-POST BED

A splendid example of Duncan's fine craftsmanship, all four posts are carved.

(*Courtesy of F. Percy Vail*)

PLATE 115. DUNCAN PHYFE'S TOOLS

Presented to the New York Historical Society by Phyfe's great-grandsons, Henry Pinkney Phyfe
and Churchill B. Phyfe.

his mouth, and keeping it there throughout the interview, is either an example of uncouth manners or of a sturdy Scotch independence which refused to recognize a difference in rank and station, or else it proves that he was so accustomed to his old friend the pipe that he was completely unconscious of the fact that he was smoking it when his noble visitor arrived. We may judge that he had a kindly heart under a rough exterior, for, together with his own large family of seven, he brought up at 193 Fulton Street the three children of Michael, who died early in life.

We can be sure, too, that Phyfe was an expert carver, for one glimpse of his own set of fine and delicate tools with ivory handles, now loaned to the New York Historical Society by Mrs. W. H. P. Phyfe, is enough to convince the passing visitor that, to make use of this outfit, he must have known every turn and trick of the chisel. These tools were once in the house of his grand-

134

son, Duncan Phyfe (son of James Duncan), where they stood, sharp ends down, set into holes in a slanting board in front of a window. Every chisel was numbered; it is said that grandfather Duncan knew each one by its number and knew exactly its place in a proposed piece of work.

After Duncan's death, the remaining members of the family moved away from Fulton Street. Two sons, William and James Duncan, went to live in Rhinebeck, and part of the furnishings from the old Phyfe residence were loaded on a boat and taken up the Hudson River. The Fulton Street property was held by the family until the Hudson Tunnels were built.

PLATE 116. JAMES DUNCAN PHYFE
James was the second son of Duncan Phyfe.
(*Courtesy of F. Percy Vail*)

Where the Phyfe workshops once stood are now the great twin buildings of the Hudson Terminals. A firehouse occupies the site of Duncan's own house on the north side of the street.

Branches of the Phyfe family are still living in New York, Pennsylvania, Connecticut, and New Jersey, and have been most coöperative in the preparation of this book. A glance at the family tree* brings to light the curious

* See Addenda.

fact that there were seven Duncan Phyfes living at the same time, for the son of Michael, Duncan's brother, bore the name of his illustrious uncle and five of Duncan's children named sons for their grandfather (this includes Duncan Phyfe Vail and Duncan Phyfe Whitlock, sons of Mary and Eliza).

In practically each direct descendant of the master is the evidence of some talent or artistic gift. Many of the men have a craftsman's love of furniture and skill in finishing or repairing it. Some of them are artists in other ways. Hal Phyfe, for example, trained as a painter and sculptor, is today devoting his skill to making beautiful camera portraits. Some of the women descendants paint, others excel in designing and executing fine needlepoint. Implanted in each and every one of them is a love of beauty and a desire to create it in one fashion or another. And this is perhaps the most important heritage that today's generation has received from the original Duncan Phyfe. It is a more significant heritage than the personal possessions left behind him, his tortoise-shell spectacle case, his snuffbox made from a spotted shell and fitted with a silver cover bearing a thistle in the center (Plate 105) —though these are interesting relics of the great man. In a sense it equals the contribution made to the life of his day by the hundreds of pieces of beautiful furniture issuing from his workshop, for the creative spirit and love of beauty is eternal, and will continue to manifest itself in various guises so long as the world is a world.

Recognition of Duncan Phyfe as our master craftsman was slow to come. His own contemporaries did not admit that he was an outstanding craftsman. His own family did not appreciate the things that he made. In some cases they are known to have thrown away some of their finest heirlooms. Not until an exhibition was organized at the Metropolitan Museum of the City of New York in 1922 to show a representative group of his best work was Duncan publicly honored with fitting appreciation.

After that, his fame spread rapidly. An important loan collection of Phyfe furniture was exhibited for the benefit of the Girl Scouts in 1929. A small group was also shown in the exhibit of New York State furniture in 1934. Meanwhile collectors and museums throughout the country began acquiring examples of his work.

One of the most interesting of these collections is that of the Taft Museum in Cincinnati, which is exhibited in a beautiful American Regency house built in 1820 for Martin Baum. The furniture and its architectural setting are therefore approximately of the same period. About forty of the pieces shown there came from the fine collection of Louis Guerineau Myers, who devoted many years to the study and acquisition of characteristic furniture made by Phyfe. The Museum is the gift of Mr. and Mrs. Charles P. Taft, who presented house and grounds and the collection of art treasures to the city of Cincinnati with an endowment of two million dollars for its continued maintenance.

The House of History at Kinderhook also has several excellent Phyfe pieces. This house, acquired by the Columbia County Historical Society in 1925, was opened to the public as a museum and historical reference library on June 25, 1937. Built around 1810 for James Vanderpoel, a prominent lawyer, afterwards appointed to the State Supreme Court, its architect was Barnabas Waterman of Hudson, New York, whose ancestors came from Newburyport. This probably accounts for the interesting combination of New England—New York State influence in the architecture. Waterman was a great admirer of Bulfinch, which explains the lovely interior woodwork in the main hall and one of the larger rooms.

In the Edison Institute at Dearborn, Mr. Henry Ford has assembled a large collection of some two hundred examples of Phyfe's work. There are occasional pieces, as well, in the Philadelphia Museum of Fine Arts. The Boston Museum is now classifying and cataloguing the important Carolik Collection, which contains many choice works of Phyfe. The Metropolitan Museum in New York has a number of the best examples of Phyfe and his nineteenth-century contemporaries in the wing devoted to American antiques, and the Museum of the City of New York has the Benkard Memorial Room, in addition to other Phyfe pieces.

The Yale Gallery of Fine Arts, in the Mabel Brady Garvan Collections, also owns many fine examples. Due to a unique request by the donor of these collections that they "should not be selfishly hoarded in Yale's own halls, but become a moving part in a great panorama of American Arts and Crafts under the leadership of Yale," individual exhibits have been and still are on loan throughout the country, either in museums or in houses like Homewood, the Carroll mansion in Baltimore, which thousands visit annually as a shrine of historic and patriotic interest.

VII

HIS WORK AND MANNER

PLATE 117. LABEL ON SEWING TABLE, PLATE 118

Duncan Phyfe probably found Sheraton's books of designs very useful when they reached America. The same year that saw young Duncan arriving in New York to make a timid beginning also saw shabby Thomas Sheraton, just turned forty, going bravely up to London from Stockton-on-Tees, to launch himself as a designer of furniture with the publication of a series of pamphlets which were to prove vastly popular among cabinetmakers. So popular were they that later on they resulted in the appearance of *The Cabinet-maker's and Upholsterer's Encyclopedia* and *The Cabinet-maker's Dictionary.*

Like any other intelligent person, Phyfe profited by these designs, but he always managed to add a personal touch which distinguished his work and raised it above the level of imitation. This is particularly noticeable in his use of the lyre and the acanthus motifs. Adam, Sheraton, English Regency, and Louis XVI French furniture all made use of the lyre as a decorative motif. It is a figure derived from the Greek *lyra,* freely used by the Romans as well, and is believed to have been suggested by the curving horns of the long-horned goats. To neoclassicists it made a special appeal because of its decorative quality and its associations. Phyfe used it to form the base of tables, to fill in the backs of chairs, to decorate the arms of sofas, and to support mirrors on dressing tables. Sometimes the pedestal of one of his larger tables is made of two crossed lyres. Usually the wires of these lyres are

PLATE 118. SEWING TABLE WITH CARVED COLONNETTES
This mahogany table, because of its style and because of the
address on the label, is to be dated around 1815.

of brass or whalebone, with a key of ebony. In some cases the curved sides are ornamented with simple reeding; usually they are carved with an acanthus leaf—delicate when the lyre is employed for lighter structural uses, sturdy when the frame is thick, and heavy to bear some weight.

139

PLATE 119. DINING-ROOM

The fine lyre-back chairs, the window seat with lyre arms, and the side tables are from Phyfe's
workshop. The cabinet is by Seymour.

(*Courtesy of Mr. and Mrs. Andrew Varick Stout*)

No other person ever carved the acanthus leaf in exactly the same fashion as Phyfe. Hagen used to say that the master "carved more like a stonecutter than like a worker in wood," and this is perhaps the most vivid and accurate description of his method, suggesting in a few brief words the clean, well-defined lines, the accents of light and shade, and the flatness of carving that might actually have been done by a sculptor of stone or marble.

The three styles of acanthus used as ornaments by the eighteenth-century architects were the prickly acanthus, the smooth acanthus, and the curled leaf. Phyfe's acanthus was none of these, nor did it bear a close resemblance to any one of the classic models. It was more like a water leaf in many ways. The design which he adopted is described as follows by Mr. Cornelius: "Phyfe's acanthus is simplified . . . into a series of rounded grooves and ridges. The depression seems to have been 'made with one curved carving-tool. This is flanked by two very narrow and shallow depressions from which the raised ridge rounds up. . . . A raised tapering ridge runs up the whole centre of the leaf, simulating the central vein of the natural form." So characteristic is this design and this manner of carving that many of Phyfe's pieces have been identified by it.

Curule chairs, like those found in Pompeii, were models used by the Adam brothers, by Sheraton, and by the French *ébénistes* of this period. Phyfe, too, made curule chairs. "Sabre legs," or curved and tapering scimitar shapes that date from the earliest Hellenic civilization, were another of

PLATE 120. PHYFE'S USE OF LYRES

These two types of chairs with lyre backs and a console table with lyre pedestal are from the Louis Guerineau Myers collection.

(*Courtesy of Mrs. Louis Guerineau Myers*)

141

the many forms revived by the neoclassic cabinetmakers. Sofas similar to the Greek *cathedra* were made in every country, including our own. All these models were due to the influence of Regency styles and proved the possi-

PLATE 121. TAMBOUR WORKTABLE
The style of its label dates this piece between 1806 and 1817. In shape and
in the details of its reeding turning it is most interesting.
(*Courtesy of Dr. Ray C. Franklin*)

bility of "designing furniture for contemporary use in the terms of an ancient tradition."

Duncan Phyfe's principal output of furniture consisted of tables, chairs, sofas, and window seats. There are also dressing tables, chests of drawers, four-post beds, sideboards, and secretaries, sometimes even wardrobes, but comparatively few so-called "case pieces." Hagen declared that this was because of the difficulty and expense of fitting the drawers and having everything work according to standards of perfection. Phyfe acknowledged that his furniture was already expensive; he feared that the cost of added labor in fittings would make the prices prohibitive.

Some piano cases and beds also came from his hands. Many of these,

PLATE 122. LABEL ON WORKTABLE, PLATE 121

like the sideboards, are late examples of his work, heavy and somewhat overpowering, quite unlike the large pieces of his early period. Now on exhibition in the House of History at Kinderhook is a fine mahogany wardrobe (Plate 141) made about 1820. Furnished with small brass paw feet, it has interior woodwork beautifully fitted with drawers and sliding trays. Although it reaches almost to the ceiling and has generous double doors, it does not seem heavy or clumsy in any way.

The beauty and suavity of Phyfe's work before 1825 reflect the prosperity of the country, the beginning of a taste that was cosmopolitan, and the broadening of America's intellectual interests. Under the influence of the Classic Revival and the revolt against the overornamentation of Adam designs, this furniture is simple and dignified, enriched by restrained carving, and outstanding mainly for the selection of choice woods and because of its beautiful craftsmanship.

For the Girl Scouts' Exhibition in 1929, Mr. Louis Guerineau Myers wrote an appreciation of Duncan Phyfe, which is quoted by permission.

Practically unknown a few years ago, the name of Duncan Phyfe has today become the plaything of every auctioneer, every furniture dealer, and every furniture buyer in the country. Every man's work during the first years of the nineteenth cen-

PLATE 123. WRITING DESK, CHAIR, AND WINDOW SEAT

Photographed at the home of the late Louis Guerineau Myers, this desk is now in the
Metropolitan Museum.

(*Courtesy of Mrs. Louis Guerineau Myers*)

PLATE 124. BENKARD MEMORIAL ROOM

This early nineteenth-century drawing-room with Duncan Phyfe furniture was given to the Museum of the City of New York by Mrs. Harry Horton Benkard as a memorial to her husband.

tury is foisted on poor Phyfe, and then he has also to shoulder many an Englishman's third rate product.

The first thing we must recognize when trying to make attributions is that no cabinet-maker with any pretense to popularity can hope to do more than design and supervise the construction of his output. This means that Phyfe worked no more with his own hand than did the famous Chippendale. Then we also know that men trained in the shop of a master to certain proportions, methods, and mechanics of construction often separate from him and continue to reproduce the things their hands are accustomed to, albeit more mechanically and less carefully.

What we may be sure of is that Phyfe refined many prevalent furniture forms; that his manner of refinement is carried to us by examples known, usually by bills of sale, to be the work of his shop. If, therefore, we find a piece rendered in the same way,

145

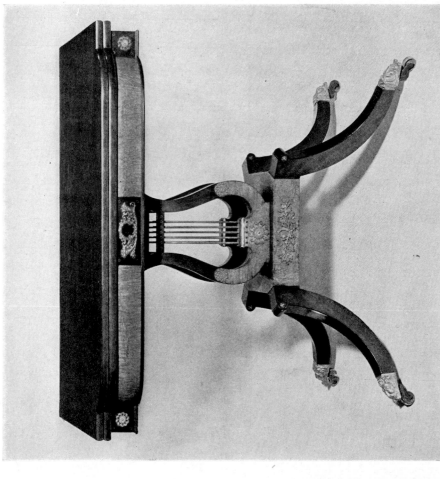

PLATE 126. LYRE-PEDESTAL CARD TABLE

A rare combination of mahogany and curly maple, the outsplayed legs terminate in brass lions' heads. The piece was formerly in the collection of Mrs. John Thompson Spencer, Philadelphia.

(Courtesy of Ginsburg and Levy)

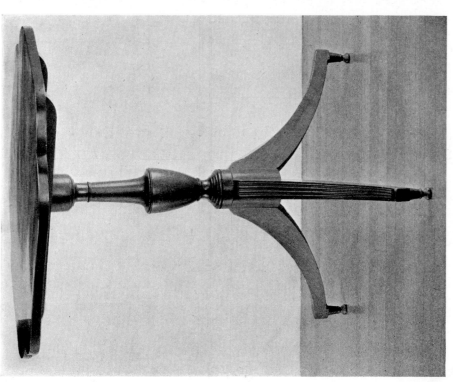

PLATE 125. SMALL MAHOGANY TRIPOD STAND

This has typical Phyfe touches in the high, vase-shaped pedestal and reeded legs. The top is in a cut-out clover-leaf pattern.

(Courtesy of Allan B. A. Bradley)

with the same touch of the carver's tool, or with precisely similar turnings, we may feel confident that it issued from the Phyfe shop or from that of a man who secured his training at this master's hands.

What we have to look for when examining a piece nominally Phyfe's is purity of form, refinement of structural dimensions, quality of wood and workmanship; with turnings patterned in a certain way, or with but the slightest variations; or if in the Empire (or classic) style, with the tool marks of an accredited piece repeated.

Contemporaries of Phyfe not trained by him and reproducers of yesterday never succeeded in closely copying these various touches. Early nineteenth century cabinet-makers in Philadelphia, Boston, and other large cities interpreted both the later Sheraton and classic styles, but not one of them ever turned a leg or carved an acanthus leaf in the Phyfe manner. Whether their methods were necessarily inferior to Phyfe's is, of course, a matter of personal predilection, but competent judges incline to this belief.

Careful study of a piece of Phyfe furniture reveals many subtle details not always apparent at first glance, except in their quiet contribution to a general air of distinction. Let us try to estimate some of them briefly. The use of veneered panels or narrow bands of wood in contrasting color is so cleverly arranged that it seems almost as if the wood grew in this fashion. This is a device frequently employed to accent and outline the edges of tables and desks and to give interest to large plain surfaces or important areas. Sometimes the panels are almost invisible except to the eye of an expert.

The fine little cock beading that binds the edge of every drawer is another detail characteristic of Phyfe. It is a raised hairline of wood, beautifully applied, which makes the difference between an edge left unfinished and one that is carefully completed. The panel of veneer on the face of corner blocks, differing in color and grain from the body of the piece, helps to give richness to the furniture and shows careful planning for effect.

The characteristic Phyfe leg often found on tables and couches has parallel circular reeding at the top, and vertical reeding along its tapering length, extending to the beginning of a plain, vase-shaped terminal. Many people have discussed the specialty of this vase-shaped terminal, but none have set out to find, as Mr. R. T. Haines Halsey did, the classic model that suggested this form. During a trip abroad he discovered it in the spokes of a wheel of an ancient chariot in the Museum of the Vatican. The dog's leg and paw, the prototype of many legs of chairs and tables made by Phyfe, he found on a classic bronze tripod in the Naples Museum.

An odd incident should be noted in connection with Phyfe's reeding of

147

PLATE 128. CONSOLE TABLE ATTRIBUTED TO PHYFE

A carved eagle with outstretched wings forms the pedestal, its claws
resting on a ball of wood upheld by four acanthus-carved legs.

*(Courtesy of the Mabel Grady Garvan Collection, Gallery of Fine
Arts, Yale University)*

PLATE 127. LIBRARY OR BREAKFAST TABLE

The base is formed by four carved colonnettes resting on four
splayed legs with acanthus carving and brass paw feet.

(Courtesy of Taft Museum)

PLATE 129. FIVE-LEGGED CARD TABLE

The center panel in the skirting has a rosewood border and fan-shaped corners, and there are rosewood borders at the top of the reeded legs.

(Courtesy of Taft Museum)

the legs of couches. As a rule, only front legs are reeded, which is quite understandable. But, if you run your hand around these front legs, you will find that *they are not generally reeded over the complete surface.* The face and sides alone are ornamented; the reeding is omitted on the back, where it would be invisible from any angle. Knowing Phyfe's painstaking care with every detail, we cannot believe that this omission is due to any lack of desire to finish a piece of furniture in the most thorough fashion possible. It is found on his finest and most elaborate sofas, and is a definite hallmark of his work.

Legs and terminals used by Phyfe were turned on a lathe. In his earliest

149

PLATE 131. SERVING TABLE WITH SHELF, CIRCA 1800–1810

The three drawers have lion's mask and ring handles and are edged with cock beading. At the corners are fluted round pilasters extending into reeded, tapered, and turned legs with small brass paw feet.

(Courtesy of Parke-Bernet Galleries)

PLATE 130. MAHOGANY CONSOLE TABLE

The vase-shaped pillar of this unusual pedestal base is reeded and carved with leaves. The four reeded legs end in wood claw feet. The table is about thirty-three inches high.

(Courtesy of Ginsburg and Levy)

furniture, practically everything except turning was done by hand. Even reeding, one of his favorite methods of embellishment, was hand grooved, as is shown by the frequent slight variations in spacing between the grooves. Nevertheless, the Bentham machines mentioned in a former chapter existed at this epoch and were capable of doing much labor in the making of furniture. Phyfe's later work shows much more turning than earlier models; possibly other parts of his cabinetmaking were done by machine before he retired from business.

Certain forms of construction often used by Duncan Phyfe are associated with his name wherever they are seen. One of these is the peculiar design of the card table with a tripod base where two of the feet swing back automatically to balance the table when the folding leaf is opened. The swivel movement is very ingeniously contrived in all of these tables. Another characteristic of Phyfe construction is the use of white-wood linings in the drawers of tables and sideboards rather than the pine linings used almost universally in America. The delicate dovetailings, the tiny mortises and tenons used to put his work together, are also regarded as identifying marks of his handiwork. So are the exquisitely made little buttons or *paterae* placed over the joinings of surfaces in chairs and sofas.

But the most satisfying proof of the individuality of Duncan Phyfe lies in his carving. It is evident from a study of his furniture that he used a limited number of designs, repeating them again and again, in varying combinations. On one of his couches we find a swag and tassel in the center panel of the top rail and laurel leaves in the side panels; on another, laurel leaves in the center and swags on the side. The designs are the same; their disposition differs.

The elements used are few and simple. Phyfe's standard designs are the bowknot and the thunderbolt, the cornucopia and wheat, the bowknot and wheat, the acanthus leaf, the drapery swag with tassels, the carved paw foot, simulated fur on the legs of chairs, the carved lyre, reeding. Least often found are carved wheat ears and oak leaves and acorns. Those who are interested in studying and comparing the use of these various motifs will be interested in the measured drawings of carving details reproduced in the Addenda to this book.

Phyfe's favorite device of reeding often serves to accent horizontal and vertical lines, and aids in establishing the balance and perfect proportion for

PLATES 132 AND 133. TWO FINE TABLES

The card table at the left, owned by Mrs. Francis P. Garvan, is one of a pair with unusual cabriole legs similar to those of the Phyfe dressing table in Plate 152. The drop-leaf library table below, from the Detroit Institute of Art, has a well-proportioned vase pedestal supported by four carved and reeded legs which terminate in brass paw feet.

PLATE 134. SOFA TABLE

Formerly in the Louis Guerineau Myers collection, this sofa table has reeded trestle supports, two drawers, and shaped drop-leaf ends with reeded edges.

(Courtesy of the Metropolitan Museum of Art)

which his early furniture is noted. His use of reeding is often identical with that in Thomas Sheraton's designs. In describing Phyfe's workshop, the old cabinetmaker Ernest Hagen once told some of his clients that the various patterns which Duncan liked best to use on his furniture were carefully drawn on stiff paper and hung from the ceiling. When there was a set of chairs to make, or some other piece of furniture that required carving, he would say to one of his skilled men, pointing to the hanging designs over their heads, "Use a combination of this and this and that."

So Duncan Phyfe systematized his designs and was responsible for the beginning of mechanical standardization in series. It is with reason that the

153

late Homer Keyes wrote in an issue of *Antiques:* "Artistically, then, Duncan Phyfe stands at the close of a great tradition whose decay is evident in most of his later productions. Mechanically and industrially he stands at the beginning of another great tradition, the promise of whose accomplishment is observable in processes of his devising."

Throughout all the work of his early period, which may be dated approximately between 1795 and 1820, runs the feeling of simplicity, great restraint, and good architectural design. The second period of Phyfe's work falls between 1820 and 1830. For the first few years of this period, the furniture was still fine; in the second half it began to deteriorate. From 1830 to

PLATE 135. SOFA TABLE WITH DROP ENDS

The support has a double stretcher and four reeded colonnettes. The legs are carved and have brass paw feet. The two drawers are outlined with inlay of rosewood. It is part of the Mabel Brady Garvan Collection.

(Courtesy of Homewood, Baltimore)

1847 was his Victorian period, when heavy rosewood and mahogany furniture took the place of the former light and graceful styles, for when Empire and Victorian fashions in furniture came into vogue, Phyfe was forced to follow these ideas. His craftsmanship was still as fine as ever, his woods were

154

PLATE 136. WRITING TABLE WITH SHELF

This table has a side drawer with a lift-up slide. It has beautifully turned and reeded half-round
pilasters at the corners, a shelf below, and two drawers with lions' masks and rings.

(*Courtesy of Edison Institute*)

still as beautiful, but the bad taste of the designs which he used, in common with all other cabinetmakers of the time, lowered his standing as an artist.

By many of his admirers these periods are called, respectively, the "Adam-Sheraton period," the "Empire period," and the "Victorian." The first two may well be called his Regency periods, as they correspond so closely to the work of the English Regency and to its interpretation of classic ideas.

When Duncan went out of business, in 1847, he was making rosewood, painted, maple, and black-walnut furniture, as well as mahogany models. The *Sale Catalogue of the Splendid and Valuable Furniture of Messrs. Dun-*

PLATE 137. SMALL DROP-LEAF TABLE
The brass drawer pull bears a design of Greek honeysuckle.
(*Courtesy of Allan B. A. Bradley*)

156

PLATE 138. FIVE-LEGGED CARD TABLE

The legs are a typical Phyfe design with reeding, a turned and tapering base, and small brass paw feet.

(From the collection of Mrs. John W. Castles, Jr.)

can *Phyfe and Son, Nos 192 and 194 Fulton Street* lists 432 lots of furniture and is an illuminating glimpse of the scope of his business at the finish of his career.

Phyfe cannot truthfully be called an originator of styles. He was rather an adapter, a translator of the popular ideas of the moment, with distinctly outstanding achievements in craftsmanship to his credit. He was, for example, the only cabinetmaker of his time who was wholly successful in repro-

157

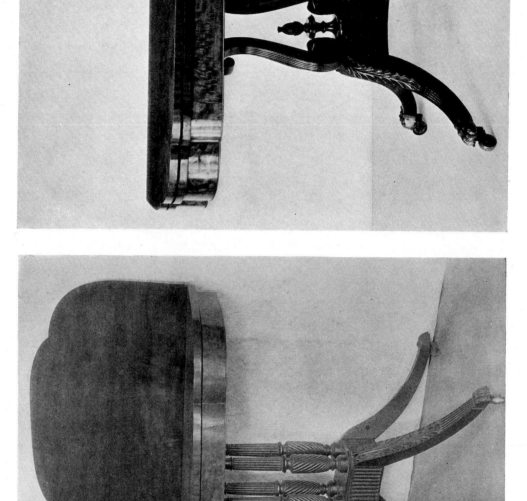

PLATE 139. COLONNETTE CARD TABLE

This table combines a clover-leaf top, four reeded and turned colonnettes, and four acanthus-carved feet with brass paws.

PLATE 140. LYRE-PEDESTAL CARD TABLE

Louis Guerineau Myers said of this table: "This is a rare design. The top and skirt have five distinct curves. The curved supports forming the pedestal suggest the crossed lyres of other tables but have a small pediment and pineapple in the center."

(Courtesy of Taft Museum)

ducing in his furniture the flowing curved lines of classic chairs. There has been much discussion as to whether Phyfe received the inspiration for his styles from England or from France. It seems quite likely that both of these countries contributed to his store of ideas, since both were working along the same lines. Phyfe never went to France. We do not know that he could speak or read French, or that he ever saw any French periodicals. Through the many French designers in New York—men like Lannuier or Gruez, for example—he may very well have gleaned some French ideas that filtered eventually into his own designs. Others came to him by way of England.

The question is often asked, "Did Phyfe ever sign his work?" We can definitely answer this query by saying "yes"; he pasted his label in many pieces of furniture. Photographs of four of these pieces with their labels are reproduced in this book. Phyfe's great-grandson, Mr. F. Percy Vail, says that practically every one of the many articles owned by them bore a label originally and that as a boy he amused himself by pulling off these labels wherever he found them. Fortunately one still remains on a console (Plate 112).

Most labeled pieces of Phyfe furniture have turned up in places outside of New York. It looks as if Duncan did not think it worth-while to label furniture that stayed in his own city. Once in a while he put his name in a piece that was shipped away, as much as to say, "Here in New York, they know me and will recognize this piece as the work of my hands, but people in a distant city may not know what workshop this furniture came from unless I mark it with my name."

The four Phyfe labels illustrated in this book are all different. The first, on Dr. Franklin's sewing table (Plates 121 and 122) *circa* 1806, reads:

D. PHYFE'S
CABINET WAREHOUSE,
No. 35 Partition-St.,
New-York

The second label (Plate 117) on another sewing table must be later than 1811 because it includes the two addresses, 33 and 35 Partition Street.

D. PHYFE,
CABINET MAKER,
33 & 35, PARTITION-ST.
New-York

The third label (Plate 234), on the Bowie secretary-bookcase, is dated 1820. By that time Partition Street had been rechristened.

D. PHYFE'S
CABINET WAREHOUSE,
No. 170 Fulton-Street,
New-York
N.B. Curled Hair Matrasses, Chair and
Sofa Cushions.
August, 1820.

The fourth label, on Eliza Vail's console table (Plate 112), is a business card, tacked to the frame of the top.

Messrs. D. Phyfe & Sons
CABINET WARE HOUSE
No. 194 Fulton Street
D. Phyfe NEW YORK
W. Phyfe
J. D. Phyfe

This label indicates that the piece of furniture was made between 1837 and 1840 when the business was known as Duncan Phyfe & Sons.

DIFFERENT TYPES OF PHYFE TABLES

Tables made by Phyfe may be classified according to their different kinds of supports. First, there are the tables with a leg at each corner, as the small boy said in describing a horse. These include certain sewing tables, card tables, and serving tables. In most cases the leg is the typical Phyfe tapering model with reeding. The card table (Plate 138) of Mrs. John W. Castles, Jr., has five such legs, one of which pulls out to support the folding leaf when it is needed. It will be noted that the vase-shaped finials on the table legs fit snugly into four-toed paw feet.

Another card table (Plate 129), which came from the Louis Guerineau Myers collection and is now in the Taft Museum, also has five legs. The top is made in the interesting clover-leaf shape, without a straight line in its design. The vase finials at the foot of the legs are extraordinarily long and slender. Mr. Myers said of this table: "Other attractive touches are the center panel with its rosewood border and fan-shaped corners, and the small

PLATE 141. WARDROBE AND NEW YORK FOUR-POST BED

The wardrobe bears all the typical Phyfe hallmarks in the interior case work, the reeding of the corner blocks, the tapering feet with small brass paws, and the choice highly figured mahogany. The bed is not by Phyfe.

(Courtesy of the House of History, Kinderhook)

PLATE 143. TAMBOUR WORKTABLE WITH SATINWOOD INLAY
This combination writing and sewing table is of inlaid satinwood
with a vase pedestal, carved and reeded legs, and carved feet.
(Courtesy of Mr. and Mrs. Wayne Johnson)

PLATE 142. TAMBOUR WORKTABLE WITH IVORY PULLS
This beautiful little table with its carved vase support has ivory
pulls and a lift-up slide in the interior.
(Courtesy of Edison Institute)

PLATE 144. EIGHT-LEGGED COUCH

The front legs are turned and reeded and the arms are double curved with reeded posts. The center panel of the cresting rail of the back is carved with the bowknot and wheat design, the side panels with the bowknot and drapery.

(Courtesy of Mrs. Giles Whiting)

rosewood-bordered panels at the tops of the legs. One of Phyfe's many mannerisms is the failure of these diminutive panels to cover the whole head of the leg above the skirt's rosewood border. This peculiarity is also found on worktables."

Cabriole legs are not often found on card tables, but Mrs. Francis Garvan owns a pair of tables (Plate 132) which defy this generality with exceptionally long cabriole legs, carved with acanthus and ending in dog's fur and paws. Small carved panels ornament the corner blocks, and there is a bowknot and drapery panels on the long side. We find the same type once more on a dressing table (Plate 152) made by Phyfe for his great-niece Emily Phyfe Dunham.

In Plate 131 we have a small serving table which is a somewhat rare example of Duncan Phyfe's casework. It has two short drawers and one long one with lion's mask heads and pulls. There is a shelf below carefully fitted into the legs, which are reeded and turned and extend all the way up to the top of the table so that they form projecting rounded corners. They have

163

PLATE 145. BENKARD SOFA

This is one of the finest of Phyfe's sofa designs, with curving arms, turned balusters, and reeded legs. With this sofa are shown two diminutive footstools with carved hair and paw feet. The side rails are reeded to match the reeding of the couch.

(*Loaned by Mrs. H. H. Benkard to the Metropolitan Museum of Art*)

vase finials and brass paw feet. This same general idea may be seen in the construction of the little combination sewing table and writing desk from the Edison Institute (Plate 136). Here, however, there is a drawer that pulls out at the end and the legs, with castors, are turned and reeded.

Dr. Franklin's tambour sewing table with a Duncan Phyfe label on the inside of the back is supported on the same type of leg. There is something very delicate and graceful about this long-suffering little table, which was found in a kitchen where hot irons had been set on it.

Pedestal tables made by Phyfe have great variety and interest. The pedestals vary from a severely plain vase, set high on three reeded legs, to an elaborately carved eagle on a four-legged base, supporting a table top with outspread wings.

PLATE 146. CANED SETTEE

The seat rail and legs of this three-paneled back settee are reeded, as are the curved arms. The cresting rail is carved with laurel in the center panel and with bowknots and thunderbolts in the side panels.

(*Courtesy of Ginsburg and Levy*)

165 ·

PLATE 147. CANED SETTEE WITH STOOL BASE

The side arms of this settee from the Mabel Grady Garvan Collection are extended to form a reeded stool-base. The top rail and arms are carved with bowknots and thunderbolts.

(*Courtesy of Homewood, Baltimore*)

Among them are drop-leaf tables with carved vase pedestals set on four legs, an unusual high console table with a reeded and leaf-carved pillar and claw feet carved in wood, and a beautiful satinwood card table (Plate 83) with a brass edge on the skirt, brass feet, and acanthus leaves on the vase and legs.

A type very rare with Duncan Phyfe is the sofa table with drop leaves and a trestle support formed by a vase-shaped pedestal at each end and connected by a stretcher. A table formerly in the collection of Louis Guerineau Myers and now in the Metropolitan Museum (Plate 134) is one of the two best examples known. Legs, vases, and stretcher are reeded and a fan-shaped motif is carved at each end of the stretcher. This table is believed to have been made between 1810 and 1815. A good sofa table, from the Garvan collection, is in Plate 135.

PLATE 148. COUCH WITH DOUBLE-LYRE ARMS

This most unusual couch has double lyres in both arms, while its reeded frame is otherwise undecorated. The saber legs almost give the effect of cornucopias.

(Courtesy of R. T. Haines Halsey and the Metropolitan Museum)

PLATE 149. SABER-LEG SOFA

This sofa from the Pendleton-Rogers family has a cresting rail carved with the motifs of bow-knot and drapery and bowknot and thunderbolts.

(Courtesy of Ginsburg and Levy)

Another type of table is that with four colonnettes and four legs. The sewing table with a Phyfe label in Plate 118 is made in this fashion. It is not in itself so pleasing as the delicate table in Plate 90, being heavy and even clumsy in effect. Its interest lies largely in the fact that it is a labeled piece. Very lovely, however, is a folding console with a similar base, carried out in a much more subtle fashion. The vases in the colonnettes are carved like twisted ropes; the legs are carved and reeded, with brass feet; and the shaped standard from which the legs spring is also enriched with reeding. There are few four-legged drop-leaf tables with colonnettes by Phyfe, but the Taft Museum in Cincinnati has one with an open pedestal of four colonnettes carved with acanthus. It was probably used as a library or breakfast table (Plate 127).

A fifth type of table made by Phyfe is the table with a lyre base or with a curved design that suggests a lyre. Mrs. John Thompson Spencer's console table of this type (Plate 126) has a folding top supported on a pedestal of double lyres that rest on a platform upheld by four outsplayed legs with brass feet. The table is further enriched with mounts of gilded metal.

A table in the Taft Museum is an unusual one of its type. The top and skirt have five distinct curves, much less often found than the tables with

PLATE 150. SOFA WITH LIONS' PAWS AND EAGLES' WINGS

The design of the carving on the back is two cornucopias from which two long sheaves of wheat stretch out to the end of the rail. The seat rail, continuing to form the side rails, is reeded. An identical sofa is owned by Charles H. Sherrill.

(*Courtesy of Taft Museum*)

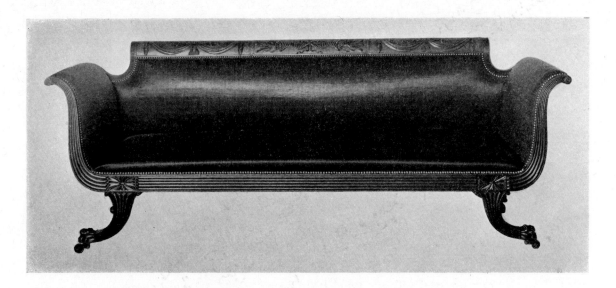

PLATE 151. SOFA WITH CARVED CORNER BLOCKS

The cresting rail of this sofa is carved and the frame reeded. The carved corner blocks at the tops
of the front legs are an interesting variation.

(*Courtesy of Charles Woolsey Lyon*)

three curves. The curved supports suggest the crossed lyres of other tables, but here the members remain separate and the little pediment and pineapple between them take the place of the usual connecting bars and strings. The symmetrical legs have acanthus carving and brass feet.

CHAIRS

Duncan Phyfe's chairs may easily be divided into groups that are characteristic of the master's three periods.

To the first or earliest period (1795–1820) belong the chairs with horseshoe-shaped seats and those with double or single crossed backs, reeded seat rails, and reeded legs. The front legs of these chairs are usually straight; the rear legs have a slight outward curve to continue the curve of the back. They follow Sheraton and Directoire lines. The best examples of this type have carved top rails. Occasional examples are found with a reeded panel instead of carving. In all of them the back panel stops some distance above the seat as in most Sheraton chairs. Examples are to be seen in Plate 157.

The question has been raised among collectors as to whether or not Duncan ever worked in the Hepplewhite style. Various people own chairs with shield backs and carved splats which they believe were undoubtedly

PLATE 152. DRESSING TABLE WITH CABRIOLE LEGS, 1815–1820

Here are the long cabriole legs which may also be seen in the card table, Plate 132. The carving of the acanthus and of the hair and paw feet follows the technique of Phyfe's lyre-back chairs. This dressing table was made for Phyfe's grand-niece, Emily Phyfe Dunham.

(Courtesy of Mr. and Mrs. Andrew Varick Stout)

PLATE 153. DRESSING TABLE, 1820–1830
Made of mahogany, this dressing table has X-supports, a stretcher, and brass feet.
(*Courtesy of the House of History, Kinderhook*)

done by Phyfe. They think that these pieces represent some of his earliest work. They have, however, no documentary evidence of this, so it is merely a belief founded on a collector's instinct or perhaps on a well-nourished hope. Certainly it is not beyond the realm of possibility that among the models given the young craftsman to copy and adapt at the outset of his career there should have been some of Hepplewhite's chairs. It is quite possible too that he carved the splats with the water leaves or acanthus which he liked so much, but a historian who wants to be meticulously accurate cannot make this statement as a proven fact without possessing more data than exist at the present time.

PLATE 154. SIDEBOARD

Beautifully figured mahogany contrasted with bands of veneer, and carved feathers on the corner blocks and feet distinguish this piece. A carved pineapple stands in the break of the pediment and on the end posts of the back. The lower rail is reeded and the drawers have lion's mask pulls with rings.

(*Courtesy of Allan B. A. Bradley*)

We do know definitely that Phyfe followed many of Sheraton's ideas. Furniture came from his hand in early Sheraton styles as well as in late Sheraton, approaching the Empire. We know too, that some of his work reproduces designs by Thomas Hope and we find among documented Phyfe

172

furniture some purely French Consulate and Directoire designs. All of these things reflected the fashions of the day. Some Hepplewhite designs may well have been included, although the beginning of Phyfe's career was contemporary with the abandoning of Adam and Hepplewhite in favor of simpler and more severe classic fashions.

Between 1800 and 1810 Phyfe made chairs with lyre backs and others with scroll arms and ovoid medallions in back held between carved scrolls (Plate 161). The legs of these chairs are sometimes carved with acanthus or

PLATE 155. SIDEBOARD WITH TAMBOUR COMPARTMENT

On the back of the tambour was found a newspaper dated 1812. The columns and the heavy feet, however, suggest a later epoch. On this sideboard again are carved pineapples, the emblems of hospitality.

(*Courtesy of Ginsburg and Levy*)

173

with hair and dog feet, as in the fine set of Livingston chairs (Plate 264). The cornucopia filled with wheat was a favorite motif of carving in this period. Curule bases were also used for chairs and sofas.

In the last period (1830–1847), a heavy double groove ornamented the seat rail and sides; the backs often had elaborate medallions of carved pineapples, baskets of fruit, etc. A reflection of Egyptian influence were the obelisk-shaped side rails and legs.

WINDOW SEATS

These little benches made to fit into the spaces under recessed windows were designed like chairs so far as arms and legs go. The lovely little caned window seat (Plate 82) added recently to the collection of the Metropolitan Museum is an example of the best type of Phyfe's first period. The two ends

PLATE 156. CHAIRS WITH DOUBLE-LATTICE BACKS, 1800–1805

These are among the rarest and most successful of Phyfe's chairs. The legs, side rails, and crestings are reeded and turned.

(*Courtesy of Taft Museum*)

174

PLATE 157. EARLY STYLE CHAIRS

These chairs also belong to Phyfe's earliest period and are among his finest work. Note the horseshoe-shaped seats, some of which have reeded rails. The bowknot-and-thunderbolt and the bowknot-and-wheat motifs are used in the carving on the cresting rails.

(Courtesy of Allan B. A. Bradley)

have top rails carved with laurel. The panels of the arms have segmental slats which intersect under a carved rosette. Seat rails are reeded. The cabriole legs are carved with acanthus and have small, brass paw feet.

Mr. and Mrs. Andrew Varick Stout own the only Phyfe window seat with lyre ends known (Plate 119).

In the Freehold Museum are a pair of Phyfe's later window benches (Plate 168). They have legs with fur and paw feet, which are gilded. Gilt also is the decoration painted on the two arms, which gives the effect of carving. Compare this late and clumsy style with the delicate window seat owned by the Metropolitan Museum.

FOOTSTOOLS

For the comfort of the ladies, Duncan Phyfe made footstools of many sorts. Few of them are preserved today. The Metropolitan Museum has two delightful examples loaned by Mrs. Harry Horton Benkard (Plate 145). Diminutive as they are, each has four little paw feet below curved hair legs;

175

PLATES 158, 159, AND 160. THREE SIDE CHAIRS

At the left is a chair with a single cross back, which is slightly canted, and reeded top and bottom panels as well as legs and side rails. In the center is one with a segmental cross back, reeded side rails, and legs with carved hair and paw feet. A similar set with carving on the top rail is in the House of History, Kinderhook. At the right is one of the rare examples of oak-leaf-and-acorn carving on a piece of Phyfe's work. It is now, appropriately enough, at Mrs. J. Amory Haskell's house, Oak Hill.

(Courtesy of Allan B. A. Bradley; the Museum of Fine Arts, Boston; R. T. Haines Halsey and the Metropolitan Museum of Art)

the joinings of the sides and the ends are covered with tiny, reeded, round buttons. In addition, the tops of the side rails are finely reeded to match the reeding of the couch which they complete. To accompany the Pearsall sofa, Phyfe made a small pair of oblong caned footstools which have tied-on pads of brocade (Plate 276).

SOFAS

Finest of the Phyfe sofas are those like the Benkard sofa (Plate 145) with carved top rails and curved arms. In these models the side rails dip down gracefully from the top of the back, curve out and in again to make a final turn-under, and rest upon posts which are set on the curving corners of the front seat rail. Mr. Cornelius believed that all sofas with double-curved arms of this sort had reeded seat rails, but the sofa owned by Mrs. Giles Whiting (Plate 144) disproves this theory, for it is completely uphol-stered over the front rail and was originally made in this manner.

The cresting rails of these sofas usually contain three panels of Phyfe's characteristic carving—wheat and bowknots, thunderbolts, drapery swags or laurel. The most unusual motif that has been found is the bow and arrow of the Akin couch (Plate 236) now in the Monmouth County Historical Asso-ciation in Freehold, New Jersey. Straight-arm sofas are more often found than curved-arm models; they have a certain reserved and dignified beauty (Plate 237).

Much caning was used by Phyfe in the making of sofas and chairs. The splendid Pearsall drawing-room sofa (Plate 280), with its curule base and its accompanying set of twelve chairs, is finished in this manner and has bro-caded, padded cushions tied over the cane. A special method of construction in these caned pieces is worth noting. There is a curve in the seat supports to allow for the elasticity of the caning and the supports are mortised into a dovetailed groove in the seat rail, "a refinement of construction which ren-ders easily distinguishable Phyfe's work from good reproduction."*

Following these types come sofas with Empire influence, many of which are carved on the top rails with Phyfe's earlier motifs; the legs, however, change into lion's paws and eagle's wings, and are often gilded. The whole effect is heavier and less graceful than that of sofas made between 1800 and 1830. The so-called "Greek couch" with its rolled-over end is a product of this late era.

* Charles Over Cornelius, *Furniture Masterpieces of Duncan Phyfe.*

PLATE 161. THREE CHAIRS WITH OVOID SPLATS, 1800–1810

These three chairs have paneled ovoid splats supported by scrolls. The center chair has the scrolled arms seen in some Sheraton chairs. Note the lateral curve of the side seat rails, used to keep the width of the cresting rail in harmony with the width of the seat.

(Courtesy of Allan B. A. Bradley)

SIDEBOARDS

Several of Phyfe's sideboards exist to show the different treatments used by him in these large pieces of furniture. Extremely interesting is the Pearsall sideboard (Plate 279), with its supporting columns of Egyptian figures and its brass feet, directly inspired by the Regency designs of Thomas Hope. This sideboard has a sliding tablet on each side of the top which can be pulled out for convenient use. Narrow lines of brass inlay frame the doors inside the band of veneer.

The Phyfe sideboard owned by Allan Bradley (Plate 154) is made of fine mahogany with two long drawers across the front, two cupboards, and two deep drawers for bottles. A band of veneer outlines the doors and drawers; the pulls are lions' masks with rings. Two small pineapples terminate the end posts of the back, and a large pineapple stands in the break of the pediment. Above the posts and on the ball feet that rest on the brass paws are small carved feathers. Carved pineapples, a symbol of hospitality, also decorate the sideboard in Plate 155. The tambour sliding doors in the center of the base have an 1812 newspaper pasted on the inside.

The sideboard made by Duncan Phyfe for his daughter Eliza (Plate 107) is an example of his late work. Beautiful crotch mahogany was employed for this piece. The design has two end compartments flanked by small Ionic columns and connected by a mirror and a long drawer. The whole structure is mounted on eight feet, the back ones plain, the front ones carved with lion's paws and acanthus leaves. Phyfe is said to be the first craftsman to attempt a crotch mahogany veneer on small round surfaces like the

PLATES 162 AND 163. TWO SIDE CHAIRS

The chair at the left again has an ovoid splat, but this time it is combined with hair and paw feet. Note that the side rails of all these chairs are designed in a long sweeping curve which runs from the front rail of the seat to the top rail of the back. At the right is a graceful lyre-back chair with grooved canted legs, and cornucopias carved on the top rail.

(Courtesy of Allan B. A. Bradley and of the Metropolitan Museum of Art)

179

PLATE 164. SIDE CHAIRS WITH X-BASES

These have segmental splats, reeded side and seat rails, cresting rails carved with laurel,
and brass paw feet.

(*Courtesy of Ginsburg and Levy*)

free-standing columns on this sideboard. It is a most difficult task, but in a hundred years not a single inch of the veneering has moved.

In his mahogany yard at 31 Harrison Street, Phyfe stored and weathered his stock of fine wood. Most of it came to him from Santo Domingo and Cuba. Hal Phyfe, whose family had a match factory in Honduras, learned during a visit there that some of the choicest mahogany from that country had also been sent to his great-grandfather Duncan. Duncan's admiration for fine woods outran his native Scottish caution, for he is said more than once to have given a thousand dollars for an exceptional log. He would keep these purchases of mahogany under sheds on Harrison Street for a year or longer until he considered them ready for use. Then the finest parts of the logs, "the flames," were sliced for veneers; the rest was used for structural parts. From Santo Domingo also came the satinwood he occasionally used and he always selected the finest and closest grains. Perhaps the hardness and compactness of the fibers of his woods has something to do with his style of carving, which is crisp, low relief more like a stonecutter's style than a wood carver's.

PLATE 165. SIDE CHAIR WITH A CARVED SCROLL SPLAT
The top rail is ornamented with a group of deeply grooved members at each side. The front legs are carved with hair and paw feet.
(*Courtesy of Edison Institute*)

181

Beds of various types were made by Duncan Phyfe. The earliest seem to have been four-posters, done under the influence of Sheraton designs. In these beds the carving is elaborate on the bottom posts, but the top posts are usually plain. An exception is the bed in Plate 114. A beautiful bed of this type is in the House of History at Kinderhook and there is one in the American Wing of the Metropolitan Museum which many experts attribute to Phyfe.

PLATE 166. DRESSING TABLE STOOL

Only four of these dressing table chairs or piano stools are known. They belong to Phyfe's second period.

(*Courtesy of Mrs. George Watson*)

182

PLATE 167. A SIMPLE CABINET DESK

The front of the upper part of this desk drops down to give writing space. The legs are
reeded and turned in typical Phyfe fashion.

(Courtesy of the House of History, Kinderhook)

PLATE 168. PAINTED WINDOW SEAT, 1830–1840

In this late example of Phyfe's work, from the Monmouth County Historical Association, gilt paint is used to take the place of carving. The carved hair and paws of the feet are also gilded.

(*Courtesy of Mrs. J. Amory Haskell*)

One of the finest documented beds is the splendid four-poster which he made for his daughter Eliza Vail (Plate 114). Like all of his mahogany pieces, it is made from beautifully figured wood. The posts rest on carved lion's feet which are now painted black, but where the paint has flaked off enough of the original finish may be seen to prove that at one time they were gilded. The fine solid footrail is very architectural in design, terminating at each side between the two footposts in a small column mounted with brass capitals and a brass base. It is unusual to find all four posts carved, and the workmanship is most remarkable. Above the footboard is a series of parallel turnings and reedings supporting a vase-shaped member carved with the acanthus pattern. Over this rises majestically a post carved like a twisted rope. The depth and beauty of this particular carving is magnificent. At the top, the post finishes in a vase-shaped form carved like the lower members. Above the tester, but not shown in the photograph, are small mahogany acorns.

An interesting French style of bed, made to stand against the wall, is the bed (Plate 286) Phyfe made for Miss Louisa Throop, now owned by Mr. Hollis Hunnewell. The front posts terminate in sphinxes' heads identical with those used on the Pearsall sideboard.

Phyfe also made "sleigh beds," large double beds (many since cut down to fit more conveniently into smaller rooms) and in at least one instance we know of a cradle made for his son James Duncan. It has solid mahogany ends and caned sides. James Duncan slept in it and it was used again for his two sons, then for his two grandsons, and is owned today by Mrs. W. H. P. Phyfe.

When Phyfe made the heavy four-poster for the Pearsall family, he also made gilt window cornices like thick, twisted ropes to match the cornice of the bed. For the drawing-room he made heavy crossed spears to hold the brocade curtains and a carved gilt shell from which draperies hung over the pier glass between the windows. All these things follow the example of the best English Regency decorators of the day.

CASE FURNITURE BY PHYFE

Among the pieces of so-called "case furniture" from Phyfe's workrooms, the secretaries, bureaus, and dressing tables are most interesting. A fine satinwood "ladies' secretary" of 1805–1810 (Plate 87), owned by Mr. and Mrs. A. V. Stout, is a charming example of the delicacy and refinement of Phyfe's best small pieces. It has ivory knobs and a fine tambour front that conceals the pigeonholes and drawers of the cabinet. The exterior is inlaid with hairlines of rosewood to outline all the surfaces. The reeded legs taper down into vase finials and round knobs.

A desk (Plate 123) from the Louis Guerineau Myers collection, now in the Metropolitan Museum, has a roll top and is made of fine mahogany; the only decoration beside the reeding of the legs is the band of contrasting veneer that outlines all edges.

Various dressing tables made by Phyfe are worthy of note. There is the

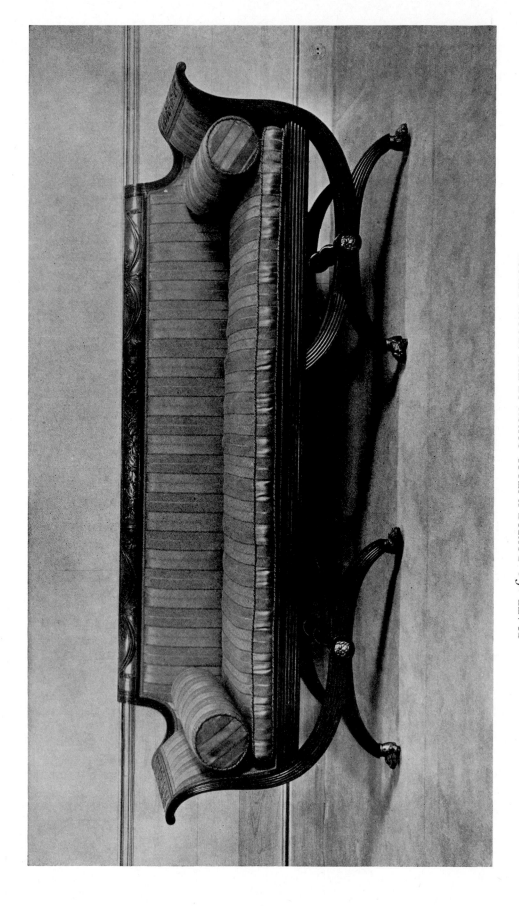

PLATE 169. DOUBLE X-STOOL COUCH OF THE SECOND PERIOD

The frame is reeded, and the carving on top rail and arms is unusually fine. This couch was found in London but has since been repatriated.

(*Courtesy of Miss Florence Cluett, Williamstown, Massachusetts*)

curious one (Plate 152) designed for his great-niece Emily Phyfe Dunham dating between 1815 and 1820. It has long cabriole front legs carved with the acanthus, hair and paw feet; the back legs are straight and reeded, with vase-shaped finials and ball feet. It has lions' masks and ring pulls on the drawers, and an attached mirror with a shaped top, held by two reeded supports.

Lyre supports are occasionally found on dressing tables of this period, but the Phyfe dressing table owned by Mrs. George E. Watson is unique in having a lyre chair stool to go with it (Plate 166).

Toward the end of his life after Phyfe retired, he amused himself by making small pieces of furniture with his own hands which he presented to various members of his family. Two little shaving stands (Plate 108) made at this time are still in the family, belonging to Mr. F. Percy Vail. Though they are designed to stand on top of a table or a bureau they are constructed from wood just as carefully chosen and as carefully veneered as in any of the larger pieces. The master kept his standard of craftsmanship to the end.

VIII

HIS COMPETITORS

By no means all the best furniture made in New York between 1795 and 1825 came out of Duncan Phyfe's workshop, nor, for that matter was all the best furniture of this period from New York City. Many parts of New England and the South had important groups of cabinetmakers with national, we might almost say international, reputations, for the brisk export trade in furniture that followed the Revolutionary War carried their names and products to all quarters of the globe.

Philadelphia, Boston, Baltimore, and Salem, to mention only four other centers of production, each made a share of fine furniture following more or less the same general styles, but with variations that added interest and distinct personality to the work of each locality. In New York City and the larger towns of the Hudson River Valley, furniture designs were dictated by the principles of simplicity, strength, and decisiveness. In Boston and Salem, cabinetmakers turned out pieces with great delicacy in form and carving.

PLATE 170. LABEL OF NEHEMIAH ADAMS OF SALEM

This label is on the secretary bookcase, Plate 171. (Text: page 200.)

188

Baltimore had much inlay work done both with wood and painted glass. In Philadelphia the opulence of eighteenth-century ideas somewhat diminished, but the furniture still kept a certain elegance that made it outstanding in the colonies.

The extraordinarily fine quality of work produced by American cabinetmakers and the important export business they developed in the early nineteenth century are not generally known or appreciated. During the

PLATE 171. SECRETARY BOOKCASE BY NEHEMIAH ADAMS
This much-traveled piece was brought back to America from Capetown, South Africa, where it was found in possession of W. R. Morrison. (Text: page 200.)
(*Courtesy of* Connoisseur)

189

PLATE 173. TRICTRAC TABLE BY LANNUIER

The backgammon points are inlaid with ivory, alternating white and green. Ivory sockets around the edge hold the scoring pegs. A chessboard slides in under the skirting. The mark "H. Lannuier" is stamped with a steel die on the edge of one of the drawers. (Text: page 215.)

(Courtesy of Benkard Memorial Room, Museum of the City of New York)

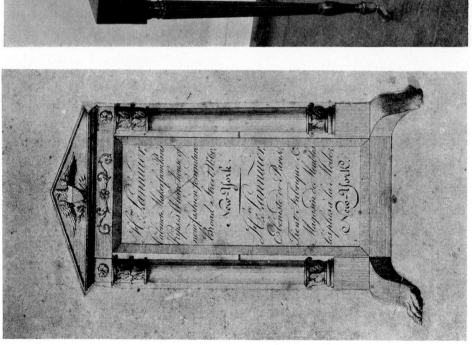
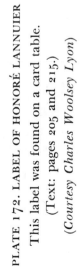

PLATE 172. LABEL OF HONORÉ LANNUIER

This label was found on a card table.
(Text: pages 205 and 215.)
(Courtesy Charles Woolsey Lyon)

years of the Revolution, when it was impossible to bring much foreign furniture into this country, and afterwards, when prejudice militated against the use of English manufactures, the craftsmen and artisans of America grew and improved in skill. It was no idle boast when Alexander Hamilton said in his treasury report in 1791: "Our cabinet wares are made little if at all

PLATE 174. CARD TABLE BY LANNUIER

This is one of a pair exhibited in the loan collection of New York state furniture at the Metropolitan Museum in 1934. It is labeled. The wood is mahogany, which is inlaid with brass. It was loaned to the exhibit by Mrs. Charles Morris Young. A similar table is owned by Miss Edith Wetmore of New York. (Text: page 215.)

(Courtesy of the Metropolitan Museum of Art)

PLATE 175. BED ATTRIBUTED TO LANNUIER

Made in New York in the early decades of the nineteenth century, the paw feet and eagles' heads
are gilded. This bed was doubtless draped with curtains in the Sheraton manner.

(Courtesy of Joseph Kindig, Jr., York, Pennsylvania)

PLATE 176. PIER TABLE BY LANNUIER

This beautifully made table of mahogany and satinwood bears the maker's label which is
unfortunately too blurred to reproduce. The table is classically pure in design.

inferior to those of Europe. Their extent is such as to have admitted of considerable exportation." To further this activity, he proposed exemption from duty of the woods used in these manufactures.

While the export trade in furniture did not equal in magnitude the trade in cotton, tobacco, and agricultural products, and while it would seem infinitesimal to a Grand Rapids manufacturer of today, it was nevertheless considerable enough to be included in the treasury reports of the last years of the eighteenth and the first years of the nineteenth century. In 1791, according to *American State Papers,* "56 carriages" of coaches, chariots, phae-

PLATES 177 AND 178. PIER TABLE BY LANNUIER, WITH LABEL.

The table is mahogany and gilt, with a marble top. Note that the spelling of Lannuier's name varies from that in Plate 172.

(Courtesy of Ginsburg and Levy)

tons, and chairs were sent to the West Indies. These "carriages" contained sixty-two desks, fifteen bureaus, twenty-six sofas and settees, thirty-four tables, and six bedsteads. In the same year four thousand Windsor chairs were shipped to the French West Indies, five hundred and thirty-three to the Dutch, one hundred and forty-four to the Danish West Indies, and twenty-four to Africa. The exports of household furniture between 1802 and 1805 varied from $92,343 to $141,008 annually. Side by side with the

PLATE 179. WORKTABLE DESK BY MICHAEL ALLISON

This table has tambour drum compartments. The tops of the carved lyres are formed by curving swans' heads, and the feet are terminated by carved eagles' heads. (Text: page 217.)

(*Courtesy of the Metropolitan Museum of Art*)

furniture shipments were always shipments of coaches which generally amounted to $25,000 or more. In 1813, after war with England had begun again largely because of the restrictions imposed on American trade with English colonies, the export record for furniture is pitifully small, amount-

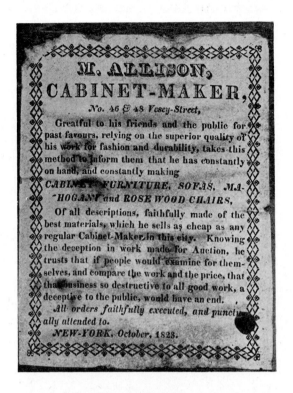

PLATE 180. LABEL OF MICHAEL
ALLISON, 1823
This labels the worktable desk, Plate 179.

ing to less than $3,000 during that year, but by 1815, after peace was declared it began to recuperate; we sent out $52,000 worth of fine furniture and steadily increased the amount until in 1821 $179,000 worth was exported.

It is interesting to trace the destination of these shipments and see where they finally came to rest. A large amount was divided among the Danish, Swedish, Dutch, French, and British West Indies. Haiti got more than $30,000 worth. To Cuba we delivered over $63,000. The Spanish South American colonies were the next largest customers, with orders for $29,000; Brazil received about $10,000 worth, and the Floridas, Honduras, Madeira, Gibraltar, and Africa took the rest.

All the seaport towns of importance shared in sending off these shipments by way of coasters and transoceanic sailing ships. In Salem, as Mrs. Mabel Swan has ably demonstrated from the study of old documents, a cooperative business venture developed for the making and exportation of furniture. Carvers, gilders, turners, joiners, and upholsterers banded together with the cabinetmakers in this venture, and references to the undertaking are frequent in the old records. One invoice of 1803 in the Essex Institute of Salem describes a cargo of mahogany furniture to the value of $5,000, made and consigned by ten well-known Salem manufacturers to be sold abroad. At another time the famous Salem merchant, Elias Hasket Derby, purchased tables, bureaus, and bedsteads for more than £177 from E. and J. Sanderson, some of which went out on the good ship *Henry,* to be sold at auction in Calcutta.

Practically all of these exportations were disposed of at vendue, or pub-

PLATE 181. EARLIER LABEL OF MICHAEL ALLISON

This label is in the top right hand drawer of the mahogany bureau, Plate 182. Another drawer has a written inscription: "Mary Mayo Scott's chest of drawers given her by her mother Elizabeth, 1806."

lic sale, and their liquidation was frequently entrusted to the captains of the ships that carried them overseas. Sometimes, as old letters show, it was difficult to get good prices. Because of the skippers' desire to be on their way home with new and profitable cargoes from foreign ports, they would have

197

PLATE 182. MAHOGANY BUREAU (1800–1812) BY ALLISON

This bureau has three short drawers and three long ones of beautifully figured wood with satin-wood stringing. Oval bail plates have an eagle and thirteen stars while the eagle on the top center drawer has sixteen stars which date the piece. The French bracket feet are connected by a valance skirting. (Text: page 217.)

(Courtesy of the Metropolitan Museum of Art)

perhaps willingly sacrificed some of these shipments of American furniture had it not been for the specific and precise instructions and restrictions issued by their owners and makers.

In various parts of the United States, outstanding cabinetmakers advertised this export business on their labels, and made a sort of "bid for favor" by their announcements. William Camp of Baltimore, on his large and important label declared, "Orders for the West Indies or any part of the Continent neatly attended to, with punctuality." Practically the same words were used by Joseph Barry of Philadelphia. Another label denoting business of a similar nature is that of John Budd of New York, who states in 1817, "Orders from Southern ports immediately attended to and all furniture warranted." Thus did American furniture manufacturers begin a worldwide expansion that scattered the products of our home towns through all the continents.

PLATE 183. WRITING TABLE BY J. CURTIS

Nothing is known of the maker of this fine little mahogany writing table with a lift-up writing pad inside the top, except scant information given in his label. (Text: page 224.)

199

The results of international trade in furniture are interesting and curious. Some of the finest pieces of American work come unexpectedly to light in far remote spots. Not many years ago a very beautiful secretary bookcase made by Nehemiah Adams of Salem turned up in Cape Town, South Africa.

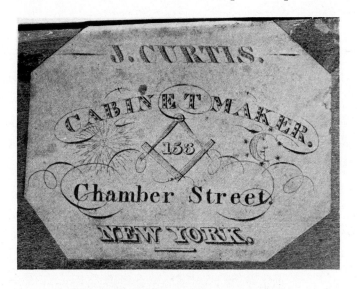

PLATE 184. LABEL OF J. CURTIS

This label is on the writing table, Plate 183. The compass and square would indicate that he was a Mason.

How it came into the possession of Mr. W. P. Morrison of that city is not known. The bookcase bears two original labels of the maker. One of them reads:

NEHEMIAH ADAMS

Cabinet-maker

Newbury Street

(near the Common)

Salem

Massachusetts.

The second label is similar, and is dated 1770. In its travels the piece suffered little except for the loss of its small brass finials which have now been replaced. It even retained part of its original glass. Records show that this bookcase sold originally for $225. By the time it was reclaimed and brought back to this country to take its place in a private collection, it had cost $5,000, plus the packing and shipping necessary for its round-the-world travels. (See Plates 170 and 171.)

In much the same fashion, an unusual American sofa (Plate 169) was discovered in London and returned here to be the pride of another collector. This is the sofa now in the possession of Miss Florence Cluett of Williamstown, Massachusetts. Instead of the usual supporting legs, there are two X-stools, which seem an integral part of the design because the side rails of the sofa flow into them in continuous curved lines which terminate in brass paws. The carving on the cresting rail is the typical design of Duncan Phyfe, a laurel branch in the center, with swags and tassels in the panel at each side.

English collectors were much interested in this piece. Turning it upside down and inside out, and studying it with the greatest care, they came to the conclusion that it could not have been made in England but was definitely American in design and workmanship. The base is, of course, similar

PLATE 185. PEMBROKE TABLE BY GEORGE WOODRUFF (1808)
This table was exhibited in the loan collection of New York state furniture at the
Metropolitan Museum in 1934.

to the curule form used in many Regency chairs and also in some of the Consulate furniture of France. It may be seen as well in the Duncan Phyfe chairs in Plate 164 and in the dressing table in Plate 153.

A settee of practically the same design (Plate 280) but with carved cornucopias in the top rail instead of swags, and caning instead of upholstery, is owned by Mrs. Henry Wilmerding Payne, and Mr. Maxim Carolik has still a third sofa of this type. Undoubtedly the three pieces were produced either in the workshop of Duncan Phyfe or by one of the workmen

PLATE 186. LABEL OF GEORGE WOODRUFF
This label, dated May 1808, at 54 John Street, is on
the Pembroke table, Plate 185.

who had been trained by him and had access to all his patterns of carving.

We have incontestable evidence that furniture made by Duncan Phyfe traveled as far as China. Mr. Abbot Low of New York, a well-known tea merchant of the early nineteenth century, received one day a letter from an American resident of China with the request to send him "some of Duncan Phyfe's furniture, as it is the only kind that will stand the rigors of this climate." It is reasonable to deduce from this that enough Phyfe furniture with its fine workmanship and meticulous finish had already found its way to China to establish the fact of its durability and resistance under Oriental weather conditions.

The West Indies became a veritable repository of New England furni-

PLATE 187. CARD TABLE BY ALLISON

One of a pair given by the Newcomb family to Lucinda Newcomb and Benjamin Leonard Johnson on their marriage, January 24, 1832, and later inherited by a grandson, Benjamin Louis Johnson. The tables are stamped with Michael Allison's name.

(Courtesy of the Edison Institute)

ture during the height of the coastal trade. They have given up many of their treasures to a shop recently opened in Boston by an intelligent antique dealer, who, recognizing the increasing difficulty of finding good examples of our early cabinetwork, made special trips to search out what existed in these islands, and bring back the pieces in triumph for profitable repatriation in their own section of the country.

THE NEW YORK GROUP

In New York, one of Phyfe's distinguished contemporaries was the French *émigré*, CHARLES HONORÉ LANNUIER (generally mispronounced *Lanier*). He came from Paris about 1804 and was twenty-six years old when he became a shopmaster. His name first appears in the *Directory* of 1804–1805 at 60 Broad Street, and thereafter regularly until the issue of 1819–

PLATE 188. DINING TABLE BY JOHN GRUEZ
Mahogany three-pedestal table with carved legs and brass paw feet. Gruez was Lannuier's successor. (Text: page 215.)
(*Courtesy of Mr. Ralph D. Cutler*)

204

1820. That he died in this latter year we may infer from the fact that the *Directory* of 1821 lists his *widow* as resident at 36 Orchard Street.

Since it was Lannuier's custom sometimes to label his furniture, and often to stamp it with his name in the manner of the old French *ébénistes,* it

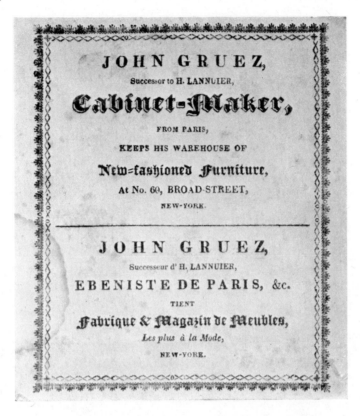

PLATE 189. ADVERTISEMENT OF JOHN GRUEZ
This advertisement in the *New York Directory* of 1821 shows that he was successor to Lannuier's shop on 60 Broad Street, New York, though not to his bad English spelling. (Text: page 215.)
(*Courtesy of the Library of the Museum of the City of New York*)

has been possible to identify many of his important masterpieces. His label was printed both in French and English. The first part reads like the broken English of a foreigner just arrived on our shores and is spelled just as it is pronounced. He informs his public that he *"Kips is Wharehouse of new fashion fourniture* at Broad Street, number 60." The second part of the label in his native tongue, runs along fluently. He is *"Ébéniste de Paris"* and has a *"Fabrique et Magasin de Meubles les plus à la mode"* (Plate 172).

205

We cannot help wondering why his sign was always bilingual. It recalls the label of John Elliot in Philadelphia, printed in English and German. For this, there was a sufficiently good reason as Elliot had among his customers many Pennsylvania Germans. It is possible that, with the influx of French *émigrés* that followed the Revolution, it was an advantage to Lannuier to print his label in his native tongue in New York City. More probably, it was done because French was the fashion; everything French was chic, which made it good business to advertise French nationality.

Washington once predicted, "The highly favored situation of New York will in the process of years attract numerous emigrants who will gradually change its ancient customs and manners." He was quite right. As early as 1794 it became necessary to establish the New York Society for the Infor-

PLATE 190. STENCILED TABLE BY JOHN BANKS

This table was made for presentation to Lafayette on his second trip to America in 1824. John Banks's name was stenciled in the bottom of one of the drawers. In the center motif on the table top is Lafayette's name and the border is a charming stenciled running vine. The base is strangely designed with a carved lyre pedestal on carved paw feet in front and turned back legs.

206

PLATE 191. MAKER'S MARK

John Banks's mark is stenciled on one of the drawers of Lafayette's table, Plate 190.

PLATE 192. CARD TABLE (1817) BY JOHN BUDD

The mahogany in this card table with twisted rope legs and cut-off corners is of exceptional quality.

(*Courtesy of Ginsburg and Levy*)

PLATE 193. LABEL OF JOHN BUDD

This label is on the card table in Plate 192, and is dated May, 1817.

mation and Assistance of Persons Emigrating from Foreign Countries. This was due to the great increase of emigration from Europe to the United States caused by the oppressions of many of the governments of Europe and by the public calamities that ensued.

The city seemed to be particularly attractive to French *émigrés*. The American letters of St. John de Crèvecoeur, published in 1787, tell how some of his countrymen founded the small borough of New Rochelle at ten leagues from New York, where during a long period of time only French was spoken and heard. Other Frenchmen built the city of Richmond and peopled Staten Island.

A visitor in 1794 to the Indian Queen, a tea-drinking house of New York, wrote back to England: "This place is filled by Frenchmen and their families. Here they all wear the tri-colored cockade, I observed, whether aristocrats or democrats."

The mother of Anthony Trollope, visiting America in 1827, wrote in her *Domestic Manners of the Americans:*

If it were not for the peculiar manner of walking which distinguishes all American women, Broadway might be taken for a French street, where it was the fashion for very smart ladies to promenade. The dress is entirely French; not an article (except perhaps cotton stockings) must be English, on pain of being stigmatized as out of the fashion. Everything English is decidedly *mauvais ton*. English materials, English fash-

PLATE 194. FINE NEW YORK CONSOLE TABLE
This marble-topped table has reeded legs and brass paw feet.
(*Courtesy of the House of History, Kinderhook*)

PLATE 195. SECRETARY DESK AND ITS LABEL BY JOHN SEYMOUR

This famous secretary desk from the Flayderman collection is one of the two known labeled
Seymour pieces and was made in Boston around 1790. (Text: page 226.)

PLATE 196. CHEST OF DRAWERS BY JOHN SEYMOUR

This fine half-round chest of drawers with lions' masks and rings is made of mahogany and maple veneer and has brass paw feet. The rounded posts are carved at the top in the fashion of Salem and Boston pieces.

(Courtesy of the Museum of Fine Arts, Boston)

ions, English accent, English names are all terms of reproach; and to say that any unfortunate looks like an English woman is the cruelest satire which can be uttered!

At the same moment many famous French designers and architects were working here on important schemes. Pierre Charles l'Enfant not only laid out the plan of Washington but also worked out the design of Federal Hall in New York, and made the open portico where Washington took the oath of office. Stephen Hallet, a Frenchman, submitted the design awarded the second place for the Capitol in Washington, and afterwards served as assistant to Thornton. John McComb with the aid of the Frenchman Joseph

PLATE 197. SECRETARY DESK BY JOHN SEYMOUR

Although lacking some of the fine details of the Flayderman desk in Plate 195, this little secretary
desk is, nevertheless, one of Seymour's best pieces. The back plates of the pulls are Bilston enamel.
Every edge of the cabinet is outlined with fine inlay work. The legs have satinwood stringings and
inlay of husk designs. (Text: page 231.)

(Courtesy of Mr. and Mrs. Andrew Varick Stout)

PLATE 198. SIDEBOARD BY JOHN SEYMOUR

This is one of the outstanding pieces of American cabinetwork. The panels of figured mahogany are outlined with bandings of satinwood and the tambour sliding front is also made of these woods. The legs, beautifully designed and carved, carry to the top in half-round reeded columns. The ivory key scutcheons are designed like small urns. A fine line of inlay outlines the top and bottom edges of this beautiful piece.

(Text: page 229.)

(Courtesy of Mr. and Mrs. Andrew Varick Stout)

PLATE 199. SATINWOOD SECRETARY BY JOHN SEYMOUR

This and the secretary in Plate 195 are the only known labeled pieces of John Seymour.

(Text: page 229.)

(*Courtesy of George A. Cluett, Jr.*)

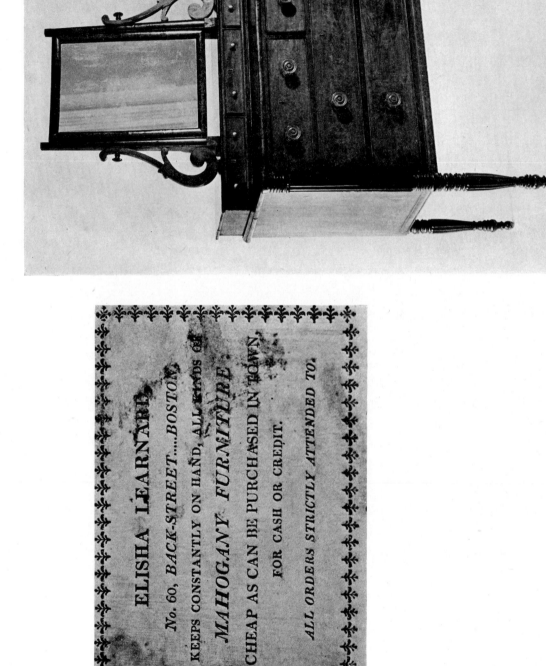

PLATES 200 AND 201. BUREAU AND MIRROR BY ELISHA LEARNARD WITH LABEL.

This simple, sturdy piece probably dates between 1820 and 1830.

(*Courtesy of Edison Institute*)

Mangin designed the new City Hall in New York, still an outstanding monument of the time. In Schenectady, Joseph Ramée built Union College, and anticipated Jefferson's ideas by adopting the form of the Pantheon as the central unit.

The *Index of American Design* has recently found records showing that Lannuier was given commissions for the new City Hall at the time of its construction. In July, 1812, he was authorized to make $409 worth of chairs for the Common Council Room. Lannuier's early furniture is very simple and purely classic. It embodies, as is natural, many of the ideas of the Louis XVI period and reflects all the classic tendencies that both France and England were adopting. The exquisitely made trictrac table (Plate 173) in the Duncan Phyfe room which Mrs. H. H. Benkard gave to the Museum of the City of New York was for years believed to be the work of Phyfe until the signature "H. Lannuier" was accidentally discovered stamped on the edge of one of the drawers. A pair of card tables purchased by Mr. Charles Woolsey Lyon in the belief that they had been made by Phyfe proved later to bear a Lannuier label (Plate 172).

This resemblance to the work of the Scotchman still continued through Lannuier's later work when he changed to the current Empire mode. In Plate 174 is a folding card table that shows the full flowering of the Regency and the beginning of Empire influence. It is one of a pair of tables with inlays of brass, the attributes of the eagle, and stars on the girdle of the carved winged figure. The feet are carved paws, with acanthus leaves.

JOHN GRUEZ took over the Lannuier establishment after his death, using the same label that Lannuier had always employed, with the substitution of his own name and rectification of the English spelling. He too is *"Ébéniste de Paris."* A half page with his announcement appears in the *New York Directory* of 1821 (Plate 189) and his label is found on a solidly made dining table with three pedestals in Plate 188.

MICHAEL ALLISON also deserves high rank among Phyfe's New York competitors. His name can be found in the *New York Directory* of 1814 at 42 and 44 Vesey Street. In 1821 he was still in the same street, but at Numbers 46 and 48. Curiously enough, two pieces of furniture made by him are today in the Metropolitan Museum bearing labels with the two different addresses. Study of the two pieces shows Allison to be a cabinetmaker of great ingenuity and no little creative ability, besides being an experienced

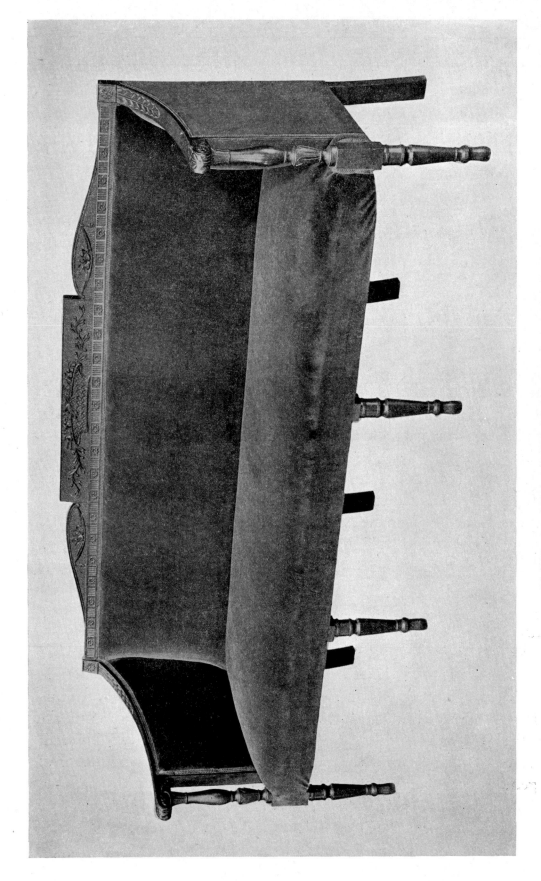

PLATE 202. SOFA CARVED BY SAMUEL McINTIRE

McIntire added two popular designs to the carving of his day, the basket of fruit and the eagle.
The former is shown on the top rail of this fine couch.

(Courtesy of Miss Katrina Kipper)

PLATE 203. HUNTING BOARD CARVED BY MCINTIRE

The center panel contains a basket of fruit, draperies are carved on the side panels, and grapes are carved on the corner blocks.

(*Courtesy of Miss Katrina Kipper*)

workman with skilled knowledge of the use of woods and the making of complicated bits of work. The chest of drawers in the Sylmaris collection (Plate 181) is a fine piece of mahogany and satinwood with inlay of an eagle and sixteen stars, which dates its manufacture between 1800 and 1812.

The other piece of furniture made and labeled by Allison is a work-

217

table and desk (Plate 179), dated October, 1823. The two supports are lyres with swans' heads turned back over the sides. The feet and legs are unusual, terminating in eagles' heads instead of paws, the upper parts of the legs being carved with acanthus leaves. On each side of the superstructure is a cylindrical compartment with tambour front. There are three simulated drawers; the top lifts to disclose a center writing pad with a ratchet and a

PLATE 204. SIDEBOARD (1809) BY WILLIAM HOOK

This sideboard, made in Salem, is of mahogany and satinwood with bandings of holly, mahogany, and ebony. The doors are inlaid with a fan-shaped design in alternating woods. (Text: page 235.)

(Courtesy of the Museum of Fine Arts, Boston)

PLATE 205. SECRETARY BY SAMUEL MCINTIRE

The basket in the pediment of this mahogany piece is typical.

(*Courtesy of Miss Katrina Kipper*)

I also give the Essex Institute The Light Stand with a turned edge to the top, a fluted pillar and small claw Feet. This is in the Parlor Chamber. The Mahogany Bureau which stands in the Front Chamber, with the Dressing Case which stands on top of it; also the Linen Scarf which is on it. They were made for my mother in 1818 by William Hook, Cabinet maker.

PLATES 206 AND 207. BUREAU BY WILLIAM HOOK AND ITS BEQUEST

According to the description in the bequest, this mahogany bureau and dressing mirror was made in 1818 by William Hook of Salem.

(Text: page 237.)

(Courtesy of the Essex Institute)

PLATE 208. DETAIL OF SOFA IN PLATE 209

compartment below in which the label is pasted. (Compare with the form of the desk in the Regency room of Buckingham Palace, Plate 42.)

STEPHEN and MOSES YOUNG also worked in the Phyfe manner. These two brothers were partners when they opened their shop at 73 Broad Street, in 1804. They were to be found for some time at 28 Market Street. Afterwards they went back to Broad Street, which was the center of the cabinet-making trade, and located at Number 79. The brothers separated in 1824,

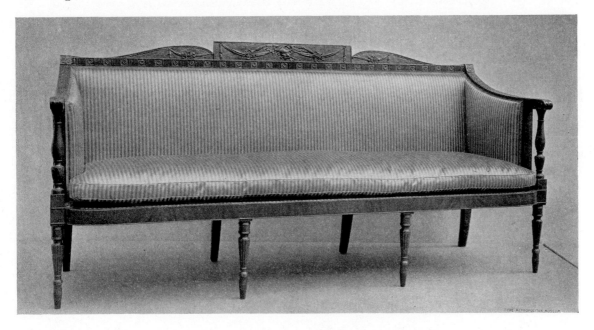

PLATE 209. SOFA BY NEHEMIAH ADAMS

The finely carved top rail of this sofa is typical of McIntire and it is believed that he did the carving for cabinetmaker Adams. The sides have wooden rails, molded and slightly carved, extending in front over turned balusters. The seat was originally a loose cushion which rested upon canvas that was laced to the frame with ropes. (Text: page 235.)

(Courtesy of the Metropolitan Museum of Art)

PLATE 210. SECRETARY BOOKCASE BY EDMUND JOHNSON

This labeled Salem piece dates between 1793–1811 and is a fine, dignified example of the
break-front style.

(*Courtesy of the Edison Institute*)

PLATE 211. BED (CIRCA 1795) CARVED BY MCINTIRE

Originally the property of Parker Cleaveland who was born in 1770 in Rowley, Massachusetts, this bed is mahogany. Two foot posts are tapered, reeded, and delicately carved.

(*Courtesy of I. Winick*)

Moses to run a mahogany yard while Stephen continued as a cabinetmaker until 1835. A table from their workshops is almost identical with that illustrated in the *Masterpieces of Duncan Phyfe* by Charles Over Cornelius. Made of a fine quality of mahogany, it has the clover-leaf form of leaves, there are turned drops at the corners, a vase-shaped pedestal carved with acanthus, and acanthus and reeding on the four legs that terminate in brass paw feet.

ASA HOLDEN of 32 Broad Street followed Duncan Phyfe's example by making "single and double cross-back chairs."

JOSEPH MEEKS, another good New York cabinetmaker, was at 61 Broad Street from 1805 to 1820.

C. CHRISTIAN of 73 Broad Street was selected in 1814 to make a desk for the Mayor's office in the new City Hall and also furniture for the Governor's room. This is perhaps the furniture about which there has been so much discussion, and which for so long was believed to have been imported from England.

J. CURTIS of 153 Chambers Street is a newly discovered craftsman of the time. Nothing much is known about him, but a charming little desk and worktable (Plate 183) shows that he worked with great distinction in the typical New York manner.

MILLS AND DEMING (1793–1798) had a shop at 374 Queen Street. A tambour secretary desk of mahogany and bird's-eye maple is known and bears their label.

JOHN HEWITT, father of Abraham Hewitt, was also one of New York's famous cabinetmakers during this period. He lived from 1777 to 1857. Some of his work is to be seen in the Museum of Cooper Union.

It is impossible to give details about all the admirable New York makers of this period. Only the outstanding ones are noted here, for contemporary makers in other cities must also be mentioned.

THE BOSTON GROUP

In Boston the noted firm of JOHN SEYMOUR & SON worked in Creek Lane from 1796 to 1842. In the collection of Mr. George A. Cluett of Williamstown there is a small sketch, of boats and a landscape, on which is written: "Falmouth, now Portland, in Casco Bay in North America—drawn by John Seymour jun., son of my very honest and worthy old friend John Sey-

PLATE 212. SECRETARY DESK BY WILLIAM HOOK

Top drawer pulls out and drops down to form the writing tablet. The half-round posts on the front are reeded, with water-leaf capitals. (Text: page 237.)

(Courtesy of Ginsburg and Levy)

mour, cabinet maker at Axminster, from whence he and his family of a wife and 8 children emigrated to America about the year 1785. [signed] *John Cranch.*" This is almost the only authentic information that we have as to Seymour's origin and provenance. It sheds much light on his early training in his métier, which must have been received in England.

PLATE 213. SIDEBOARD BY HENRY CONNELLY
Made for Stephen Girard about 1830, this piece has legs that end in a
rounded spade typical of this maker.
(*Courtesy of Directors City Trusts for Girard College*)

A fine secretary (Plate 195) from the collection of Philip Flayderman sold for $30,000 at the American Art Galleries in January, 1930. It is one of two known labeled Seymour pieces. Probably one of the finest examples of American cabinetwork in existence, it came originally from the collection of Judge George A. Emery of Saco, Maine, and is unequaled for quality, condition, and design. *The American Art Gallery Catalogue* describes it as follows:

A cabinet of two long drawers with a hinged folding flap above, on four tapered legs with pierced scrolled brackets at the corners; superimposed by a cabinet of arched pigeonholes and small drawers, enclosed by a pair of sliding tambour shutters. It is constructed in variously figured mahogany of the finest quality. The shutters are inlaid with husk festoons in light wood. Flanking the shutters and the drawers is inlay simulating pilasters. The edges of the top and of the folding writing flap are inlaid with checkered bandings of similar shaded holly, the tapered square legs inlaid with delicate pendant sprays of husk ornament and cuffed at the base. Drawer fronts are panelled with stringings of holly or satinwood, enriched with four contemporary beaded ring handles, framing circular plaques of Battersea enamel painted with female figures emblematic of the Four Seasons. Pasted on the bottom of the lower drawer is the maker's original label which reads: John Seymour & Son, Cabinet-makers, Creek Lane.

Mr. George A. Cluett owns the other labeled piece, a secretary (Plate 199) made entirely of feathered satinwood. The color of the wood is unbe-

PLATE 214. ARMCHAIR (CIRCA 1805)
BY EPHRAIM HAINES
The feet and legs and carving are typical
of the work of this cabinetmaker.
(*Courtesy of the Philadelphia Museum of Art*)

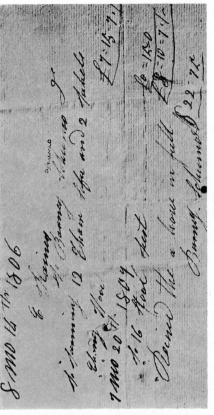

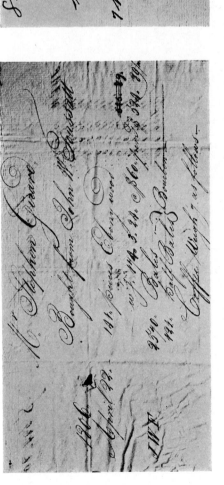

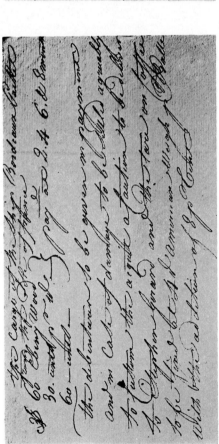

PLATE 215. BILLS FOR FURNITURE MADE BY EPHRAIM HAINES FOR STEPHEN GIRARD IN 1806

These bills cover the complete history from wood to finished furniture of a large purchase. (Text: page 244.)

(Courtesy of Directors City Trusts for Girard College)

lievably lovely and the workmanship exquisite. Its tambour sliding fronts are so perfectly made and matched that they seem to be one piece of wood. Seymour's label is on the back of the cabinet. This piece, the secretary known as the Flayderman secretary and a Seymour sideboard (Plate 198) owned by Mr. and Mrs. Andrew V. Stout are three of the most distinguished examples of American cabinetmaking.

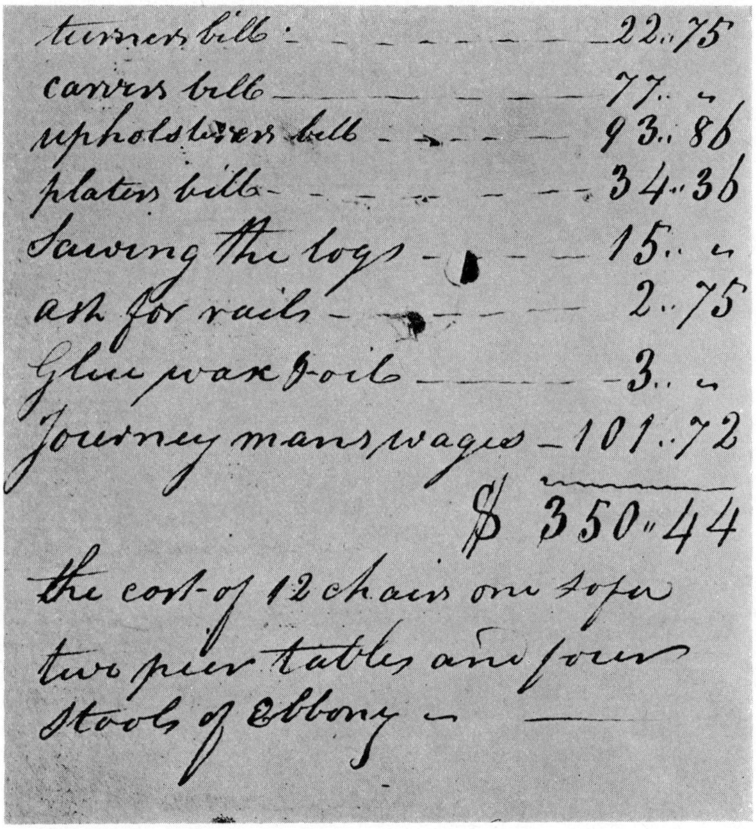

turners bill : _ _ _ _ _ _ 22..75
carvers bill _ _ _ _ _ _ 77. „
upholsterers bill - „ - - _ 93.86
platers bill _ _ „ _ _ -, 34..36
Sawing the logs - , _ _ 15.. „
ash for rails - „ _ - _ 2..75
Glue wax & oil _ _ _ -3.. „
Journey mans wages - 101..72

$ 350..44

the cost of 12 chairs one sofa
two pier tables and four
stools of Ebbony „ _____

PLATE 216. LISTING OF BILLS IN PLATE 215

The superb sideboard has reeded legs carried up to the top as engaged columns and finished there with a carved panel in a fashion similar to that seen in some of the Salem pieces. The tambour doors are flanked with small inlaid pilasters. A fine and delicate inlay outlines the top and bottom edges. The ivory scutcheons are in the forms of vases; a key turned in the lower keyhole, in the wheat-carved apron, locks the entire sideboard. As is usual with Seymour pieces, the interior of the cupboard is painted robin's-egg

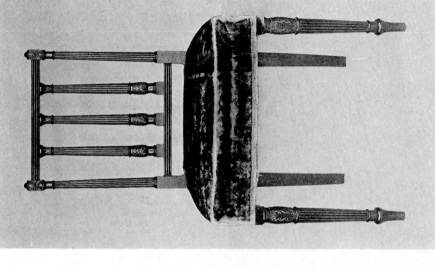

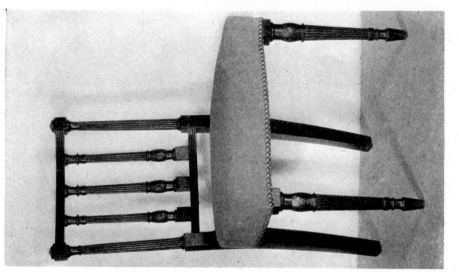

PLATE 217. SIDE CHAIR (1810) BY HENRY CONNELLY

This upholstered chair has a mahogany back and legs. (Text: page 244.)

(*Courtesy of the Philadelphia Museum of Art*)

PLATES 218 AND 219. EBONY CHAIRS BY EPHRAIM HAINES

Ten side chairs with a pair of matching arm chairs were made for Stephen Girard. The bills are seen
in Plates 215 and 216. (Text: page 244.)

(*Courtesy of the Directors City Trusts for Girard College*)

PLATE 220. CARD TABLE ATTRIBUTED TO CONNELLY

The spade foot and the carving at the top of the legs of this mahogany piece are characteristic of this Philadelphia craftsman. (Text: page 242.)

(*Courtesy of the Taft Museum*)

blue. In addition to all the exquisite detail that marks this fine piece, the mahogany of which it is made is most beautifully figured and is superior in quality.

Mr. and Mrs. Stout are also the fortunate possessors of a Seymour secretary desk (Plate 197) believed to have been made between 1790 and 1800, with Bilston enamel drawer pulls, ivory scutcheons, and tambour doors. This is not unlike the famous Flayderman secretary in form, but lacks some of its distinction of detail. The interior is also in the curious Seymour blue. The same collection also boasts a Seymour cabinet (Plate 119).

231

PLATE 221. THREE-PIECE DINING TABLE BY CONNELLY

This piece from the Louis Guerineau Myers collection is a splendid example of Henry Connelly's work. Few American tables are carved on both leg and stile as in this instance. (Text: page 242.)

(Courtesy of Israel Sack)

THE SALEM GROUP

Just as New York, Boston, and Philadelphia furniture had its special and individual characteristics, Salem furniture of this period is distinguished by certain traits not found in the work of other localities. While New York Regency furniture depends for its ornamentation on reeding and occasional carving and relies even more on the color and figure of the mahogany from which it is made, Salem furniture is built around beautiful carved designs which seem to be the chief reason for its existence. There is scarce a sofa without carved rails and a carved panel in the top rail of the back; there is hardly a bookcase without a carved central motif in the pediment, and its chairs and tables are handsomely embellished in the same manner. This special characteristic is perhaps accountable to the residence in Salem of a great family of wood carvers, the five McIntire brothers, of whom Samuel is the

232

most famous. His architectural work is discussed in Chapter V. Samuel McIntire died in 1811 at the early age of fifty-four. Unlike Duncan Phyfe, he accomplished his best work in the later years of his life. As Mr. Edward Hipkiss says, "Although the practice of his art was restricted within a somewhat narrow compass, McIntire attained outstanding distinction in his time. He marks the end of an epoch in style, which was followed by the Greek Revival."

McIntire's son did his best to carry on the tradition of this family of carvers, but lacked the creative genius of his father. The extent and variety

PLATE 222. WRITING DESK BY HENRY CONNELLY

This piece is mahogany with spade foot and carving typical of this Philadelphian's work.

(*Courtesy of Arthur Sussel*)

233

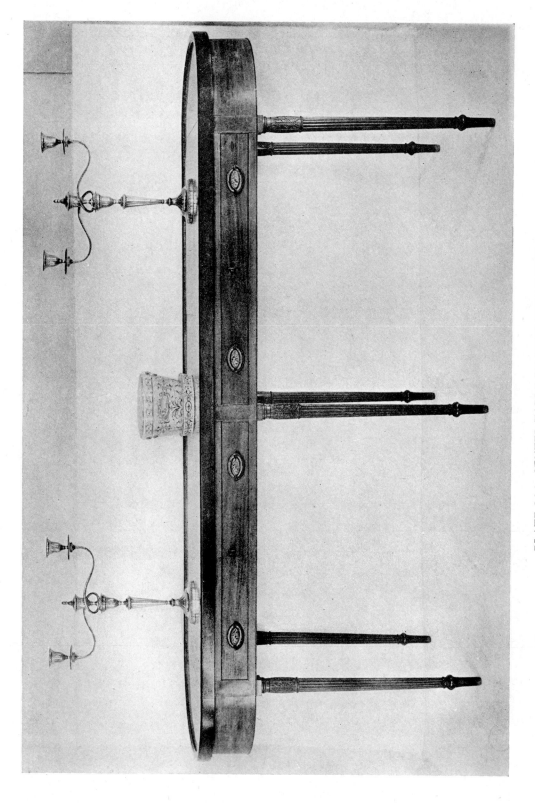

PLATE 223. CENTER TABLE BY EPHRAIM HAINES

This table is one of two included in the order for Stephen Girard in 1806. (Text: page 244, also
see Plates 215, 216, 218, and 219.)

(Courtesy of the Directors City Trusts for Girard College)

of his work is shown in an advertisement of 1815 in which he offers to carve "Ship heads, Eagles of all sizes, Brackets, Draperies. A variety of figures, Butter and Cake Stamps."

ELIJAH and JACOB SANDERSON were perhaps the most prominent cabinetmakers in Salem. Elijah left his native Watertown in 1751 for Salem, where he died in his seventy-third year. His brother, six years his junior, lived until 1810. With their partner, Josiah Hastings, they were most active in the making and exportation of furniture.

Mrs. Mabel M. Swan, who has thrown so much light on this particular period in Salem through her excellent research, says: "One of the most valuable contributions of Sanderson papers and bills is the surprising revelation of the co-operative nature of the making of Salem furniture. In fact there appears to have been a spirit similar to that in Roxbury, where so many craftsmen gathered together in order to obtain work from the Willard clockmakers." Mrs. Swan discovered bills from McIntire to the Sandersons and other cabinetmakers for carving chairs, beds, and sofas.

Next to the Sandersons, "Deacon Adams" was probably the most outstanding among the Salem cabinetmakers. This is the NEHEMIAH ADAMS (1769–1840) who made the secretary bookcase (Plate 171) that traveled to Cape Town. Like the Sandersons he availed himself of McIntire's skilled hand for much of the carved finishing ornament for his work. An imposing eagle sofa (Plate 209), often described as a McIntire sofa, was probably the product of such collaboration between the "Deacon" and McIntire. WILLIAM HOOK (1777–1867), another fine cabinetmaker, moved from Roxbury to Salem in 1796 and developed such excellence in his work that his furniture was in great demand. Because of his popularity it was sometimes necessary to place orders with him a year in advance. None of his labeled pieces have been found, but it has been possible to obtain photographs of two pieces that are authenticated in such a fashion as to leave no room for doubt that they were made by his hands. Both of these were bequeathed to Museums with documentary proof that they were made by William Hook. A sideboard (Plate 204) was left to the Museum of Fine Arts in Boston by Mabel H. F. McInnes. She inherited it and stated: "It was made by William Hook of Salem as a wedding present for his sister, Hannah Hook, who married Peter Folsom of Exeter, New Hampshire in 1809." The donor herself was a granddaughter of this marriage. This sideboard is a combination of

235

beautifully figured wood, with a richly veneered swell front. Two long drawers are below the cupboard whose doors are inlaid with bands of alternating mahogany and satinwood which taper fan-fashion to a center in a sunburst. On the edge of each ray is a tiny inlay of holly and ebony. The delicate finish at the edges of the sideboard, the waterleaf carving at the top of the corner pilasters, and the bands of inlay around the drawers are also distinguished details of this really beautiful piece.

When we study the minute and careful work of this piece of furniture, we are not surprised to learn that, although it was promised as a wedding gift, the sideboard took so much longer than Hook had calculated that he

PLATE 224. SIDEBOARD BY HENRY CONNELLY

This beautiful serpentine sideboard is the only known piece of Connelly which still has a label.
(Text: page 239.)

(*Courtesy of Dr. John Carson*)

was several months late, so that the young couple started housekeeping without it.

In 1910 the Essex Institute of Salem was bequeathed a bureau and mirror by William Hook (Plate 207) with the following document from the

PLATE 225. LABEL OF HENRY CONNELLY
This label is in the sideboard, Plate 224.

donor, Mr. George R. Curwen (Plate 206): "I also give the Essex Institute The Light stand with a turned edge to the top, a fluted pillar and small claw feet. This is in the Parlor Chamber. The Mahogany Bureau which stands in the Front Chamber, with the Dressing Case which stands on top of it; also the linen scarf which is on it. They were made for my mother in 1818 by William Hook, Cabinet Maker."

This bureau is not so unusual in design as the sideboard just mentioned. It even breathes somewhat of Empire decadence and goes to prove that William Hook, like most human beings, could do bad work almost as well as good. A secretary desk (Plate 212) attributed to him has many of the fine details that characterize his best work and somewhat restores our confidence in him. *Pax vobiscum,* William Hook.

237

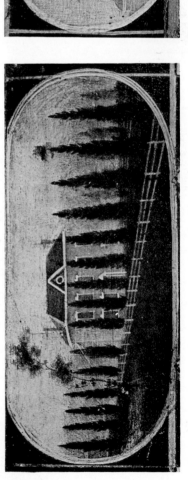

PLATE 226. PAINTED SCENES ON CHAIRS MADE BY JOHN FINDLAY

The houses pictured are all Maryland residences. Reading from top to bottom, left column first, they are: Woodville, which belonged to Captain Yellot; Homewood, residence of Charles Carroll of Carrollton; Montebello, residence of Gen. Samuel Smith; Mount Clare, home of the barrister, Charles Carroll; the residence of L. Pierce; Mount Deposit, built by David Harris and afterwards renamed Surray. (Text: page 246.)

(Courtesy of Mrs. William De Ford)

In Philadelphia the interest in American Regency furniture was not nearly so vivid as in the elaborately carved Chippendale furniture of the preceding century. Ephraim Haines and Henry Connelly, Daniel Trotter and Joseph Barry, however, created enough fine mahogany furniture in our period to make a distinguished Philadelphia group.

PLATE 227. ANOTHER CHAIR-BACK OF THE SET BY FINDLAY
This represents Greenwood, the home of Philip Rogers.
(*Courtesy of Mrs. William De Ford*)

HENRY CONNELLY was a member of the Society of Friends. Born in Philadelphia in 1770, he died in Mill Creek Hundred, near Newark, Delaware, in 1826. He worked at 16 Chestnut Street and at 44 Spruce Street. The particular furniture leg which is recognized almost as a Connelly trademark is the leg ending in a rounded spade. It is often reeded vertically and sometimes has bands of parallel horizontal reeding at the top, almost like Duncan Phyfe's. Often it is carved at the top in the manner of Salem furniture, but the terminal at the foot is entirely distinct and different. There is a sideboard by Connelly (Plates 224 and 225), belonging to Dr. John Carson of Philadelphia, which is the only labeled piece known. On the label Con-

PLATE 228. BALTIMORE CARD TABLE

The black-glass inset is typical of Baltimore decoration. This piece is now owned by
Mrs. J. P. Walker. (Text: page 246.)

(Courtesy of Ginsburg and Levy)

PLATE 229. BALTIMORE SECRETARY BOOKCASE (1800)
This bookcase is of mahogany with satinwood inlay, but the medallions
are of black glass with classical figures in gilt. (Text: page 246.)
(Courtesy of the Metropolitan Museum of Art)

PLATE 230. BALTIMORE MIXING TABLE (1800)

The wood is brown mahogany with inlaid panels of satinwood. The side drawers are for decanters and a tambour roll-top closes over the central portion. (Text: page 246.)

(Courtesy of the Metropolitan Museum of Art)

nelly describes himself as "Cabinet and chair-maker." The sideboard has rounded ends and a serpentine front, is made of fine mahogany, and has characteristic Connelly legs and feet.

The Taft Museum has a fine mahogany card table (Plate 220) attributed to Connelly. A three-part dining table (Plate 221) from the Louis Guerineau Myers collection is described by Mr. Myers as follows: "This table is a splendid example of Connelly's work. Few American Sheraton tables are carved on leg and stile as in this instance, and the writer knows of no other dining-table so decorated."

The Philadelphia Museum of Art owns a pair of side chairs by Con-

PLATE 231. BALTIMORE ROLL-BACK SIDE CHAIR

This chair resembles some of Phyfe's models but the roll at the top of the back resembles English chairs. The paw feet are carved from wood.

(*Courtesy of Homewood*)

243

nelly, similar in design and carving to ten EPHRAIM HAINES ebony chairs owned by Girard College. This Girard College group is extremely interesting being entirely documented by bills (Plates 215 and 216). First comes the bill for 141 pieces of ebony wood bought abroad from John W. Foussatt, then a bill for shipping this wood by Bordeaux packet, followed by Haines' bill for making twelve chairs (Plates 218 and 219), sofa, and two tables (Plate 223). There are also the turner's bill, the carver's bill, the upholsterer's bill, and even a bill for sawing the logs. Another Haines piece of this same epoch is in the Metropolitan Museum of New York—a fine secretary bookcase.

PLATE 232. SIDEBOARD BY JOHN SHAW (1797)

This Baltimore piece in Hepplewhite style is of mahogany with inlay of satinwood. The label in the top center drawer dates the sideboard. (Text: page 245.)

(*Courtesy of the Baltimore Museum of Art*)

PLATE 233. LABEL OF JOHN SHAW
This label is in the top center drawer of the sideboard in
Plate 232. The date is written by hand.

THE BALTIMORE GROUP

Between 1746 and 1820 there were in Maryland approximately 330 cabinetmakers. Baltimore boasted a cosmopolitan group including English, German, Dutch, Irish, Italian, and French names. In Annapolis the cabinet-makers were all English. Native walnut and mahogany were the favorite woods used by these artisans. Cherry was popular in Annapolis and maple, a favorite of the early days, returned to vogue after 1820.

The name of JOHN SHAW, cabinetmaker, is outstanding in Annapolis. A sideboard with his label may be seen in the permanent collection of the Baltimore Museum of Art in the Maryland Wing (Plates 232 and 233). Many authorities, including Mr. Halsey and Dr. Berkeley, believe that Shaw was merely an importer and not a maker of furniture. He may have restored and altered pieces that came to him from abroad but it certainly would be very difficult to certify that the Hepplewhite sideboard in the Baltimore Museum was made by him, even though it bears his label.

Nineteenth-century Baltimore furniture, although it kept the simple lines characteristic of this period, used elaborate decorative treatments peculiar to the locality, such as the insertion of black-glass panels decorated with classical figures in gold. This treatment may be seen in the secretary bookcase (Plate 229) in the Metropolitan Museum and also in a serpentine card table (Plate 228) now owned by Mrs. J. P. Walker. Both pieces are of mahogany inlaid with lines of satinwood and both have the inset glass panels. In Plate 230 is a Baltimore mixing table with marble top made about 1800. It is of a light tone mahogany with a restrained satinwood inlay on the front of the legs. Straight lines emphasize the structural quality of the design. The side drawers are for decanters. Over the center part is a tambour roll-top.

Much painted furniture also was made in Baltimore. Robert Fisher is renowned as the maker of a fine painted set with Maryland mansions in its design. A settee made by Thomas Renshaw was decorated by John Barnhart with Maryland mansions and another set of chairs made by John Findlay was painted in the same manner by an unknown English artist (Plates 226 and 227). So popular was this style of decoration in the neighborhood that several different cabinetmakers used the designs.

Although this is by no means a complete list of American cabinetmakers of the early nineteenth century, it is perhaps comprehensive enough to give an idea of the number of men who ranked as Phyfe's peers and competitors. To them all honor for a fine American interpretation of the classic tradition.

IX

HIS CUSTOMERS

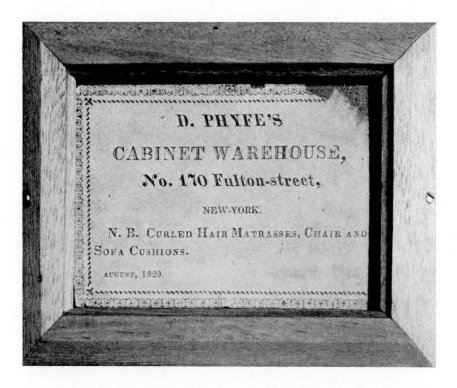

PLATE 234. LABEL ON BOWIE SECRETARY, PLATE 251

No account books of Duncan Phyfe's have been preserved. Certain old wills and inventories, however, tell us the names of people for whom he made some of his superlatively fine furniture. A few bills still exist and occasional members of old families are able to furnish an exact genealogy of their possessions. From these scarce records we can deduce the fact that Duncan was cabinetmaker for the fashionable world of his day. Orders for some thirty-six distinguished clients have been carefully traced and are recorded here under the name of the original purchasers with all available data.

Most accounts of Phyfe's work ignore the furniture of his later periods and confine themselves to the work he did between 1800 and 1820. After all, the review of a man's work during his lifetime should reasonably include all the different types that came from his hand and, since commissions from the people mentioned in this chapter begin early in the century and run on to 1847, a number of later pieces are included among the photographs. It is interesting to see how Phyfe was obliged to change his style in order to follow the changing fashion, and how his earlier delicacy of line thickened as Victorian ideas prevailed.

The list does not in any way pretend to be a complete record. Doubtless hundreds of additional names will come to light after the publication of this book. I hope so. I hope, too, that descendants of other original Phyfe customers will send information that will aid in rounding out the register which has been begun here.

PLATE 235. PAINTING OF WILLIAM AKIN
Attributed to Ezra Ames, this painting on wood is from the
collection of Miss Alice Irwin.
(*Courtesy of the Frick Art Reference Library*)

248

PLATE 236. MR. AKIN'S SOFA, 1797

Mr. Akin was married on Christmas Day, 1797, and had Duncan Phyfe make this sofa for his Greenbush home. It is now loaned to the Monmouth County Historical Association.

(*Courtesy of Mrs. J. Amory Haskell*)

WILLIAM AKIN, Greenbush. When William Akin (Plate 235) married Caroline Matilda Cary on December 25, 1797, Duncan Phyfe made for them a beautiful couch which was sent to their home in Greenbush, New York. Greenbush, across the river from Albany and originally called East Albany, is today known as Rensselaer. William Akin came there from Pawling, Dutchess County, in about 1810 and purchased, from John J. Van Rensselaer, land which was known as "Akin Mile Square." He built his house on it at the corner of Broadway and Mill Street in about 1818. The beautiful couch (Plate 236) was one of the treasures of the Akin home. William Akin, Lafayette, and Citizen Genêt often sat on it together to discuss the events of the day. By 1844 this couch was owned by Jacob Van Benschoten Teller; his daughter, Anna Teller Irwin, inherited it and left it to Anna Irwin Chamberlain, who exhibited it at the Albany Institute of History and Art.

It is now the property of Mrs. J. Amory Haskell, who has loaned it to the Monmouth County Historical Association in Freehold, New Jersey.

The shape, design, and carving of this piece of furniture are most unusual. In the center panel of the top rail is a crossed bow and arrow with a drapery swag on each side. The bow and arrow motif is practically a stranger in Phyfe ornament and it may have been used on this particular wedding piece as a symbol of the God of Love. Two long panels, formed by reeding, flank this carving on the top rail. The arms have a double curve and are reeded to within a short distance of the post. Acanthus leaves are carved over the final downward curve. The posts and the two corner legs repeat the reeding but the two center front legs are plain. All four finish in small brass feet. This sofa is 6 feet 6 inches long.

JOHN ALLING, Newark. The first mahogany sofa (Plate 237) to come into the town of Newark, New Jersey, was made by Duncan Phyfe for John

PLATE 237. JOHN ALLING'S SOFA

This piece of furniture by Phyfe is reputedly the first mahogany sofa to penetrate the town of Newark. Identical sofas were made for Jeremiah Halsey Pierson (Plate 281) and Theodore Frelinghuysen.

(Courtesy of Miss Sarah Alling Wheeler)

PLATE 238. JOHN JACOB ASTOR'S ARMCHAIR

Mr. Astor lived near Phyfe's warehouse and was one of his regular customers.
Compare with chair in Plate 40.

(*Courtesy of Miss Katherine Langdon Wilks*)

Alling. At this time the Alling Homestead stood on the corner of Broad and Market Streets, surrounded by ample acres and orchards. Newark was still a simple village with a town pump in the center street. There were few mansions where fine mahogany furniture was suitable. Later on John Alling built a house in East Park Street, not far from the Training Common. After his death, the sofa was taken from this residence to Chimney Manor in West Orange, the home of his granddaughter, Caroline Matilda Crane Van Wagenen. In 1919 Mrs. Van Wagenen gave the sofa to a great-granddaughter,

Mary Louise Wheeler, living in Llewellyn Park, and it is now owned by her sister, Sarah Alling Wheeler.

The sofa (Plate 237), an excellent example of Phyfe's early period, has a top rail carved with a drapery and tassel swag in the middle panel and bowknots and thunderbolts in the two side panels. The side rails and posts are reeded as are also the four front legs. Identical to it is a sofa in the Taft Museum, Cincinnati, and, with the exception of the corner blocks, it is also exactly like one made for Jeremiah Halsey Pierson (Plate 281) and also for Theodore Frelinghuysen.

PLATE 239. MR. ASTOR'S CONSOLE TABLE
This folding table has acanthus carved legs and paw feet.
(*Courtesy of Miss Katherine Langdon Wilks*)

JOHN JACOB ASTOR, New York. In Ernest Hagen's notebook, now owned by Mr. R. T. Haines Halsey,* we find a memorandum saying that the son of Duncan Phyfe's brother Michael was "mostly employed about the ware-rooms dusting and delivering the furniture by pushcart. He took many loads of it to the Astors who were their best customers." At that time the Astors lived in Vesey Street, so Duncan's nephew did not have far to push from the warerooms in Partition Street. There was no trace of the furniture delivered there by him when search was begun for this record, but some of it has been tracked down to Canada. An armchair (Plate 238) and console table (Plate 239) are among the pieces ordered by the great fur trader from Duncan Phyfe, and are authenticated by his great-granddaughter Miss Katherine Wilks, who writes, "I know that the two pieces of which you have photographs belonged to John Jacob Astor."

John Jacob Astor came to this country from the little German town of Waldorf in 1784, the same year Duncan set sail from Scotland with his family. Six years later, by the time the Scotch lad had finished his apprenticeship and was ready to begin work as a cabinetmaker, John Jacob Astor had already laid the foundation for his great fortune.

The resemblance of Mr. Astor's armchair to the form of the Thomas Hope Egyptian chair owned by Mr. Knoblock (Plate 40) is striking. Similarities of this sort prove how closely the Regency styles of England are linked with early nineteenth-century cabinetwork in this country. The Astor console (Plate 239) is similar to the one made for Miss Louisa Throop in 1806 (Plate 287), which is an indication of the date of its manufacture.

MATTHEW WILKS, Ontario, Canada. In 1842 Matthew Wilks, an Englishman, married Eliza Langdon, the granddaughter of John Jacob Astor, at the home of her parents in Hyde Park. At first the Wilkses lived in New York and at this time Duncan Phyfe, who was nearing retirement age, made a number of pieces of furniture for them. The dressing table (Plate 240), a dining-room sideboard, a four-poster bed, and various other things came from Phyfe's workshop for the bride's new house. At a later date, Matthew Wilks purchased an estate in Cruickston Park in Galt, Ontario, as a summer residence but he became so fond of the place that he eventually settled there, moving all his furniture from New York. On the death of his wife's mother,

* See Addenda.

253

PLATE 240. MATTHEW WILKS' DRESSING TABLE, 1842

In 1842 Mr. Wilks married Mr. Astor's granddaughter. The dressing table is one of several pieces made for him at this time by Phyfe and represents the late period of the master's work. Note the obelisk mirror supports.

(Courtesy of Miss Katherine Langdon Wilks)

Mrs. Walter Langdon, he also bought the furniture from her old house at 61 Lafayette Place and sent it to Ontario.

Miss Katherine Langdon Wilks inherited the estate and the furniture from her father and lives there now. She says, "I have the furniture bought by my parents when they were married and I recollect my father's saying 'Made by Phyfe.' "

PLATE 241. BILL ADDRESSED TO CHARLES N. BANCKER
Sketches of two types of chairs with alternative prices for cane or upholstered seats make this bill of particular interest.
(*Courtesy of R. T. Haines Halsey and the Museum of the City of New York*)

CHARLES N. BANCKER, Philadelphia. A bill of January 4, 1816, from Duncan Phyfe to Mr. Charles N. Bancker of Philadelphia was discovered by Ernest Hagen and presented to Mr. R. T. Haines Halsey, who has loaned it to the Museum of the City of New York. This document (Plates 241 and 242) bears on the reverse side rough sketches of two chairs and gives the alternative price for making them either with cane seats and cushions or with upholstered seats.

Charles Nicoll Bancker was born in 1777 and died in February, 1869.

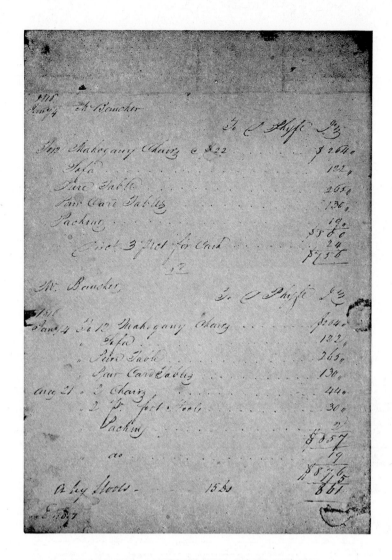

PLATE 242. REVERSE SIDE OF PLATE 241

In 1840 he was president of the Franklin Fire Insurance Company of Philadelphia. His marriage to Sarah Upshur Teackle of Virginia resulted in a
family of five sons and four daughters, one of whom married John Cad-
walader as her second husband.

Phyfe, according to the evidence contributed by the bill, made a first
shipment amounting to $800 in the month of January. He offered his client
a discount of 3 per cent for cash. Mr. Bancker, however, did not avail himself of this offer as we can see by the second bill of August 21 which cites the
first order (still unpaid) and adds two chairs and a pair of footstools to the
list. Seven months was a long time to wait for payment, but it saved Phyfe

256

more than his 3 per cent for there is an error in subtraction which would have made him lose $20 had the bill been discounted. The bookkeeping of the Phyfe establishment cannot have been too exact, for another error is found in the bill to George MacCulloch (Plate 269). This time it is a dollar in Phyfe's favor, but he was up against another Scotchman and the bill was corrected.

Mr. Bancker's bill gives a good idea of Phyfe's prices at the time. The mahogany dining chairs—a set of twelve was undoubtedly for the dining room—cost $22 apiece. The Phyfe sofa, which probably had a carved rail, does not seem too dear at $122 in the light of present-day prices. The "Piere Table," probably elaborately carved, for the best parlor, seems expensive at $265. Card tables at $65 apiece undoubtedly had carved bases and fine veneer like the tables illustrated in former chapters.

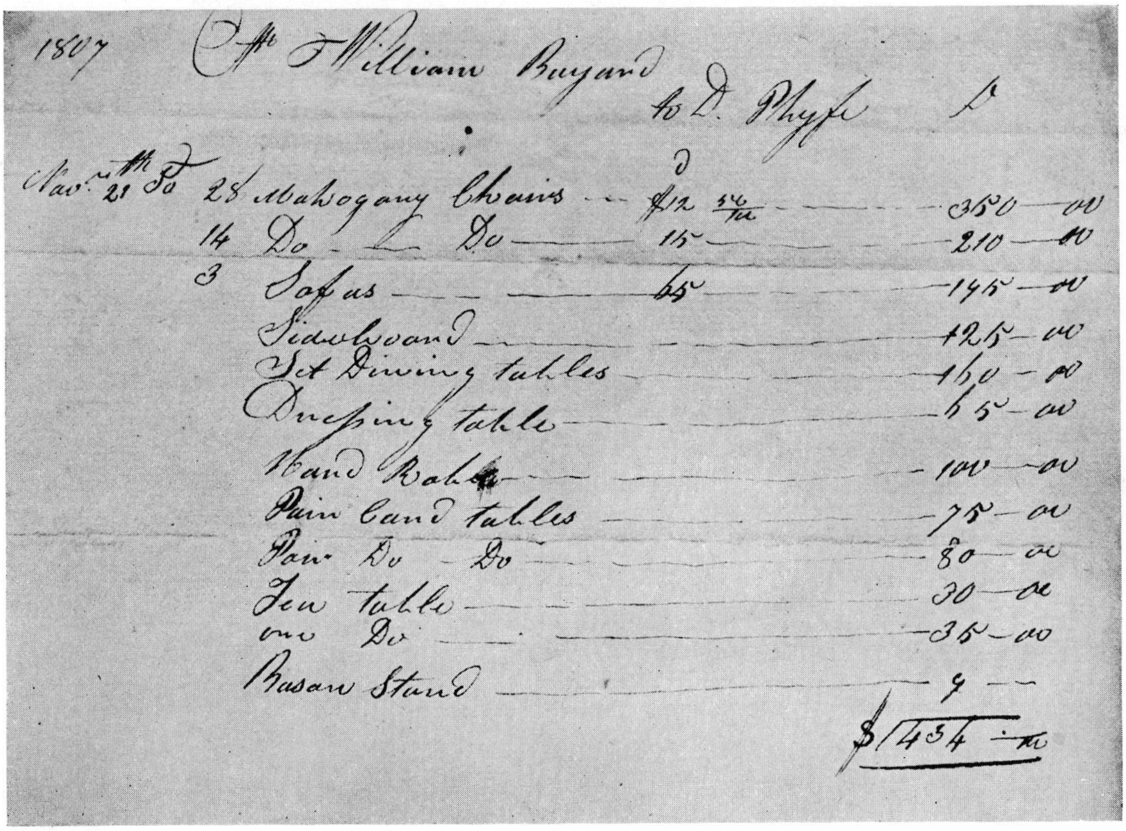

1807 Mr William Bayard

to D. Phyfe Dr

Nov. 21th	28 Mahogany Chairs	$12 50/100	350—00
	14 Do L Do	15	210—00
	3 Sofas	65	195—00
	Sideboard		125—00
	Set Dining tables		160—00
	Dressing table		65—00
	Ward Robe		100—00
	Pair Card tables		75—00
	Pair Do Do		80—00
	Tea table		30—00
	one Do		35—00
	Bason Stand		9 —
			$1434 —

PLATE 243. BILL ADDRESSED TO WILLIAM BAYARD

Practically all the items on this bill have been identified and their present owners established.

WILLIAM BAYARD, New York. The Phyfe bill (Plate 243) of November 21, 1807, was found among the papers of Mr. Bayard after his death and is now in the possession of the present owner of the chairs (Plates 244 and 245). Twelve of these were originally in the old William Bayard house on Broadway. From there they moved to 170 Fifth Avenue. They were inherited by Miss Marie Louise Campbell, a granddaughter of Mr. Bayard, and sold from her estate in 1912 to the late Horace Townsend. Some of the other fur-

PLATE 244. WILLIAM BAYARD'S SIDE CHAIR, 1807

This is among Phyfe's finest models and is one of a set of twelve chairs.
The bill in Plate 243 values it at $12.50.

258

PLATE 245. MR. BAYARD'S ARMCHAIR, 1807
One of the set made for William Bayard and billed at $15.

niture listed on the bill is still in the Bayard family. In her Washington house Mrs. Bayard Cutting has the sideboard and wardrobe that were among Mr. Bayard's purchases and she also owns a bureau and a large four-poster bed which do not appear on the bill.

One of the pair of card tables made for Mr. Bayard had a curious history. When he organized the Bank of America in 1812, he convened a small group of men to discuss plans with him and serve as directors. The council table which they used was one of these Phyfe card tables. At a later date when the Bank of America merged with the National City Bank, Mr. Bay-

259

PLATE 246. MR. BAYARD'S CARD TABLE

This is one of a pair. The other was presented to the Bank of America in 1812, when
Mr. Bayard organized it.

(Courtesy of Dr. Howard Townsend)

ard presented the card table to the museum of the bank. In some unexplained fashion it has disappeared and cannot be traced today. We know, however, what it was like, for the other table of the pair (Plate 246) is owned by Dr. Howard Townsend of Poughkeepsie.

PLATE 247. PORTRAIT OF SOPHIA MILES BELDEN
Duncan Phyfe made her wedding furniture.
(*Courtesy of Mrs. Giles Whiting*)

SOPHIA MILES BELDEN, New York. Sophia Miles Belden (Plate 247) bequeathed to her daughter, Mrs. Laura Belden Field, long resident at 86 Gramercy Park, the wedding furniture made for her by Duncan Phyfe. In

261

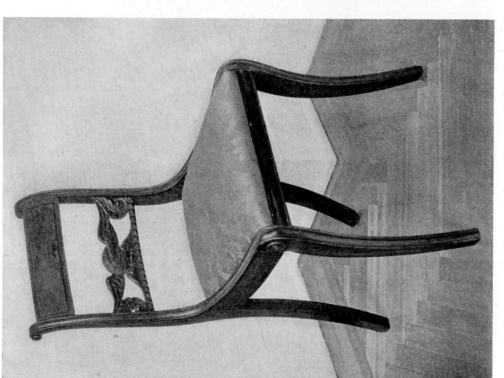

PLATES 248 AND 249. MRS. BELDEN'S CHAIRS

The chair with the spread-eagle splat is one of a set of eight. That with the swag and double eagle-head splat is entirely different from most of Phyfe's designs.

(*Courtesy of Mrs. Giles Whiting*)

the collection are chairs with a spread eagle in the splat (Plate 248). They are similar to a set owned by Mr. R. T. Haines Halsey, usually believed to have been made by Lannuier about 1815–1820. There is also a beautiful set of ten chairs (Plate 249) with double-eagle splat. The eagles hold draperies in their beaks. This model has not been found elsewhere. A fine butler's desk (Plate 250) also belonged to Mrs. Belden and is one of the rare examples of "case furniture" by Duncan Phyfe. All of these articles are now the property of Mrs. Giles Whiting of New York.

PLATE 250. MRS. BELDEN'S BUTLER'S DESK
This is one of the rare examples of Phyfe's case furniture.
(*Courtesy of Mrs. Giles Whiting*)

263

PLATE 251. THOMAS LATTIMER BOWIE'S SECRETARY DESK, 1820

This desk, made for Mr. Bowie of Philadelphia, bears two of Phyfe's labels, one of which is reproduced in Plate 234.

(*Courtesy of Mr. and Mrs. Bayard Bowie*)

THOMAS LATTIMER BOWIE, Philadelphia. A simple secretary bookcase (Plate 251) made by Duncan Phyfe in 1820 for Thomas Lattimer Bowie of Philadelphia was shipped directly to the old Bowie house at 1710 Walnut Street and was always there during the lifetime of its owner. It is today in the possession of Mr. and Mrs. Bayard Bowie. Thomas Lattimer Bowie (1808–1838) was a lawyer, born in York, Pennsylvania. He moved to Phila-

PLATE 252. HENRI CHRISTOPHE, BLACK EMPEROR
OF HAITI

This is a Torchiana engraving from a drawing by
Dridier. The Emperor ordered a carved bed from
Phyfe for the royal bedroom.

(Courtesy of the Print Room, New York Public Library)

265

delphia with his mother to study and practice law in that city and in 1836 married Catharine H. Ashurst.

The secretary is one of the rare Phyfe pieces with a label (Plate 234). In fact it has two labels—one in the upper cabinet and one in the lower part, in a drawer. From them we are informed that the exact date of the piece is 1820.

HENRI CHRISTOPHE, Black Emperor of Haiti. About 1815 Duncan Phyfe received a commission which interested him so much that he gave it a great deal of his personal attention and even, it is said, did some of the

PLATE 253. PORTRAIT OF DE WITT CLINTON

This portrait by John Trumbull shows the long legs of the Governor which Phyfe provided for in his long-legged armchair in Plate 255.

(*Courtesy of the Art Commission of New York*)

266

PLATE 254. GOVERNOR CLINTON'S CHAIR
This stunning eagle-back chair is on exhibit at the Metropolitan Museum. It is one of a set made for Governor Clinton.
(*Courtesy of Mrs. Henry Wilmerding Payne*)

carving himself. The order was for a four-poster bed for Henri Christophe, the Black Emperor of Haiti (Plate 252). The bed was destined to go into the magnificent palace of Sans Souci with its turquoise tiles from Seville, its fountains and waterfalls running through Pompeian-red waterways, and its clear yellow stucco walls that gleamed in the sun like dull gold.

The Black Emperor ordered Phyfe's bed for the royal bedroom in his palace. It was in this very room, after a stroke had deprived him of the ability to mount his horse and after the desertion of his own picked troops, the Dahomeys, that he bade farewell to his family and pulled the trigger which sent a silver bullet through his brain.

The magnificent palace, with all its contents, was destroyed during the revolution that was the occasion of Christophe's death.*

* The information about Phyfe's order for this bed came originally from Mrs. Duncan Phyfe Vail, Eliza's daughter-in-law. It is confirmed by Mr. F. Percy Vail, great-grandson of Duncan Phyfe, who distinctly remembers family conversation about this order.

PLATE 255. GOVERNOR CLINTON'S OWN ARMCHAIR
This chair with extra long legs has a double-cross back
and upholstered seat.
(*Courtesy of Charles Woolsey Lyon*)

PLATE 256. H. G. CLOPPER'S DESK SEWING TABLE, CIRCA 1816

It is not to be assumed that this distinguished ex-commissariat of the British army kept his needle and thread provisions here, but at any rate this table was one of his purchases made from Duncan Phyfe about 1816.

(Courtesy of the Edison Institute)

De Witt Clinton, Mayor of New York, 1803–1815, and afterwards Governor. A fine set of chairs with carved eagles in the backs was made by Phyfe for this distinguished citizen. Two of the set are now on exhibition at the Metropolitan Museum (Plate 254). They are owned and loaned by Mrs. Henry Wilmerding Payne, into whose family Clinton married. Phyfe also made for the same client a double-cross back armchair (Plate 255). The excessive length of the legs of this chair, when compared with the height of the imposing figure of De Witt Clinton in Trumbull's portrait (Plate 253) indicates that the chair was specially made for his comfort.

PLATE 257. EDWARD DELAFIELD'S COUCH
This is one of Phyfe's finest couches, made for one of New York's finest physicians.
(*Courtesy of the Edison Institute*)

H. G. Clopper, President of the Central Bank of New Brunswick. The combination sewing table and writing desk from the Edison Institute Collection (Plate 256) was made by Duncan Phyfe about 1816 for H. G. Clopper, who for many years was a commissariat officer in the British army and was stationed at Fort Cumberland. Founder of the Central Bank of New Brunswick, he was its first president, a position which he held until his death in 1838. His likeness is still to be seen on the five-dollar bills of the People's Bank, Frederickton, New Brunswick.

DR. EDWARD DELAFIELD, New York. Dr. Edward Delafield, the best-known physician of his time, was also a patron and customer of Duncan Phyfe. In his day President of the College of Physicians and Surgeons, he married Miss Julia Floyd, a granddaughter of one of the signers of the Declaration of Independence. His beautiful sofa (Plate 257) with rounded ends was made by Duncan Phyfe. It was left to his son, Dr. Francis Delafield, who in turn willed it to his daughter, Elisabeth Ray Delafield, from whom it was purchased for the Edison Institute in Dearborn, Michigan.

VICTORINE DU PONT, Eleutherean Mills, near Wilmington. Miss du

PLATE 258. PORTRAIT OF SAMUEL A. FOOT
(*Courtesy of Miss Olive W. Whittredge*)

271

PLATE 259. MR. FOOT'S CONSOLE
This is one of a pair.
(*Courtesy of Miss Olive W. Whittredge*)

Pont married Ferdinand Bauduy, but her romance had a sad ending. She was a widow in less than a month after her wedding day. Duncan Phyfe made for her a beautiful little sewing table, which now belongs to her great-niece, Mrs. Francis B. Crowninshield of Boston. There is a bill for this table, which has been mislaid, and also a letter from Madame Bauduy's sister-in-law, saying: "Mr. Phyfe has been very slow about finishing the table which he was making for Victorine, and I have been to ask him to hurry it. It is very pretty and he will have it soon."

SAMUEL A. FOOT, New York. In July, 1819, Samuel A. Foot (Plate 258), eminent New York lawyer, was, on the recommendation of Governor Clinton, appointed to the highly responsible office of District Attorney for Albany County. He bought a house in Albany in 1821 and in 1837 built another at 678 Broadway in New York. This he sold ten years later, moving from New York to Geneva, New York, in order to obtain rest from his daily work and give his fifteen children opportunity for out-of-door exercise and sunshine. Here he built a Greek Revival house, planted a garden, and stocked a farm on his property. This house is now used as a school. It was natural that Mr. Foot should go to the best cabinetmaker of his day to order furniture for his New York house. He had a large number of Phyfe pieces. All of the furniture in Plates 259, 260, and 261 was made for him in 1837 and is interesting because it still has its original covering of crimson mohair with white woven designs (Plates 260 and 261) which matched the borders on the drawing-room curtains. Some pieces were inherited by his daughter Euphemia Whittredge, and later by Miss Olive W. Whittredge of Camden, South Carolina; Mrs. L. Emery Katzenbach of New Canaan, Connecticut also inherited pieces.

PLATE 260. MR. FOOT'S CHAIRS AND STOOL

Phyfe made four chairs and four stools for Mr. Foot's drawing room. The upholstery is original and matched the curtains of the room.

(*Courtesy of Miss Olive W. Whittredge*)

Theodore Frelinghuysen, Newark (1786–1861). Theodore Frelinghuysen was Chancellor of New York University, President of Rutgers College, and Senator from New Jersey during his lifetime. He had a couch which is in every way a duplicate of the one made for John Alling of Newark (Plate 237). The design seems to have been a favorite one of Duncan Phyfe. He made it again for Jeremiah Halsey Pierson and it is also to be seen in the Taft Museum in Cincinnati. The Frelinghuysen sofa is now owned by a great-grandson.

William Gaston,* Savannah, Georgia. Almost identical with the larger Phyfe dining table in the Metropolitan Museum is the three-pedestal table which Mr. William Neyle Habersham of Savannah saw one day standing in the yard of the Montgomery House loaded with vegetables (Plate 262). Being a connoisseur of beautiful furniture, he purchased the table and

* The historical notes about William Gaston are taken from an article by Thomas Gamble, in the Savannah *Morning News*.

PLATE 261. MR. FOOT'S SOFA, 1837

This is one of a pair made for Mr. Foot's drawing room. As with the furniture in Plate 260, the upholstery is original.

(*Courtesy of Miss Olive W. Whittredge*)

PLATE 262. WILLIAM GASTON'S DINING TABLE

The table of this Savannah citizen is identical with one in the Metropolitan Museum except for the turnings on the columns.

(*Courtesy of Mrs. Clarence G. Anderson*)

took it to his home at White Bluff, where it has been ever since. The accompanying photograph shows clearly the design of the four turned colonnettes resting on a platform supported by four splayed feet which are reeded and carved with acanthus terminating in carved paws. There must originally have been two extra leaves, as each section has supports with brass knobs to hold them, but the leaves themselves are missing. The table is so designed that each of the three parts may be tipped up and stood out of the way when not in use. The length of the three sections together is nine feet, the width four feet, and the height 29½ inches.

Mr. Habersham's investigations proved that this table was made by Duncan Phyfe for Mr. William Gaston, a native of New Jersey, who went to Savannah and became an outstanding citizen. He was known as "the Prince of Savannah Merchants" and "the friend and citizen-host of strangers," and entertained lavishly in his handsome house. He became President of the Planter's Bank in July, 1822. While on a visit to New York in 1837, he died suddenly. The bells of the Presbyterian Church and the City Exchange tolled when the news of his death reached Savannah and the citizens were summoned to a mass meeting where they decided to build a tomb in Bona-

PLATE 263. JOHN LIVINGSTON'S CHAIRS

These chairs are still in the Livingston house in Greendale, New York. They are similar in style, except for the legs, to Governor Clinton's chair in Plate 255.

(*Courtesy of Mrs. Herman Livingston, Sr.*)

venture Cemetery for his remains and as a receiving vault for strangers who died in Savannah.

After Mr. Gaston's death his furnishings, silverware, and wines were sold "at public outcry." The table was purchased by the British Consul, Mr. Molyneux, who later sold it to Mr. Habersham. Today it is owned by Mr. Habersham's granddaughter, Mrs. Clarence G. Anderson.

WILLIAM HINMAN, Brooklyn. When Mr. William Hinman was living in Brooklyn, before his marriage in 1841, he ordered from Duncan Phyfe some dining-room furniture which is now owned by his daughter, Miss Jennie Hinman of New York and Southbury. The dining table has a central part and two end sections, which may either be added to extend the table or used by themselves to form a smaller table. Curiously enough, the legs of the two end pieces are entirely different in design from the legs of the center table. Mr. Hinman was advised to send them back when they were delivered, but he apparently liked the oddity of the combination and refused to return them to Duncan Phyfe. The eight chairs accompanying this table are examples of Phyfe's later and heavier work. Miss Hinman has also one of the fine mahogany card tables of Phyfe's earlier period with the curious swivel mechanism for which he was justly celebrated, to move the legs at the back, and there are also two beds which have been cut down for use in single bedrooms.

PLATE 264. JOHN LIVINGSTON'S SOFA

Bowknot and thunderbolt design is in the central panel of the back, flanked in the side panels by carved drapery swags.

(*Courtesy of Mrs. Herman Livingston, Sr.*)

277

MRS. RALPH IZARD, New York. Mrs. Ralph Izard, who was Miss Alice Delancey, went to live in Charleston after her marriage. Besides their town house, the Izards also had a plantation outside of the city. Miss Delancey's father furnished the plantation house for her and must have sent down from New York a whole boatload of furniture made by Duncan Phyfe. Still in existence today is a large dining table in three parts, with reeded legs and brass paw feet, which now belongs to Mrs. Joseph E. Jenkins of Charleston. A fine Phyfe sofa table with a double stretcher and old brasses was also part of the furnishings of the great Izard house.

PLATE 265. JOHN LIVINGSTON'S CONSOLE TABLE AND CHAIRS
The base of the table is heavily carved and gilded.
(*Courtesy of Mrs. Herman Livingston, Sr.*)

JOHN LIVINGSTON, Oak Hill, Greendale, New York. Only a few years after Duncan Phyfe had opened a shop in New York, John Livingston built his big house at Greendale on the Hudson on property known as Oak Hill. The house, with some alterations, is still standing and in it is still some of the Phyfe furniture (Plates 263, 264, and 265) made for it around the time when it was built. At the gate of this old Livingston manor, is a sign placed

278

there by the New York State Education Department which reads: "Built in 1793 by John Livingston, son of the 3rd Proprietor, and home of succeeding generations of the Family."

WILLIAM LIVINGSTON, Governor of New Jersey. Duncan Phyfe made furniture for more than one governor. The chairs bought from him by De Witt Clinton have already been mentioned. In addition, there is Governor Manning's furniture in South Carolina. There is also a set of twenty-four chairs made for William Livingston, Governor of New Jersey. This fine set (Plate 266) was widely scattered. Ten were recovered from Mrs. Robert Gardner, a member of the Livingston family, and three others have been

PLATE 266. WILLIAM LIVINGSTON'S CHAIRS

Duncan Phyfe made twenty-four of these chairs for William Livingston, who was Governor of New Jersey.

(*Courtesy of Mr. and Mrs. Andrew Varick Stout*)

found in different places. The seat rails bear numbers indicating that the set originally contained twenty-four, for, although some numbers are missing, one chair is marked 23.

These chairs were reassembled by Louis Guerineau Myers and are now in the possession of Andrew Varick Stout. They are among the most interesting of Phyfe's designs, for they have carved lyres in the backs, reeded seat rails, and legs carved with fur and dog's paws. They are identical with the set made by Phyfe in 1808 for Miss Louisa Throop (Plate 287).

PLATE 267. CHARLES LUDLOW'S CHAIR

One of a set of seventeen lyre-back chairs made for the Ludlows. Five of the set are in the Metropolitan Museum, and the rest of the set are at the Edison Institute.

(*Courtesy of the Edison Institute*)

280

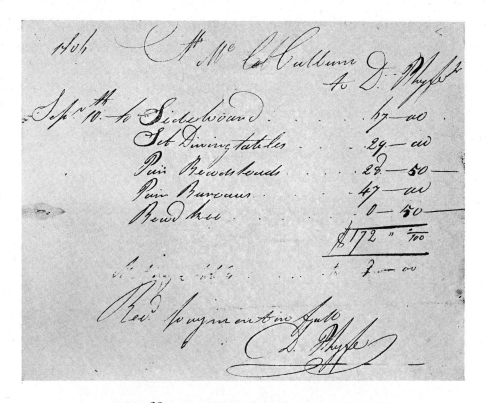

PLATE 268. BILL RECEIPTED BY DUNCAN PHYFE
The reverse side of this bill is shown in Plate 269.

CHARLES LUDLOW, New York and Flatbush. A set of seventeen chairs with lyre backs, reeded rails, and front legs carved with acanthus was made by Duncan Phyfe for the Charles Ludlow family of New York and Flatbush.

Edward P. Chrystie, a great-grandson of Charles Ludlow, tells me that his mother when she was a very little girl remembers seeing Duncan Phyfe when he came to Windsor Hill on a business visit which concerned a lawsuit about his property at 193 Fulton Street.

The Ludlow chairs were inherited by Mrs. Maria Phillipse James of Norwalk, Connecticut. On her death she left twelve of them to her lifelong friend and attorney, Mr. John P. Treadwell; these twelve chairs are now in the Edison Institute in Dearborn. The other five are in the possession of the Metropolitan Museum in New York (Plate 267).

GOVERNOR MANNING, South Carolina. In the early nineteenth century, Duncan Phyfe furnished Millford, the home of Governor Manning. He made not only all the furniture but also the curtains and cornices for the rooms on the main floor. A granddaughter of the Governor, Mrs. Cato Glover, owns several tables, dressing tables, beds, ottomans, and corner cupboards from the old mansion as well as the dining-room chairs. The bills for this furniture are still in existence. The borders of the curtains are exactly like the borders on the furniture covering on the sofas (Plate 261) made for Samuel A. Foot of New York.

WILLIAM WALLACE McCAY, Bath, New York. A pair of very late console tables, made after 1830, were ordered from Duncan Phyfe by William Wallace McCay for his house in Bath, New York. One of the pair is now the property of his great-granddaughter, Mrs. Milton Tootle 3d, the other belongs to Senator Truman Newberry of Detroit. They are florid Empire in style with heavy gilt carving.

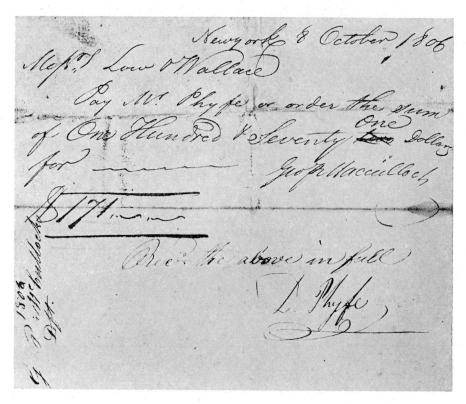

PLATE 269. GEORGE P. MACCULLOCH'S BILL FROM PHYFE

Pity the poor customer! Not only was Mr. MacCulloch overcharged, but his name was misspelled in two different ways in the above, and in yet another way in the first proofs of this book.

(*Courtesy of Emil Hurja*)

282

PLATE 270. CHARLES MARCH'S SIDE CHAIR
This is one of a set of eighteen chairs, six of which are exhibited
at the House of History, Kinderhook, New York.
(*Courtesy of James E. Leath*)

GEORGE P. MacCULLOCH. Nothing is known about this client. Indeed, that Phyfe knew little more than we is shown by the fact that the bill (Plates 268 and 269) is made out in somewhat hesitating form to "Mr. McCullum." Besides the misspelling there is a misaddition which was caught and corrected by the careful client in his order to his bankers to pay the bill. The draft is dated 1806. These two documents have never before been published and are the property of Emil Hurja of Washington.

CHARLES MARCH, New York. The chair illustrated (Plate 270) is one of a set of eighteen made by Duncan Phyfe for Charles March of New York, whose town house was at 16 Warren Street. Mr. March was a prominent wine importer, proprietor of the old firm of March & Benson. When business encroached too much on his residence, he built a house at 23 Fifth Avenue, where he lived across the street from his friends the de Rhams. On his death the chairs were inherited first by his son, John Pyne March, later by his grandson, the late Clement March, who lived for forty-five years at 25 North Washington Square before moving to Kinderhook, and now belong

PLATE 271. MRS. WILLIAM MINTURN'S ARMCHAIR, 1806

A carved seat rail is most unusual in Phyfe's chairs.

(Courtesy of Mrs. Harry Horton Benkard and the
Museum of the City of New York)

284

PLATE 272. MRS. MINTURN'S SIDE CHAIR, 1806

Mrs. Minturn's side chairs have horseshoe-shaped seats, brass
paw feet, and reeded seat rails.

(*Courtesy of Mrs. Harry Horton Benkard*)

to Clement March's foster son, James Edward Leath, who is President of the
Columbia County Historical Society. Six of them are on exhibition in the
House of History in Kinderhook.

The chairs show Directoire influence and belong to Phyfe's second
period. They have a double open splat holding between its two sections a
center carved roundel. The side rails and seat rail are deeply grooved; the

cresting rail has a group of five incised grooves at each side. The Edison Institute has a duplicate set, differing in the front legs which have carved hair and paw feet.

Mr. and Mrs. William Minturn, New York. In 1806 Mrs. William Minturn purchased from Duncan Phyfe some chairs which are among the most distinguished work of the nineteenth century. These chairs were inherited by Mr. and Mrs. Henry Post and finally came into the possession of their granddaughter, Mrs. Harry Horton Benkard. At one time they were in her Ninth Street drawing room.

PLATE 273. PORTRAIT OF PRUDENCY TELFORD MORTON
Mrs. Morton ordered a slipper chair from Phyfe
to fit her needlework.
(*Courtesy of Miss Mary Vincent*)

286

The single cross-back armchair (Plate 271), now loaned to the Museum of the City of New York, is most unusual because of the rarely found carving on the front of the seat rail. The cresting rail is carved with the bowknot and thunderbolt design and the carving on the seat rail repeats this design. Next

PLATE 274. MRS. MORTON'S SLIPPER
CHAIR
This little mahogany chair measures
only fifteen inches from seat rail to
floor.
(*Courtesy of Miss Mary Vincent*)

it are small carved blocks like corner blocks, but they are not set squarely over the legs, as is usual. The side chairs (Plate 272) have horseshoe-shaped seats and single cross backs in reeded frames. The front legs terminate in small brass paw feet.

Mrs. John Morton, née Prudency Telford, New York. A rare chair (Plate 274) by Duncan Phyfe is the low "slipper chair" made for Prudency Morton (Plate 273), wife of John Morton, a merchant and importer who made a fortune in New York. "Aunt Dency," as she was called by her relatives, was much interested in needlework and with her own hands she worked the cover for the seat of this chair which she ordered made according to specifications to fit her needlework. From the top rail of the back to the floor this little chair is only two feet six inches high and from the seat rail to the floor it measures fifteen inches. The seat, however, is surprisingly deep and comfortable for such a small piece of furniture.

The Mortons, when they were first married, lived in Canal Street, but later moved to Fourth Street. John Morton's niece, Mrs. John W. Vincent inherited the chair, which is now the possession of her daughter, Mary Vin-

PLATE 275. PAINTING OF THOMAS CORNELL PEARSALL
BY JOHN OPIE
(*Courtesy of Mrs. Henry Wilmerding Payne*)

cent. It is the only example of a Duncan Phyfe slipper chair known to the author. The design of the splat is identical with that of the full-size dining-room chairs made by Phyfe for Charles Gustavus Smedberg (Plate 283).

DUNBAR PAUL, Charleston. Mr. Paul had Duncan Phyfe make a set of dining-room furniture for him which is now owned by Miss Marian Paul of Charleston, South Carolina. There are two console tables, one of which bears a label of 1820 identical with that in Plate 234. In addition to these console tables, there is a large center table with two drop leaves, which can be opened into a dining table or a tea table. It has the same base as the consoles. There are also seven side chairs and a pair of armchairs.

THOMAS CORNELL PEARSALL, New York. An extraordinary group of Phyfe's work, never divided since it was made, and never out of the posses-

PLATE 276. MR. PEARSALL'S DRAWING-ROOM CHAIRS
This set included ten side chairs, two armchairs, two footstools, and a caned couch (Plate 280).
(*Courtesy of Mrs. Henry Wilmerding Payne*)

289

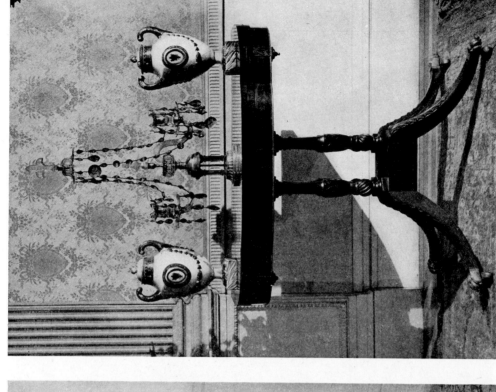

PLATE 278. MR. PEARSALL'S CONSOLE

Duncan Phyfe made a pair of these consoles with four
colonnettes for Mr. Pearsall.

(Courtesy of Mrs. Henry Wilmerding Payne)

PLATE 277. MR. PEARSALL'S CARD TABLE

This is one of a pair of five-legged card tables.

(Courtesy of Mrs. Henry Wilmerding Payne)

sion of the family, is the furniture made for Thomas Cornell Pearsall, now owned by Mrs. Henry Wilmerding Payne. There is a set of two armchairs and ten side chairs (Plate 276), a great four-poster bed, and a sideboard. These all descended from the original owner through Mrs. Payne's great-aunt, Miss Phoebe Pearsall, to her mother and then to Mrs. Payne. With the chairs is a long sofa (Plate 280) that matches them and has a double curule base and, like the chairs, a caned seat and back. Two small footstools (Plate 276) complete the set.

PLATE 279. MR. PEARSALL'S SIDEBOARD

The shelves at the back are a later addition. This should be compared with some of Thomas Hope's designs.

(Courtesy of Mrs. Henry Wilmerding Payne)

PLATE 280. MR. PEARSALL'S SOFA

This sofa with X-stools was part of the drawing-room set in Plate 276.

(*Courtesy of Mrs. Henry Wilmerding Payne*)

PLATE 281. JEREMIAH PIERSON'S SOFA, 1810

Except for the lack of cushion, this sofa is identical with that made for John Alling in Plate 237.

(*Courtesy of Israel Sack*)

The sideboard is unlike any other known to be from this maker's hand. It has Egyptian figures as supports, lion's-mask handles, and paw feet which might well mislead one to the belief that it is a Regency sideboard made in England by Thomas Hope but for its authentic American history. In each drawer is carefully stamped in ink the words: "Thomas Cornell Pearsall. Made for him by Duncan Phyfe" (Plate 279). Not too successful additions have been made to this sideboard. The shelves on the top were installed within the recollection of Mrs. Payne, who says that the low brass rail on the sides was originally there, but no shelves at the back. The Pearsalls' fine country place was at Fifty-seventh Street and the East River, and it was for this dwelling that Phyfe made the furniture.

JEREMIAH HALSEY PIERSON, New York. Mr. Pierson built and furnished a large house called The Homestead in 1810 at Ramapo, Rockland County, New York. In it he put the Duncan Phyfe sofa in Plate 281. Mr. Pierson departed this life in 1856, but the sofa remained in the house until

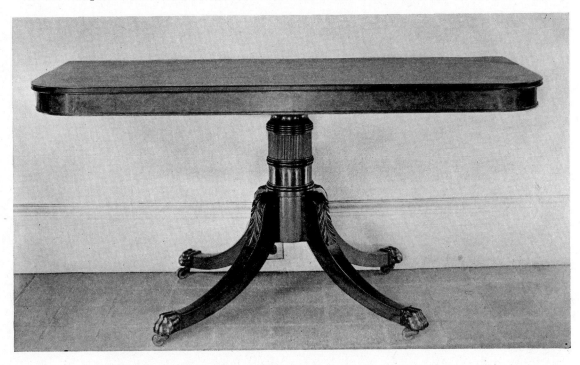

PLATE 282. CHARLES GUSTAVUS SMEDBERG'S DINING TABLE

This shows one end of the table, which has been divided between two descendants. The legs are carved with acanthus and finish in brass paw feet.

(*Courtesy of Mrs. Carl G. Smedberg*)

293

PLATE 283. MR. SMEDBERG'S CHAIRS
These chairs are part of a set of twenty-four which accommodated the purchaser's
large family and many friends.
(*Courtesy of Mr. and Mrs. Adolphus Smedberg*)

1915. It is identical in design with two others made for John Alling and Theodore Frelinghuysen (Plate 237).

CORNELIUS SCHOONMAKER, New York. Duncan Phyfe made various pieces for this old Knickerbocker Dutchman, among them a fine couch which was later inherited by Marius Schoonmaker. Death and financial difficulties brought many changes in the family's condition. The couch was eventually given by Julius Schoonmaker, son of Marius, in settlement of a lawyer's bill of $17. It was sold at the Anderson Galleries in 1928 for $2,600.

PLATE 284. LOUISA THROOP'S SECRETARY DESK, 1808
Empire in feeling, it has half-round columns, brass lion's-mask pulls, and carved paw feet.
(*Courtesy of Mr. and Mrs. Hollis Hunnewell*)

CHARLES GUSTAVUS SMEDBERG, New York. Charles Gustavus Smedberg came to this country in 1812 as representative of a British bank, at a moment when an English agent would not have been acceptable. Being a Swede, he could come in where Angles feared to tread. He was most successful in his work and became so enamored of this country and of a certain Isabella Renwick that he decided to marry here and settle in New York. In due time he headed a family of twelve children. It is said that he once did a great favor

PLATE 285. MISS THROOP'S BREAKFAST TABLE

This table has drop leaves, turned colonnettes, carved acanthus on the legs, and paw terminations.

(*Courtesy of Mr. and Mrs. Hollis Hunnewell*)

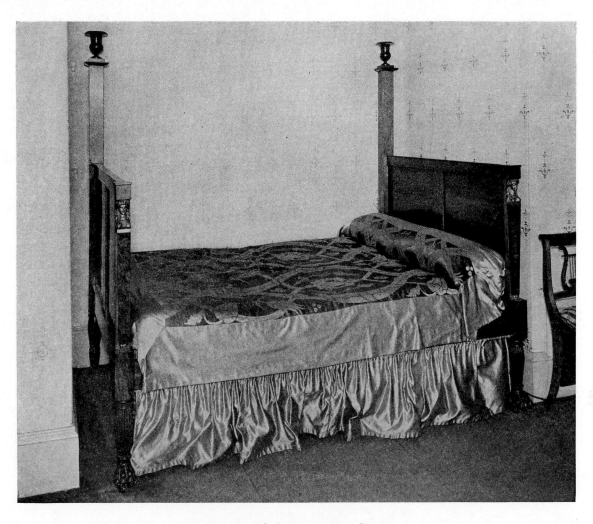

PLATE 286. MISS THROOP'S BED

This Phyfe bed is as French in style as that attributed to Lannuier (Plate 175).
(Courtesy of Mr. and Mrs. Hollis Hunnewell)

for Duncan Phyfe who, to show his appreciation, presented him with a sideboard, a dining table, and twenty-four chairs. The two ends (Plate 282) of the dining table are today owned by Mrs. Carl G. Smedberg of Summit, New Jersey. The center part belongs to Mrs. Edwin Carnes Weeks, another member of the family, who, alas! has cut it down. Twelve of the chairs (Plate 283) are in the possession of Adolphus Smedberg of New York and twelve belonged to his brother, the late Edmund Morton Smedberg of Quogue, Long Island. The sideboard, which in the division of the original estate went to John George Smedberg, was sold at auction in Saugerties in 1874 and is said to have been purchased by a member of the Livingston family.

Miss Louisa Throop, New York. The maiden daughter of Governor Throop, who lived at the corner of Twenty-sixth Street and Fifth Avenue and died there in 1883, had her house furnished in 1808 with the best of Duncan Phyfe's furniture. After her death the furniture went in part to her nephew, Frederic Bronson of Greenfield, Connecticut, but the lion's share was sent to the late Mrs. Hollis Hunnewell of Wellesley, Massachusetts, and is now divided among her heirs. A console table with a pedestal and four colonnettes is owned by Mrs. Hunnewell's daughter, Mrs. Walton Martin. Mr. Bronson Griscom inherited a caned couch with X-stool base, identical in every way with Mrs. H. W. Payne's sofa (Plate 280), eight lyre-back chairs carved with fur and dog's paws, a charming little claw-footed "bason stand," and two armchairs with upholstered seats and back panels. In addi-

PLATE 287. MISS THROOP'S CONSOLE TABLE AND LYRE-BACK CHAIR
The top to the console table is folded. The chair frame is identical to those of
Mr. and Mrs. Andrew V. Stout in Plate 119.
(*Courtesy of Mr. and Mrs. Hollis Hunnewell*)

298

PLATE 288. MISS THROOP'S COUCH
This couch has double-lyre arms, carved lion's paws with gilded eagle's wings, and
its back is caned in three panels.
(*Courtesy of Mr. and Mrs. Hollis Hunnewell*)

tion to these original pieces, Mr. Griscom has the "dozend of dining arm-chairs" copied by Ernest Hagen for Mr. Frederick Bronson.*

Mrs. Hollis Hunnewell's son owns the interesting bed, with two high posts to stand against the wall and two low posts at the front, finishing in carved gilt Egyptian heads. The front feet are lion's paws of carved wood. This bed should be compared with the Lannuier bed in Plate 175 to see the strong French influence. Lyre-back chairs similar to those of Mr. and Mrs. Stout's (Plate 287), a caned couch with two lyres in the arms like Mr. Halsey's (Plate 148), a handsome secretary desk in the Empire style, and two tables with supports of four colonnettes are also part of the Throop furniture.

DR. JAMES TUPPER, Nantucket. This eminent physician was born on the island of Nantucket in 1754 and was one of the first medical men to

---

* See Addenda, *Memorandum* by Ernest Hagen.

advocate the open-air treatment for tuberculosis. During his frequent trips to New York and to Charleston, South Carolina, where his sons lived, he became greatly interested in furniture and in paintings. On one of his visits to New York he ordered Duncan Phyfe to make twelve dining-room chairs for him with lyre-backs and top-rails carved with a twisted rope (Plate 289). The original bill for them was still in existence a few years ago, but has recently disappeared. Mrs. Nonie Tupper Gregg of Boston owned three of these chairs, but two of them were stolen and every effort to trace them failed.

STEPHEN VAN RENSSELAER, the Seventh Patroon. A fine lot of furniture

PLATE 289. JAMES TUPPER'S CHAIR
A set of twelve of these dining-room chairs were
made for Dr. Tupper by Duncan Phyfe.
(*Courtesy of Mrs. Nonie Tupper Gregg*)

300

PLATE 290. STEPHEN VAN RENSSELAER'S CHAIRS

This set has six side chairs and one armchair. The frames are grooved and they have a
twisted rope as a cresting rail.

(*Courtesy of Miss Cornelia Livingston Van Rensselaer Strong*)

was made for Catharine Livingston, daughter of Philip Livingston, signer
of the Declaration of Independence. She married Stephen Van Rensselaer,
the Seventh Patroon. Much of this furniture has descended in a direct line
to the Strong family of New Brunswick.

A set of six side chairs and one armchair (Plate 290) with twisted rope
motifs in the top panels are among these inherited treasures, and belong to
Miss Cornelia Livingston Van Rensselaer Strong. A fine center table (Plate
292) with vase-shaped pedestal and carved acanthus on the feet is the prop-

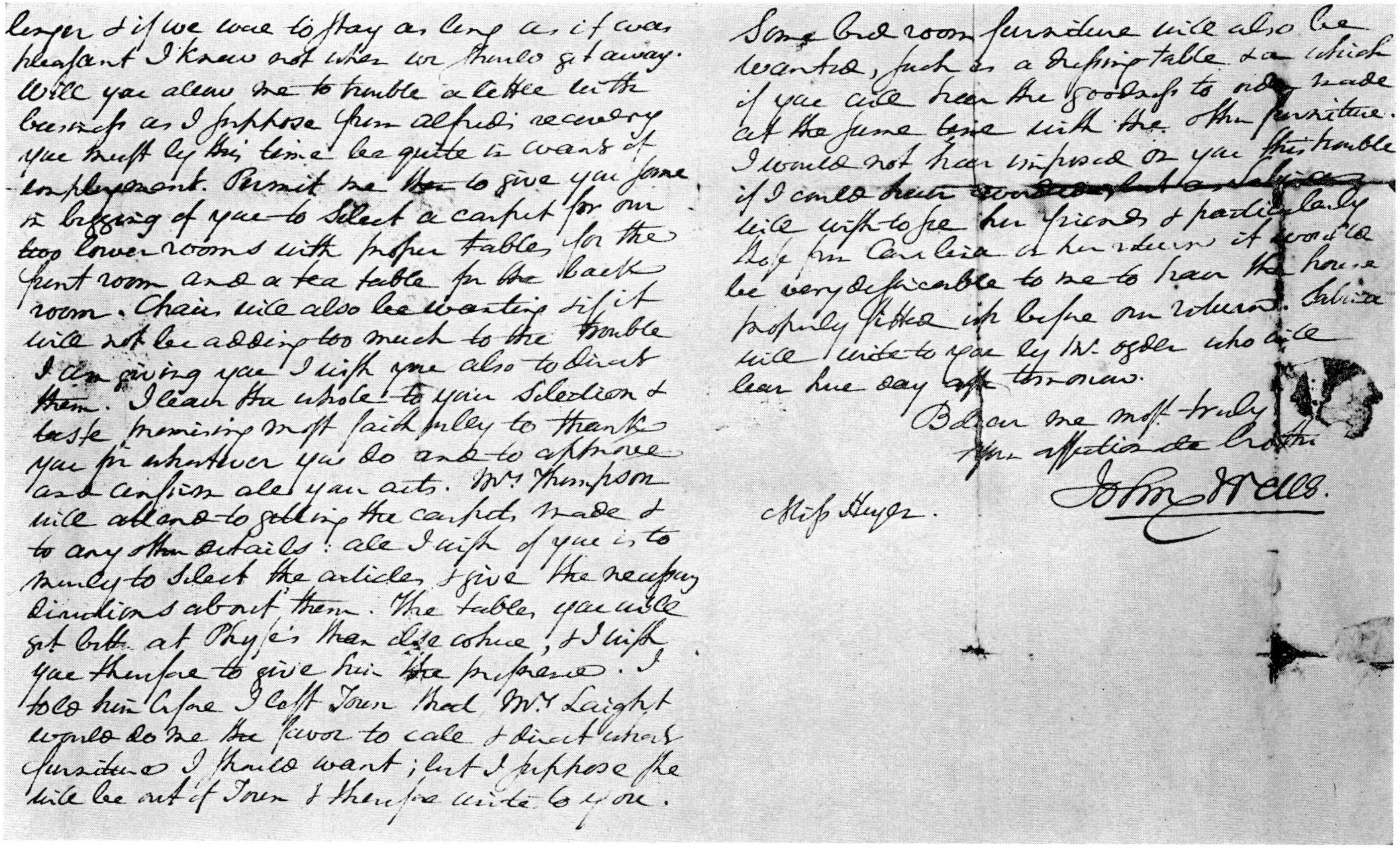

longer & if we were to stay as long as it was
pleasant I know not when we should get away.
Will you allow me to trouble a little with
business as I suppose from Alfred's recovery
you must by this time be quite in want of
employment. Permit me then to give you some
in begging of you to select a carpet for our
two lower rooms with proper tables for the
front room and a tea table for the back
room. Chairs will also be wanting & if it
will not be adding too much to the trouble
I am giving you I wish you also to direct
them. I leave the whole to your selection &
taste promising most faithfully to thank
you for whatever you do and to approve
and confirm all your acts. Mr Thompson
will attend to getting the carpets made &
to any other details: all I wish of you is to
[illegible] to select the articles & give the necessary
directions about them. The tables you will
get better at Phyfe's than else where, & I wish
you therefore to give him the preference. I
told him before I left Town that Mrs Laight
would do me the favor to call & direct what
furniture I should want; but I suppose she
will be out of Town & therefore write to you.

Some bed room furniture will also be
wanted, such as a dressing table &c which
if you will have the goodness to order made
at the same time with the other furniture.
I would not have imposed on you this trouble
if I could have [illegible]
will wish to see her friends & particularly
those from Carolina on her return it would
be very desirable to me to have the house
properly fitted up before our return. Sabina
will write to you by Mr Ogden who will
leave here day after tomorrow.

Believe me most truly
your affectionate brother
John Wells.

Miss Huger.

PLATE 291. LETTER FROM JOHN WELLS

He writes his sister-in-law, Miss Huger, in New York, asking her to select some furniture for him at Duncan Phyfe's shop. The letter is dated July 25, 1815.

(Courtesy of Mrs. Edward Rutledge)

erty of Mrs. Theodore Strong. A sofa, not illustrated here, has lion's paws with carved fur for the four supports. The front legs have carved eagle's wings above the lion's paws. Mrs. Strong also owns a fine Phyfe couch (Plate 293), with very unusual carving and reeding in the top panel, which came from Fort Crailo, in Greenbush, where Jeremiah Van Rensselaer lived for many years. Instead of the bowknot and thunderbolts in the top panel (a more usual design of Phyfe's), this couch is carved with a bowknot and wheat. There are five stalks of wheat on each side of the ribbons, exactly like the design on the Delafield sofa (Plate 257). The side panels are formed by simple lines of reeding. The front legs also are reeded.

PLATE 292. MR. VAN RENSSELAER'S TABLE
This finely proportioned pedestal table is an excellent example of acanthus carving.
(*Courtesy of Mrs. Theodore Strong*)

PLATE 293. MR. VAN RENSSELAER'S SOFA

The middle panel of the back is carved with a bowknot and wheat; the side panels are reeded.

(Courtesy of Mrs. Theodore Strong)

JOHN WELLS, New York (1770–1823). John Wells was such a famous lawyer that one of the large ships going to foreign shores was named for him. He married Sabina Elliott Huger, daughter of the Honorable Daniel E. Huger of Charleston, South Carolina, and arranged to take her to New York to live. On his honeymoon trip he wrote from Boston to his sister-in-law Miss Huger at 340 Broadway, about the furniture for his house. The letter is dated July 25, 1815. A photostat of part of it follows (Plate 291):

. . . and if we were to stay as long as it was pleasant I know not when we should get away. Will you allow me to trouble you a little about business as I suppose from Alfred's recovery you must by this time be quite in want of employment. Permit me then to give you some in begging you to select a carpet for our two lower rooms with proper tables for the front room and a tea-table for the back room. Chairs will also be wanting: if it will not be adding too much to the trouble I am giving you, I wish you also to direct them. I leave the whole to your selection and taste, promising most faithfully to thank you for whatever you do and to approve and confirm all your acts. Mrs. Thompson will attend to getting the carpets made and to any other details; all I wish of you is merely to select the articles and give the necessary directions about them.

PLATE 294. JOHN WELLS' PIER TABLE, 1815

This was procured for him by his sister-in-law while he was away on his wedding trip. Exhibited in the Charleston Loan Exhibit, 1939.

(*Courtesy of Miss Sabina Elliott Wells*)

The tables you will get better at Phyfe's than elsewhere, and I wish you therefore to give him the preference. I told him before I left town that Mrs. Laight would do me the favor to call and direct what furniture I should want; but I suppose she will be out of town and therefore write to you.

Some bedroom furniture will also be wanted, such as a dressing table and a —, which if you will have the goodness to order made at the same time with the other furniture. I would not have imposed on you this trouble if I could have avoided, but as

PLATE 295. MRS. JOHN ZABRISKIE'S CHAIR, 1830

This was given to Abigail Lefferts Lott by her father on her marriage to John Barrea Zabriskie, together with seven others.

(Courtesy of Miss Louise G. Zabriskie and the Index of American Design)

306

Sabina will wish to see her friends and particularly those from Carolina on her return, it would be very desirable to me to have the house properly fitted up before our return. Sabina will write to you by Mr. Ogden who will leave here day after tomorrow.

Believe me most truly
your affectionate brother

Miss Huger.   John Wells

Mr. Wells and his bride lived in New York, but had a country house in Brooklyn, the old Stone house formerly occupied by Samuel Jackson. Mr. Wells died of yellow fever in 1823 when both Brooklyn and New York were swept by the scourge.

One of a pair of pier tables (Plate 294) made for him by Duncan Phyfe was exhibited in March, 1939, in a loan exhibit at the rectory of St. Phillips Church in Charleston. A photograph of it will be of great interest to students of style, for the letter above indicates that it was made in 1815, though it is a design commonly believed to be of later date. Much of the furniture made by Duncan Phyfe for the New York house is now owned by descendants in Charleston and in Washington. The mate to the pier table in the photograph belongs to Miss Fanny Wells of Washington, who also owns the dressing table mentioned in the letter of 1815.

Both Mrs. Edward Wells of Ontario, Canada, and the Honorable Mrs. Anthony Methuen of Corshall, Wilts, England, inherited Phyfe card tables, while Miss Julia Wells, of New Brunswick, New Jersey, has a set of a dozen Phyfe chairs.

Phyfe also made for the Wells house seven large bookcases—two triple, three double, and two single. They are perfectly plain and unornamented and have nothing in particular to distinguish them as his handiwork. Two are in Charleston, at the house of Mrs. Edward Rutledge. Of the three double bookcases with sliding doors, one is at the house of Miss Julia Wells in New Brunswick, one is now owned by the New Jersey College for Women, and one by Mr. Tileston Wells of New York.

Mrs. John B. Zabriskie, New York. Many of the finest wedding presents given in New York in the first half of the nineteenth century came from Duncan Phyfe's workshop. Miss Louise Zabriskie and her brother, Dr. Edwin G. Zabriskie of New York City, have six of a set of eight chairs presented as a wedding gift to Abigail Lefferts Lott by her father upon her mar-

307

riage to Dr. John Barrea Zabriskie in 1830. These chairs (Plate 295) have typical Phyfe curves; the back and the side rails appear to be in one single piece; the carving of the splat represents two cornucopias, each filled with two pineapples and carved leaves with the points of the pineapples touching.

In summing up Duncan Phyfe's life and lifework we become aware that it foreshadows much that is now traditional in our culture. His furniture masterpieces, though derived from and inspired by European style and traditions, were thoroughly American—made for the needs and personality of this country. We are fortunate to be able to focus and particularize that personality in a small degree by this study of Phyfe's customers. Many of these were leaders in act and in taste in a country that, having uprooted its social structure and thought patterns in a revolutionary war, was in a mood for intellectual reëvaluation and creative initiative.

As his furniture interpreted foreign traits in an American way, so did the character of Phyfe himself. His Scottish acumen found American expression in mass production so that his activities extended beyond those of a carver and cabinetmaker and he became one of the first businessmen in furniture making. Even in the career of such an early pioneer in mass production the compromise this involves is apparent. Craftsmanship was not sacrificed, but Phyfe was no longer free artistically. In his later years, in order to maintain the establishment that his life endeavor had built, he was forced to follow the dictates of changing tastes by manufacturing in styles which he himself contemptuously referred to as "canal-boat furniture."

Like many, he came to America a poor boy and died a comparatively rich man, but in honestly gaining his physical wealth he contributed immeasurably to the artistic wealth of his adopted country.

ADDENDA

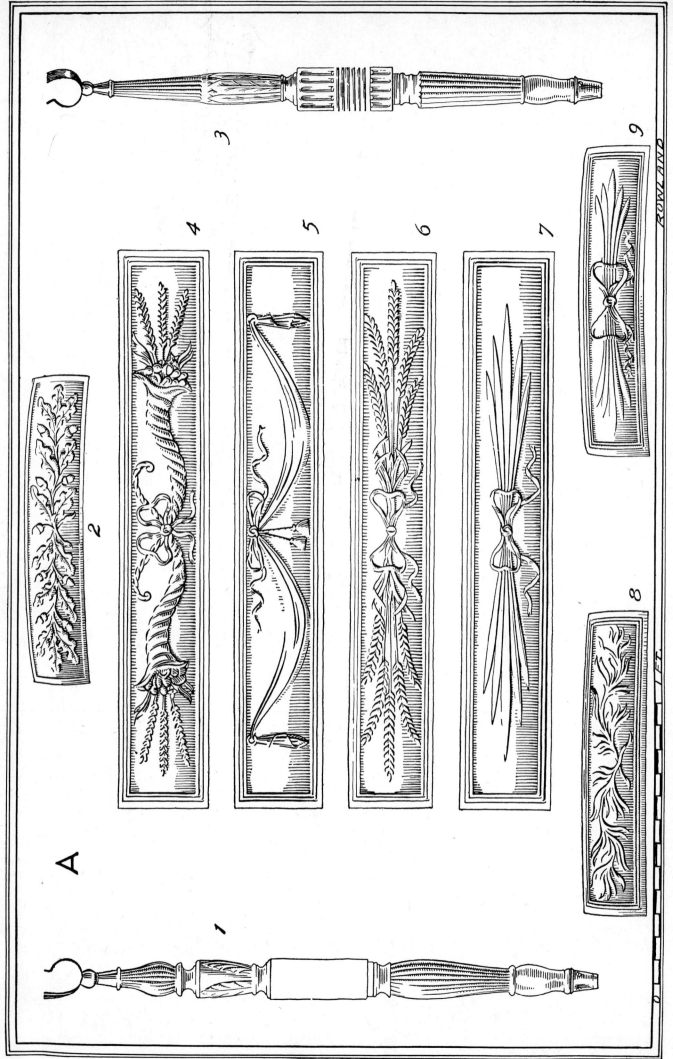

DETAILS OF SOFA ARMS AND LEGS. CARVED PANELS FROM SOFAS AND FROM CHAIR-BACKS

(From Furniture Masterpieces of Duncan Phyfe by Charles Over Cornelius, copyright 1922 by Doubleday, Doran & Co.)

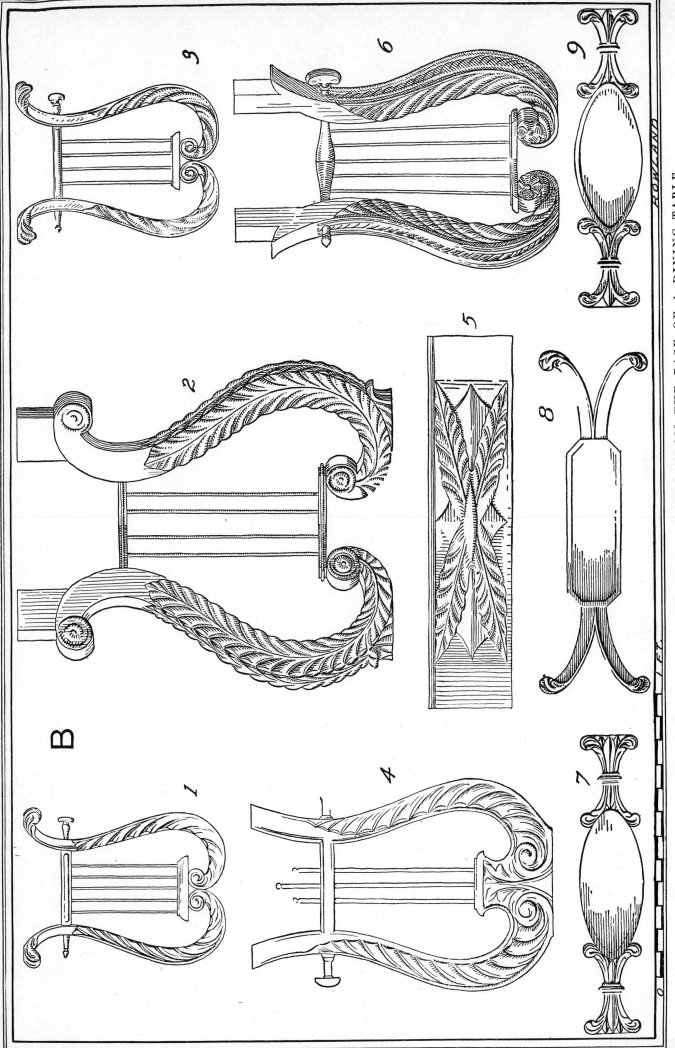

TYPICAL LYRES AND CHAIR SLATS WITH A PANEL FROM THE BASE OF A DINING-TABLE

(From Furniture Masterpieces of Duncan Phyfe by Charles Over Cornelius, copyright 1922 by Doubleday, Doran & Co.)

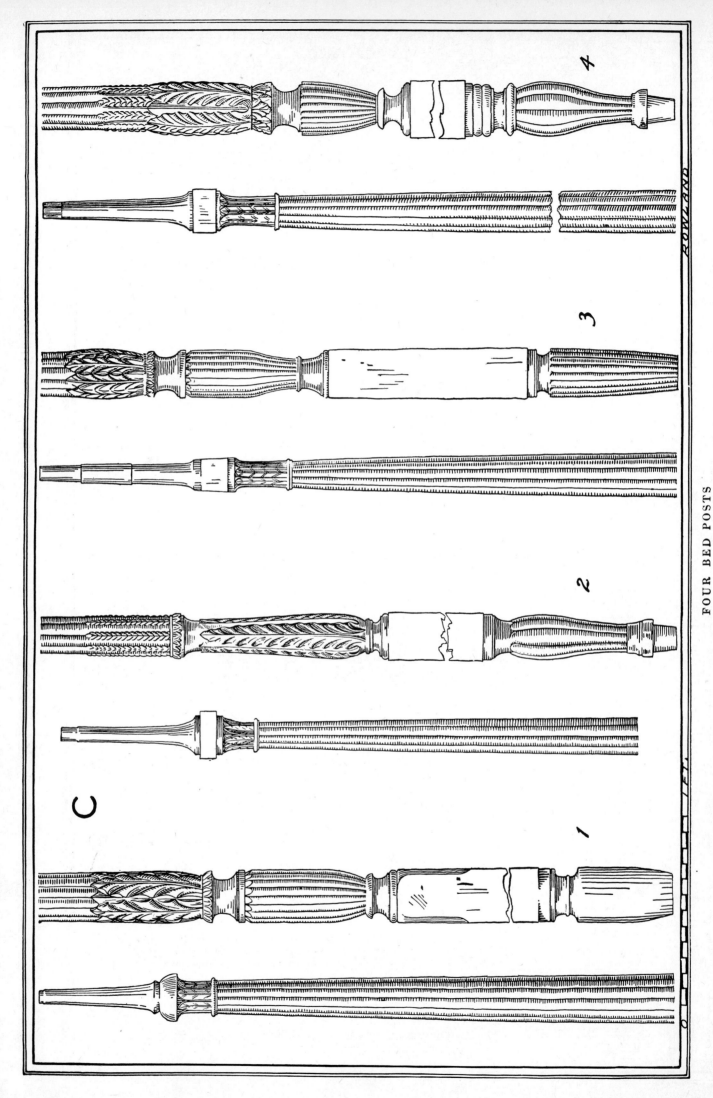

FOUR BED POSTS

(From Furniture Masterpieces of Duncan Phyfe by Charles Over Cornelius, copyright 1922 by Doubleday, Doran & Co.)

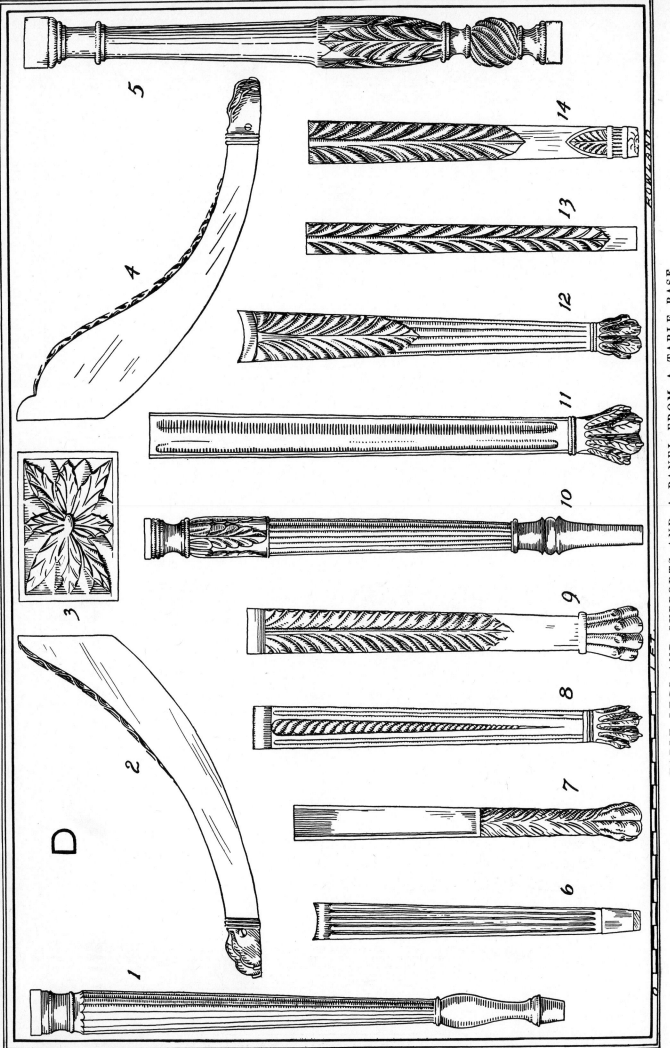

TABLE LEGS AND SUPPORTS AND A PANEL FROM A TABLE BASE

(From Furniture Masterpieces of Duncan Phyfe by Charles Over Cornelius, copyright 1922 by Doubleday, Doran & Co.)

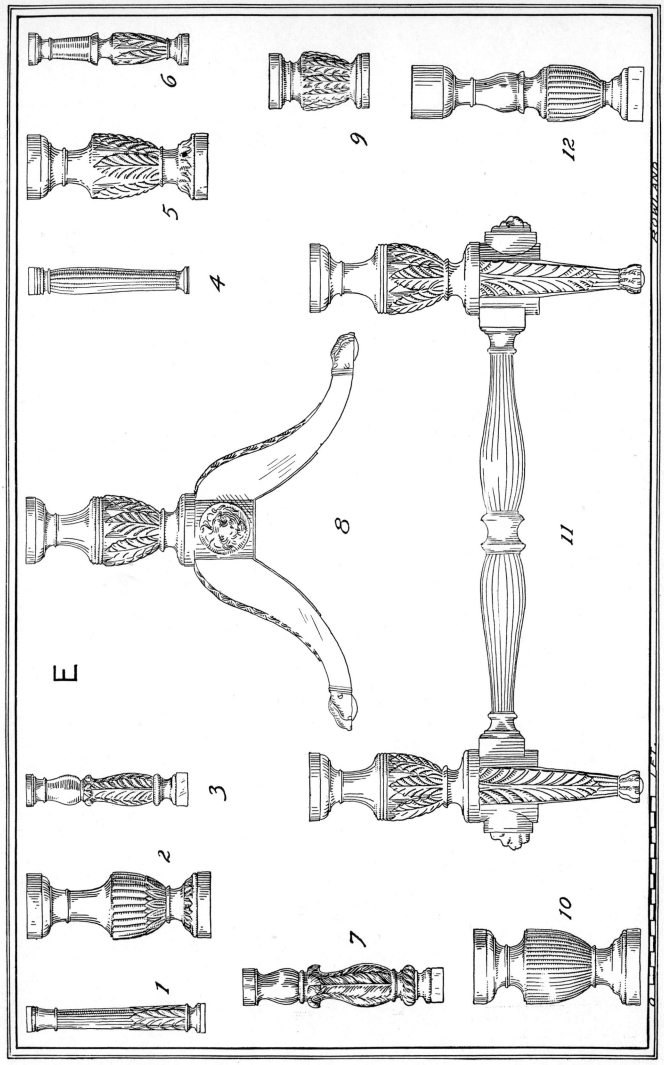

A PIANO TRESTLE AND VARIOUS DESIGNS OF TABLE POSTS AND URN-SHAPED SUPPORTS

(From Furniture Masterpieces of Duncan Phyfe by Charles Over Cornelius, copyright 1922 by Doubleday, Doran & Co.)

MEMORANDUM ON PHYFE BY THE CABINETMAKER ERNEST HAGEN. WRITTEN IN 1907.

(Included in this book by the kind permission of R. T. Haines Halsey, Esq.)

[The spelling and punctuation in this copy are that of the original. Various inaccuracies of statement exist in the document, viz.: Five brothers, not four, came over from Scotland; one child, not two, died on the trip to America; Mrs. Langdon, Mr. Astor's daughter, was only eight years old when Phyfe was located in Broad Street; Duncan's wife was Rachel Lowzada, not Rachel *Salade*.]

Duncan Phyfe and his brother, Harry Phyfe who live at #12 East 43rd Street are the sons of James D. Phyfe who was the son of Duncan Phyfe the founder of the firm, they are Bachelers and a Miss Pinkney a Cousin keeps house for them.

Duncan Phyfe of 83 Summit Avenue Jersey City now 93 years old is the son of Michael Phyfe the oldest of the 4(the) brothers that came from Scotland who died early and Duncan his brother brough up the family at 193 Fulton Street, he was mostly employed about the ware rooms dusting and delivering the furniture by pushcart and took many loads of it to the Astors who were their best custumers, he now lives with his Daughter Mrs. L. Purdy at 83 Summit Ave Jersey City.

There was a brother of Mrs. Purdy, Mr. William Phyfe conected with the "E.H. Purdy Manufacturing Company at 42 to 48 West 13th Street through whom I obtained the first information about the Phyfe family as we had some business transactions with them. The[y] were in the looking glass frame business, I have a letter from him dated May 31. 1892 about some furniture his sister Mrs. Purdy wanted to sell of the heavy veneered 1833 kind which she still has on storage some where

Loughlin Phyfe, the youngest of th 4 brothers, who was the best Cabinet maker in his brothers shop died Oct. 6. 1869. 92 years old. They have a picture of him in 43rd Street.

In 1783 or 1784 just after the close of the revolutionary war a Scotch family by the name of Phyfe left their home of Loch Fannich 30 miles N W of Inverness with 6 or 8 children of whom 2 died on the long voyage in the old slow sailing vessel and coming here settled in or near Albany N. Y.

The Second oldest son "Duncan" then about 16 Years learned the Cabinet makers trade in Albany, and after a time set up a small shop for himself—but he could not find work enough to make it pay in Albany so he moved to New York and tried it here down in Broad Street where most of the Cabinet makers were then located—he got some work from Mrs Langdon the daughter of John Jacob Astor which done to her satisfaction got more orders, but after all it was not Enough and he concluded that he would go back to Albany and try it there a second time, when Mrs Langdon heard of this she pursuased him to stay here and promised to help him where ever she could and recomend him to her friends—

he remained in New York and after several moves finally settled in #35 "Partition Street" which was then that part of Fulton Street which lies west of Broadway, that part of Fulton Street east of Broadway being called Fair Street this was in 1795 in 1816 the name of the Street was changed to Fulton Street and renumbered, his new number being 192 and 194 with his dwelling house opposite 193

in 1837 the firms name changed to Duncan Phyfe and *sons*
in 1840 it again changed to Duncan Phyfe and *Son* the sons name (name) being James D. Phyfe. 1847 he sold out and retired, but still lived at 193 Fulton Street until his death which ocured August 16 1854 in the 86th Year of his age and was buried in the family vault in Greenwood Cemetery his wife Rachel (nëë Salade) was born in Holland and died July 17 1851

there were quiet a number of other Phyfes of the side lines in business in New York and some in the upostery business in Maiden Lane and continued so for a long time after, but they had nothing to do with Duncan Phyfe in business Matters

Duncan Phyfes chief merrit lies in the
carring out and Especially *improving*
of the "Sheriton" style of Settees,
Chairs and tables in his best period
the work about 1820 although the workmanship was perfect gradually degenerated in style at first to the questionable "American Empire" and after 1830 to the abominable heavy and Nondescrip veneered style of the time when the Cholera first appeared in New York 1833 to 1840–1845 when the overdecorated and Carved rosewood style set in which Phyfe himself called the "Butcher furniture"

Phyfes Shop #192 & 194 Fulton Street was at the South west corner of Church Street and the whole block on Church Street (1907) is now being pulled down to make room for the new tunnel to Jersey City.

#193 opposite, where he lived, is now occupied by the fire department for an Engine house—within a stones throw of the old shop in the Sextons office of St Pauls Church is one of Phyfes Sofas, 2 Chairs which they had to match it Where lost—at 12 East 43rd Street they have water colour picture of the Shop made by an apprinteze and Mr Phyfe of 43rd Street will allow us to take a Photograph of it at his house, but will not let it go out of his hands

Duncan Phyfe of 83 Summit Avenue Jersey City (now 93 years old) who knows more about the old affairs then any of the other members of the family says that his uncle was a very plain Man always working and allways smoking a short pipe in 1842 a Lord John Hays visited his shop to get some information concerning Cabinet woods when

316

he would not even take the pipe out of his Mouth he was very strict in his habits and all the members of the family had to be in bed by 9 O'clock, and after retiring from business kept on working at the bench making small things for his folks which they still preserve

Mrs Purdy showed me a toy bureau with glass which he made for her when a little girl, and Mr William Phyfe at 48 West 13th Street showed me a work box which he made—they have a number of very slightly made pieces of furniture, such as little desks and tables of no artistic merritt whatever both at the 43rd St house and at Jersey City which no doubt Came from the old shop, but of the kind of furniture that made Phyfes name famous the[y] have no Idea whatever so much so that they even threw away some handsom old Chairs that a relative who died had left they only have some Chairs of the 1833 period of Phyfes make now

Mr Phyfe of Jersey City has on his wall hanging a water color picture of the old Scudder Museum on Broadway and says the he with other Boys used to play marbles in front of it—
after the concern broke up in 1847 he worked at the Harness making business, went west and south and returning to New York settled on a farm at Madison New Jersey until a few Years ago the moved to Jersey City

to get there take the Montgomery Street Car until you get on top the hill, get out at Summit Avenue—turn to left and walk about 5 blocks

---

Miss Throop the maiden Daughter of Gov Throop who was born 1790 got her house furnished on her 18th birthday 1808 by Duncan Phyfe with best of his Make—Miss Throop died in her house N.W. Corner of 26th Street and 5th Aven in 1883—in 1881 we reproduced for her Nephew Frederic Bronson a Dozend of Phyfes Dining Arm Chairs, and through her I got the *first* information of Duncan Phyfe—after her death the furniture in part went to Mr Bronson and the best part to Mrs Hollis Hunnewell of Wellesley Park, Massachusetts. Mr Egerton Winthrop, another heir, did not Care for any of it; the bulk, about a R R car load, went to Massachusetts

furniture in the Governors room City Hall
it would be very interesting to know where the furniture that was made about 1812 cam from—it of the Shereton style but not as light and graceful as Phyfes, Valontine's Manuel 1845 page 337 says temporary City Hall corner of Nassau & Wall St finnished in 1700 cost L 1185 or L 18, 6d less than the furniture of a single room 1845 in 1787–1789 this building was enlarged & altered for the U.S. Congress it was taken down in 1811
the New City Hall was finnished in 1812 at a cost of a half million of Dollas *Exclusive of the furniture*

317

THREE GENERATIONS OF THE PHYFE FAMILY

1. Duncan, His Brothers and Sisters

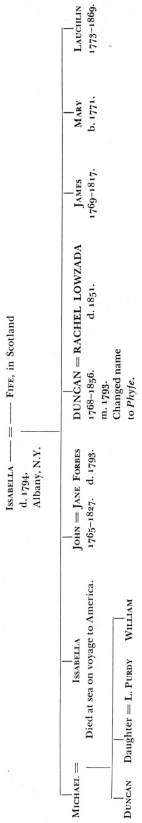

ISABELLA ════ ──── ════ FIFE, in Scotland
d. 1794,
Albany, N.Y.

ISABELLA ═══

JOHN = JANE FORBES
1765–1827. d. 1793.

DUNCAN = RACHEL LOWZADA
1768–1856.   d. 1851.
m. 1793.
Changed name to *Phyfe.*

JAMES
1769–1817.

MARY
b. 1771.

LAUCHLIN
1773–1869.

MICHAEL =
Died at sea on voyage to America.

DUNCAN   Daughter = L. PURDY   WILLIAM

2. His Children

DUNCAN PHYFE = RACHEL LOWZADA
1768–1856.   d. 1851.
Born *Fife;* changed name to *Phyfe,* 1794. m. Feb. 17, 1793, in First Presbyterian Church, New York.

MARY
b. Sept. 2, 1795.
m.
CAPT. SIDNEY B. WHITLOCK

JAMES DUNCAN
b. June 26, 1797.
m.
JULIA MATILDA PINCKNEY

WILLIAM
b. July 7, 1799.
m.
ANN ───

ELIZA
b. Jan. 31, 1801–
d. 1890.
m.
WILLIAM VAIL
1802–1875.

MICHAEL
d. before 1840.
m.
───
1. DUNCAN
2. WILLIAM
3. MARY JANE
m.
DAVID WINTRINGHAM

ISABELLA
Lost from Hudson River boat at age of 16 or 18 (about 1823).

EDWARD DUNCAN
m.
MARY F. WESTLAKE

HARRY E. PHYFE
1871–1933.
m.
ALICE EATON
d. 1927.

HEROLD RODNEY EATON PHYFE
b. 1890.

3. His Children's Children

Mary Phyfe = Capt. Sidney B. Whitlock
b. Sept. 2, 1795.   1794–1849
Daughter of
DUNCAN and
RACHEL.

Sidney   Fred   George   Walter B.   Charles   Edward   Eliza   Isabel   Sarah

Duncan Phyfe Whitlock
m.
Margaret P. Ronaldson

Mary Whitlock   Elizabeth Whitlock   James
m.
Heyward Cornell
Margaret Cornell
m.
Polk E. K. Flower

James Duncan = Julia Matilda Pinckney
b. June 26, 1797.
Son of DUNCAN
and RACHEL.

Duncan Phyfe
m. his cousin
Grace Huntington Pinckney

William Henry Pinckney Phyfe
Author and educator.
m.
Edith Bell

Henry Pinckney Phyfe
m.
Elizabeth D. Pancoast

Churchill B. Phyfe

Eliza Phyfe = William Vail
b. Jan. 31, 1801–   1802–1875.
d. 1890.
Daughter of
DUNCAN and
RACHEL.

William Harry Vail   Sarah Whitlock Vail   Issabella Phyfe Vail   Elizabeth Garretson Vail
1832–1884.   m.   1834–1901.   1839–1871.
m.   William Mitchell   m.
Emma Van Derveer   Nelson Runyon
                                           1821–1900.

Duncan Phyfe Vail
1829–1894.
m.
Mary Francis Onderdonk
1839–1924.

Frederick Percy Vail b. 1861.
m.
Ida Mary McLaurie
b. 1867.

Virginia Adelaide Vail
b. 1887.
m.
J. Bertram Howell
b. 1893.

Glorianna Howell
b. 1929.

Frederick Howell
b. 1924.

William Phyfe = Ann ———
b. July 7, 1799.
Son of DUNCAN
and RACHEL.

Albert   Samuel   Lilla   William D.   Mary   Belle   Anna   Charles

Duncan

RECORDS OF DUNCAN PHYFE'S MARRIAGE AND THE BIRTH AND BAPTISM OF FOUR OF HIS CHILDREN

(From the Archives of the First Presbyterian Church, New York.)

THE FIRST PRESBYTERIAN CHURCH
in the City of New York
Church Office—12 West 12th Street

New York, December 3rd, 1938.

Nancy McClelland, Inc.,
　15 East 57th Street,
　　New York City.

My dear Miss McClelland,
　　I can, according to the records of the First Presbyterian Church, New York report that on February 17th, 1793, by the Rev. Dr. John Rodgers, (please note Dr. Rodgers spelled his name with a d) were married

DUNCAN FIFE AND RACHEL LOWZADA—(her name is poorly
written: this is the best I make of it)

Before 1795, Mr. Phyfe changed the spelling of his name, for the baptismal record contains the following:

Mary, daughter of Duncan and Rachel Phyfe,
　　born September 2nd, 1795　　　　baptized Sept. 29th, 1795
James, son of Duncan and Rachel Phyfe,
　　born June 26th, 1797　　　　　　baptized July 30th, 1797
William, son of Duncan and Rachel Phyfe,
　　born July 7th, 1799　　　　　　baptized September 1st, 1799
Eliza, daughter of Duncan and Rachel Phyfe,
　　born January 31st, 1801　　　　baptized April 9th, 1801
　　　　They were all baptized by Dr. Rodgers.

It is probable they were also church members but our membership record for that period has been lost.

Yours very truly,

(signed) Florence P. Weiss,
Church Secretary.

December 6th, 1938.

Nancy McClelland, Inc.
15 East 57th Street,
New York City.

My dear Miss McClelland,

The exact wording of the record is: FEBRUARY 17th, 1793—DUNCAN FIFE AND RACHEL LOWZADA.

Dr. Rodgers had a way of heading pages with the year, and *"by Rev. Dr. J.R. were married,"*—then the page was filled up with just the dates and the names of the parties.

There was no Second Presbyterian Church in 1793. The First Church was located Nos. 14 to 20 Wall Street. Its branch was the Brick Church, located on Beekman Street. Probably the reference to Second Church refers to the Brick Church, which is still in existence and is now building a new house of worship at Park Avenue & 92nd Street. Dr. Rodgers served as pastor to both the First Church and the Brick Church.

Yours truly,

(signed) Florence P. Weiss
Church Secretary.

COPY OF DUNCAN PHYFE'S WILL
HALL OF RECORDS, NEW YORK

I Duncan Phyfe of the City of New York late Cabinet Maker, being of sound and disposing mind memory and understanding, do make publish and declare this to be my last Will and Testament—First—I order and direct that all my just debts and funeral expences be paid by my Executors hereinafter named, as soon as conveniently may be after my decease—Second—I give, devise and bequeath unto my two daughters, Mary widow of Sidney B. Whitlock, and Eliza wife of William Vail, all my silver ware, china & glass-ware, curtains, *both* Bed and window, all beds, bed linen and bedding of every kind, table linen, set of Knives and forks and box containing them, which box was made by me, to be divided equally between my said daughters—Third—I give devise and bequeath to my brother Lauchlin Phyfe the yearly sum of four hundred & twenty dollars to be paid to him by my Executors in half yearly payments for and during the term of his natural life, and that my Executors retain in their hands

out of my personal estate so much as will be sufficient to produce said annual sum, and after the death of the said Lauchlin Phyfe I order and direct that the said sum so retained by my said Executors for him shall sink into and form part of my residuary personal estate, and go and be applied in the same manner as I shall hereafter direct as to my said residuary personal estate. Fourth—I give devise and bequeath unto Duncan Phyfe, William Phyfe and Mary Jane Wintringham wife of David Wintringham, children of my deceased son Michael, each the sum of fourteen thousand dollars and do direct that the same be paid to them as soon as practicably may be after my decease. Fifth—I give devise and bequeath all the rest residue and remainder of my Estate Real and Personal equally to and amongst my Children Mary widow of Sidney B. Whitlock, Eliza wife of William Vail, William Phyfe James D. Phyfe and Edward D. Phyfe to have and to hold the same to them my said children their heirs and assigns forever. Lastly I make nominate constitute and appoint my said sons William Phyfe, James D. Phyfe and my son in law William Vail Executors of this my last Will and Testament, hereby revoking all former and other wills, by me at any time heretofore made. In Witness whereof I have hereto subscribed my name and affixed my seal this twenty fourth day of January one thousand eight hundred and fifty four.
(certified Nov 8th, 1854)   D. Phyfe (L.S.)

Signed sealed published and declared by the above named testator Duncan Phyfe as & for his last Will and Testament in the presence of us who at his request and in his presence and in the presence of each other have hereunto subscribed our names as witnesses thereto etc.

Livingston K. Miller   135 Livingston St. Brooklyn
Stephen Burkhalter   191 Fulton Street, N.Y.

In the matter of proving the
last Will and Testament of
Duncan Phyfe deceased as a
Will of Real and Personal
Estate.

Examination of Witnesses Sworn and
examined in the above entitled matter—County of New York to wit: Livingston Miller of the City of Brooklyn Kings County being duly sworn as a witness in the above entitled matter and examined on behalf of the applicant to prove said Will says, I was well acquainted with Duncan Phyfe *now* deceased. I knew the above named decedent for more than two years before his death. etc.

(Burkhalter knew Duncan Phyfe 30 years.)

A LIST OF REAL ESTATE BELONGING
TO DUNCAN PHYFE

(Copies of deeds in the New York, Brooklyn, and Connecticut Halls of Records.)

New York

Liber 65, page 314, 9/30/1803.

. . . from James Walker New York Merchant and his wife Ann, on September 30th, 1803, for the sum of $1625.00, land situated on Southerly side of Partition Street. Bounded Northerly side in front by Partition Street, Easterly by ground now or late of Martin Ryerson, Southerly in rear by ground now or late of Dirck Dey, Westerly by ground now or late of John Van Winklen.

Liber 65, page 311, 9/30/1803.

. . . from Peter De Riemer of Poughkeepsie, farmer, and his wife Else, on September 30th, 1803, for the sum of $2500.00,—Southerly side Partition Street and known and distinguished in a certain chart or map made by Francis Marschalk, late one of the sworn surveyors of the said City bearing date the first of May in the year 1748, by lot number 13. Bound North Easterly in front by Partition Street and in the rear by a lot of ground now or late of John Gasner. On the South Easterly by lot number 12 belonging to Peter De Riemer and on the North Westerly by lot 14 belonging to Isaac Vanderbeck. [A dwelling house is mentioned in the last part of the deed—not listed in the section of deed giving location of land.]

Liber 67, page 336, 8/11/1804.

. . . from Isaac Vander Beck Esquire [this name at the end of the deed is mentioned as being signed Vanderbeck] and his wife Rachel, on August 11th, 1804, for the sum of $3500.00 on the Southerly side of Partition Street, bound in front by Partition Street by a house and lot of ground late of Peter De Reimer now belonging to the said part of the second party. Southerly in rear by a lot of ground belonging to Jacob Bauman and on the Westerly side by a lot of ground belonging to Benjamin Romaine.

Liber 78, page 493, 12/9/1807.

. . . from Ann Rose De Kater Duclos, widow, for the sum of $4500.00, dwelling house and lot of ground number 29 bounded in front on Partition Street; in the rear on ground now or late of Henry Tiebout, on the Easterly on ground now or late of Isaac Vander Beck and on the Westerly by ground now or formerly belonging to John Ryerson. [Copy of signature reads: Anne Rose De Kater veuve Duclos.]

Liber 109, page 358, 7/1/1815.

. . . from Charles Ludlow of Windsor Hill County of Orange, State of New York,

Esquire, and Margaret Thornton late Margaret Thornton Machaness his wife for the sum of $9250.00 dwelling house and lot of ground whereof the later Thomas Machaness of the City of New York deceased Father of the now Margaret Thornton Ludlow was seised at the time of his death, situate lying and being in the now Third Ward of the said City on the Northerly side of Partition Street being part of the lands commonly known by the name of the Church Farm and also being the center equal third part of several lots of ground which in a map or chart formerly made of the said Church Farm were known and distinguished as the lots of numbers 33, 34, 35 being bounded Southerly in front by Partition Street, Northerly in the rear by a lot of ground formerly belonging to the Rector and Inhabitants of the City of New York in communion with the Protestant Episcopal Church in the City of New York now occupied by William Brown and in part by the rear of another lot of ground formerly belonging to the New York Manufacturing Society and or company but now of Frederick Depeyster and Easterly on the side of the house and lot of ground formerly of Jacob Van Vleck now owned by Leonard Kip and Westerly on the other side by the house and lot of ground formerly of George Stanton now owned or in possession of Duncan Phyfe.

Liber 130, page 592, 11/3/1818.
. . . from Gurdon S. Mumford merchant New York and Letitia his wife and James Caze of the same place merchant for the sum of $9500.00 . . . dwelling house and lot on a certain street formerly called Derick Dey's Street and now called Dey Street lot number 38.

Liber 141, page 26, 10/14/1819.
. . . from Isaac Lowzada and Catherine his wife, for the sum of $2000. . . . Fifth Ward being part of the land commonly known by the name of the Church Farm and distinguished in a map or chart thereof by lot 580 bound northerly in front by Reed Street, Southerly by rear of lot 597, Westerly by lot 581 and Easterly by lot number 579.

Liber 157, page 23, 12/24/1821.
. . . from Isaac Concklin of the City of New York merchant and Elizabeth his wife, for the sum of $9000. dwelling house and land thereto conveyed by Robert Benson of the City of New York to the said Isaac Concklin, situated in the Third Ward of the City of New York on the South side by Fulton Street late Partition Street at present distinguished in the City of New York by the number 163 formerly 23 Partition Street.

Liber 193, page 162, 6/11/1825.
"For and at the request of Teunis Quick" . . . from Isaac Vanderbeck, gentleman and Duncan Phyfe for the sum of $6500. "Ground, dwelling house and premises now

in the possession of Robert Kelly formerly known as No. 25 Partition Street but by this alternative of the name of said City is at present known as 164 Fulton bounded Northerly in front on Fulton Street, Westerly by the house and lot of ground 165 now belonging to the said Isaac Vander Beck, Easterly by the house and lot of ground known as 163 . . . are the same as hereto conveyed by John Lawrence late of the City of New York Esquire to John Coleman of the same City mariner by deed bearing date 2/20/1801 and by the said John Coleman devised unto his wife Margaret and her heirs and with her late husband Lawrence Powers conveyed to Robert Kelly of the City of New York cabinet maker by deed and afterwards mortgaged by him unto John Van Blarcom Jr. late of the City of New York gentleman for securing the payment of the sum of $6000. and since his death released and conveyed by him the said Robert Kelly and Elizabeth his wife unto Teunis Quick and Andrew C. Zabriskie unto said Isaac Vander Beck."

Liber 241, page 168, 10/7/1828.
. . . from Benjamin Romaine and Mary his wife for the sum of $6000.—near the Kings Farm and known as lot number 15 on Marschalk's map of Partition Street, now known as 198 Fulton Street.

Liber 327, page 121, 3/3/1835.
. . . from Leonard Kip Esquire and Maria his wife for the sum of $22,500. land and buildings at the corner of Fulton and Church Streets, lots 33–34–and 35, known as Church Farm land.

Liber 372, page 244, 2/17/1837.
. . . from John Turnbull and Michael Phyfe (land belonged to William Rhinelander deceased in and by a certain indenture bearing date of 5/1/1826 deed grant demise lease and to farm let unto one miner Butler. . . .) Easterly Washington Street, Southerly Jay Street and Westerly by land belonging to estate of Rhinelander deceased and Northerly by land leased to Turnbull and Phyfe.

Liber 420, page 490, 11/22/1841.
. . . from Rector Church Wardens of Trinity Church . . . for the sum of $10,000. lot number 35 (Church Farm land) on map bound Southerly Fulton Street, Westerly lot number 68, Northerly in rear lot number 40 and 39, and Easterly by lands now or late belonging to Duncan Phyfe.

Liber 549, page 189, 8/8/1850.
. . . from John Phyfe ivory turner and Jane his wife, Church Farm land lot number 414, for the sum of $16,000. known as 71 Murray Street.

Liber 636, page 360, 7/9/1853.

. . . from William Phyfe of Stamford and Ann his wife, number 192 Fulton Street.

Liber 636, page 243, 5/2/1853.

[This is a record of land sold by Duncan Phyfe to Edward D.—198 Fulton Street.]

BROOKLYN

June 4, 1835.	*Grantee*—Phyfe James	(Liber 50, p. 373.)
	William F.	
	Robert	
	Grantor—James E. Underhill	

Property—Lots adjoining Parmentier's Garden belonging to James E. Underhill and those situate in the City of Brooklyn filed in the Office of the Clerk of the County of Kings by James E. Underhill March 30th, 1835 by the numbers in numerical figure 593, 594, 595, 596, 597, 598, 611, 612, 613, 614, 615, and 616 which said lots taken together are bounded as follows—Westerly by Covert Street as laid down on said map, Easterly by Clinton Avenue as laid down on said map, Northerly by lots numbers 599–601–602–603–604–605– and 606 on said map and Southerly by lots number 592– and 610 on said map. *And also* all those 24 certain other lots, pieces or parcels of land situate lying and being in numerical figures 283–284–285–286–287–288–289–290–291–292–293–294–295–296–297–298–299–300–301–302–303–304–305–306 which said last mentioned lots lying together and forming a block of land are Bounded as follows Westerly by the Turnpike Road leading from the City of Brooklyn to Flatbush, Northerly by Denton Street as laid down on said map, Easterly by Vasques Street as laid down on said map and Southerly by Lafayette Place, as laid down on said map TOGETHER with the land lying opposite to and adjoining said lots extending to the center of said Covert, Denton and Vasques Streets and Clinton Avenue and Lafayette Place. . . .

This property was sold by Robert Phyfe (merchant) and his wife Helen T. Phyfe of Philadelphia to Charles Christmas of Brooklyn, on July 8, 1846 (Liber 149, p. 467).

August 13, 1842.	*Grantee*—Duncan Phyfe	(Liber 104, p. 201.)
	Grantor—Sidney B. Whitlock	

This indenture made the 18th day of July, 1842 between Sidney B. Whitlock of the City of Brooklyn, County of Kings and City of New York, merchant, and wife Mary, of the first part, and Duncan Phyfe of the City of New York Cabinet maker of the second part WITNESSETH that the said parties of the first part for and in consideration of the sum of $100. . . .

326

All that certain dwelling house and those four certain lots of ground situate lying and being in the City of Brooklyn aforesaid and described as follows viz Two lots fronting on Sands Street commencing on the Southerly side there of 50 feet Easterly from the corner of Adams Street and running 55 feet Easterly along the Southerly side of Sands Street and in depth parallel to Adams Street 100 feet being in breadth front and rear 55 feet and in length on each side 100 feet and being lots numbers 278–279 55' of the Easterly side of lot number 280 as laid down on the map of the said city, formerly village. Also the two lots on High Street commencing on the Northerly side there of 50' Easterly from the corner of Adams Street and running Easterly along High Street 47' 6" more or less being in breadth front and rear 47' 6" and in length on each side 100 feet and also the alleys running along said lots as laid down on the map of the said city formerly village.

———————

The records of October 14, 1844, show that the last two lots were sold by Duncan Phyfe to Matilda Hilton, wife of William Hilton of the City of Brooklyn (Liber 114, p. 145).

The dwelling house and first said lots were sold by Duncan Phyfe to Sarah Richards February 20, 1845 (Liber 128, p. 177).

February 26, 1844.   *Grantor*—Duncan Phyfe   (Liber 117, p. 24.)
                          Grantee—Mitchell S. Mitchell

Property—4 brick houses and lots and other buildings—Jackson and Nassau Streets, sold to Mitchell S. Mitchell of Southbury, Conn.

———————

The deed reads that this was bought on a foreclosure in a suit by the Court of Chancery, for the foreclosure of mortgage to Edward Phyfe—"bidded in and purchased by Duncan Phyfe, the party hereto of the first part, to enable himself to perform the condition to his aforesaid Bond to the said Mitchell. . . ."

In looking up the record, it shows that Edward D. Phyfe had the mortgage on the property owned by Sidney B. Whitlock.

There are also records of mortgages held by Duncan Phyfe on properties owned by Sidney Whitlock and I. Lowzada (his wife's brother or father?).

William Phyfe & wife
To
Duncan Phyfe

THIS INDENTURE, made the *Eleventh day of July* one thousand eight hundred and *fifty three,* Between WILLIAM PHYFE of Stamford in the State of Connecticut and *Ann* his wife of the *first* part, and DUNCAN PHYFE of the City of New York late Cabinet

Maker, (father of the said William Phyfe.) of the second part, WITNESSETH, That the said parties of the first part, for and in consideration of the sum of *Ten Dollars* lawful money of the United States of America, to them in hand paid by the said party of the second part, at or before the ensealing and delivery of these presents, the receipt whereof is hereby acknowledged, have granted, bargained, sold, aliened, remised, released, conveyed and confirmed, and by these presents do grant, bargain, sell, alien, remise, release, convey and confirm, unto the said party of the second part, and to his heirs and assigns, for ever, ALL That certain Lot, piece or parcel of Land, situate, lying and being in the *Third Ward* of the City of New York on the *Southerly side* of *Fulton Street,* and known and distinguished by the *Street Number (192) One Hundred and ninety two, on Fulton Street* aforesaid, *Bounded Northerly* in front by Fulton Street, *Southerly* in the rear by land now or late of James Fellows, *Easterly* by Lot Number One Hundred and Ninety Fulton Street belonging to James D. Phyfe, and Westerly by Lot Number One Hundred Ninety four Fulton Street, belonging to Eliza Vail *Containing in breadth in front and rear Twenty five feet and in length on East side Seventy seven feet.*

TOGETHER with all and singular the tenements, hereditaments and appurtenances thereunto belonging, or in any wise appertaining, and the reversion and reversions, remainder and remainders, rents, issues and profits thereof. AND also all the estate, right, title, interest, *dower and right of power* property, possession, claim and demand whatsoever, as well in law as in equity, of the said parties of the first part, of, in or to the above described premises, and every part and parcel thereof, with the appurtenances. To HAVE AND TO HOLD all and singular the above mentioned and described premises, together with the appurtenances, unto the said party of the second part, his heirs or assigns, for ever.

IN WITNESS WHEREOF the parties to these presents have hereto set their hands and seals this day and *year first above written*
Sealed and delivered. In presence of
(signed) LIVINGSTON K. MILLER

(signed) WILLIAM PHYFE
ANN PHYFE

[This is the end of the first page of the deed. The following is on the inside page.]

City & County of New York: On the 7th day of July 1853 before me came William Phyfe and Ann his wife. Known to me to be the persons described in, and who executed the within conveyance and acknowledged to me that they executed the same, and the said Ann on a private examination by me apart from her husband acknowledged that she executed the same freely without any fear or compulsion of her husband.

signed by Com. of Deeds James Girdby

DUNCAN PHYFE
To
ELIZA VAIL

Deed 194 Fulton Street

This Indenture, made the *Second* day of *May* one thousand eight hundred and fifty *Three* Between DUNCAN PHYFE, of the City of New York, late Cabinet Maker of the *first part*, and ELIZA VAIL, wife of *William Vail, Junior, of Middlesex County, in the State of New Jersey (daughter of the said party of the first part.)* of the second part, WITNESSETH, That the said party of the first part, for and in consideration *of the natural love and affection which he hath and beareth to his said daughter, and of the* sum of *One Dollar,* lawful money of the United States of America, to him in hand paid by the said party of the second part, at or before the ensealing and delivery of these presents, the receipt whereof is hereby acknowledged, hath granted, bargained, sold, aliened, remised, released, conveyed and confirmed, and by these presents doth grant, bargain, sell, alien, remise, release, convey and confirm, unto the said party of the second part, and to her heirs and assigns, for ever, ALL *That Certain Lot, piece or parcel* of Land, Situate, lying and being on the *Southern side of Fulton Street,* in the Third Ward of the Said City of New York, and known and distinguished, by the Street Number (*194*) *One Hundred and Ninety four, Bounded Northerly* in front by Fulton Street, as foresaid, Southerly in the rear by land now or late of John D. Wolf, *Easterly* by Lot Number (192) One Hundred and Ninety Two conveyed to William Phyfe and *Westerly* by Lot Number One Hundred and Ninety Six, conveyed to Mrs. Mary Whitlock, by the party hereto of the first part, by Deeds bearing even date herewith, *Containing in breadth* in front and rear *Twenty five feet,* and in length on Each Side *Seventy seven feet.*

TOGETHER with all and singular the tenements, hereditaments and appurtenances thereunto belonging, or in any wise appertaining, and the reversion and reversions, remainder and remainders, rents, issues and profits thereof. AND also all the estate, right, title, interest—property, possession, claim and demand whatsoever, as well in law as in equity, of the said party of the first part, of, in or to the above described premises, and every part and parcel thereof, with the appurtenances. TO HAVE AND TO HOLD all and singular the above mentioned and described premises, together with the appurtenances, unto the said party of the second part, her heirs or assigns, for ever.—

IN WITNESS WHEREOF the parties to these presents have hereto set their hands and seal the day and year *first above written.*—
Sealed and delivered, In presence of

D Phyfe

[This finishes the first page of the Deed. On the inside is the following.]
     City & County of New York;
               On this Second day of May 1853 before me personally appeared Dun-
     can Phyfe known to me to be the same person described in and who exe-
     cuted the within conveyance and acknowledged to me that he executed the
     same.
                                                  (signed) Wm. F. Clarke
                                                                Com. of Deeds

Recorded in the Office of the Register of the City & County of New York in Liber 646
of Conveyances page 24 May 6th 1853 at 25 Mins past 10. O'Clk A.M.

                                                  Ex. by G. Dyckman
                                                              Register

Vol. 11, p. 480

Warrantee

Dated—Sept. 30, 1843

Recorded—Oct. 13, 1843

Mitchell S. Mitchell   To   Duncan Phyfe
                                                              Cabinetmaker of the
                                                              City of New York

One certain tract of land situated in said Southbury, Being the homestead & the present Residence of the said Mitchell S. Mitchell & contains one hundred & ten acres of
land more or less, with all the buildings thereon standing, and bounded as follows

     North—On Nathan C. Monson—Nathaniel Beecher & the heirs of Abel Stiles.
     West & South—On Highway
     East—On Highway & said Monson, Beecher & Stiles Heirs.

[Note on back of above.]
Copy of early deeds
affecting Southbury
property of Charlotte B. Woodward.

_____

Original search made by
Clarence Stiles in 1932
for State of Connecticut
of which this is a copy.

Vol. 14, p. 78

N.Y.—Deed

Dated—May 2, 1853

Recorded—June 29, 1853

Duncan Phyfe
of the City of New York
late Cabinetmaker

TO

Mary Whitlock
Widow of Sidney B. Whitlock
of Southbury, etc.
(daughter of the said party
of the first part)

All that certain piece of land situated in Southbury aforesaid, being the former Homestead & Residence of Mitchell S. Mitchell, containing one hundred & ten acres of land, more or less, with all buildings thereon standing & bounded as follows—

North—On land now or late Nathan C. Munson–Nathaniel Beecher & the heirs
of Abel Stiles
West & South—On the highway
East—On the highway & land now or late of said, Minson–Beecher & Stiles heirs.

[Note on back of above.]
Southbury Property.

INVENTORY OF CONTENTS OF DUNCAN PHYFE'S HOUSE AT 193 FULTON STREET MADE AFTER HIS DEATH. DATED SEPTEMBER 8, 1854

(In Hall of Records, New York.)

HOUSEHOLD FURNITURE AT DWELLING HOUSE
Number 193 Fulton Street, New York Viz:

FIRST FLOOR
FRONT OFFICE

1	mahogany closet marble slab	$ 6.00
1	mahogany hat stand	1.00
1	mahogany Book Case	10.00
2	mahogany Chairs	1.50
1	Fancy Rosewood Chair	.75
1	Oilcloth on floor	2.00
1	Umbrella stand	.75
1	window shade	.25
1	checker board	.25
1	Lamp	—
1	Picture	3.00
1	Picture	.20
1	Set Window Blinds	.20
1	Slate	.20

FRONT PARLOR

8	mahogany French Chairs	12.00
	(Over)	$ 38.10

(Amount brought over) $ 38.10

FRONT PARLOR (Continued)

2	Mahogany window seats	3.00
1	Mahogany pier table, marble slab	5.00
1	Mahogany Writing secretary	5.00
1	Mahogany Armchair stuffed	5.00
1	Mahogany Small rocking chair	2.50
1	Mahogany Work table	2.50
1	Pier Glass	20.00
1	Mantle Glass	10.00
3	Candelabra in bronze	2.00
2	bronze lamps glass drops	4.00
1	gilt clock	20.00
2	pictures	2.00
1	carpet on floor	5.00
1	rug on floor	1.00
1	mahogany sideboard and cellaret	20.00
1	East India wood tea caddy	5.00
2	alabaster vases	10.00
1	plated solar lamp	1.50
1	rosewood center table	10.00
1	rosewood center table	7.50
1	mahogany sofa and pillows	15.00
8	mahogany chairs Broad rail	16.00
2	rosewood armchairs	15.00
1	mahogany stand (top)	1.50
1	mahogany work table (marble top)	2.50
1	rosewood work table	3.00
4	tea trays	.75
1	alabaster clock	20.00
2	large gilt lamps (glass drops)	7.50
	(Over)	$258.35

Amount Brought down	$258.35
1 mantle glass	10.00
1 mirror	10.00
1 picture	2.00
1 plated tea urn	2.50
1 Lot books in parlor	15.00
1 carpet on floor	15.00

LOWER HALL

1 oil cloth on floor	5.00
1 stove and pipe	3.00
4 mahogany chairs	3.00
1 Hall table and Book Shelf	2.50
1 Hat Stand	1.00
1 Hall Lantern	2.00
1 Bust and Bracket	.50
1 Refrigerator	2.00
1 mat	.10

DINING-ROOM

1 carpet on floor	2.50
1 mahogany sideboard table & book shelf (marble slab)	5.00
1 mahogany sofa	5.00
6 mahogany chairs	3.00
1 mahogany old armchair	.50
1 mahogany oval table	2.50
1 set mahogany extension tables	10.00
1 lot books	2.50
5 pictures	5.00
1 piece glass	10.00
	$379.95

(Over)

Amount brought down	$379.95
One mantle glass	5.00
One spittoon	.10
2 sets Window Blinds	.25
One Astral Lamp and Marble stand	2.00
One piece oil cloth	.25
2 Plated Branches	2.00

DINING-ROOM CLOSET

1 Folding Fire Screen	.50
2 mahogany trays	.50
1 mahogany knife box	.50
1 Lamp Stand	.10
1 Closet bench	.10
2 mahogany bottle racks	.20
1 Plated Castor	1.00
1 tea tray, candle box and rings	.25
1 Closet step	.10
1 lot baskets	.20
1 lot bottles	.10
1 old lamp, shade and chimney	.10
Plated fish knives and butter knife	2.00

KITCHEN

1 oil cloth on floor	.20
3 kitchen tables	.25
4 chairs	.25
3 benches	.20
1 lot tin ware	.50
3 brass kettles	2.00
	$398.60

(Over)

Amount Brought down	$398.60
1 lot iron ware	.50
2 iron coal scuttles	.50
1 copper coal scuttle	.12
1 square Salt box	0.00
Lot Lamps	.10
1 Glass Lantern	0.00

BACK STOOP

Lot Tubs and Pails	.25
2 Step Ladders	.25
1 Clothes Horse	.50
1 Foot Pail	.10
1 Portable Irong Table	.50
1 Lot Spittoons	.25
1 Oil Cloth	.10

BACK SHED

1 lot old Iron	1.00
1 lot Croton Hose	.50
3 Iron Cramps	.50
2 Iron Vices	.50
1 Grind Stone	1.00
1 piece East India Wood	.50

FIRST FLOOR OF SHOP

4 Unfinished Foot Benches	.50
1 Unfinished Work Box	.10
1 lot Brass	5.00
1 Nail Box	.10
1 Knife Box	0.00
	$411.47

(Over)

Amount brought down	$411.47
1 Grind Stone Complete	2.00
1 Veneer Cutting Board	1.00
1 lot Mahogany Veneers sold to Mr. Buckley	100.00
1 lot Locks and Screws	.50
1 Chest of Tools	25.00
1 Old Maple Writing Desk	.50
1 Pine Press	1.00
1 Small Press	.50
1 lot French Ornaments	2.00
1 lot Castors	2.50
1 lot Locks and Screws	2.50
1 box Glue	.50

UPPER SHOP

1 box Tools	10.00
1 Stove and Pipe	.50
1 Work Bench	2.00
1 lot Culls for Cabinet Makers	.50
4 Benches	.25
1 Wooden Cramp	1.00
1 Iron Cramp	2.00
2 Wooden Vices	.50
1 Iron Vice	1.00
1 lot Writing Blocks and Slate Boards	.50
1 lot Small Sliding Covered Boxes	.25
1 lot Hand Screws large and small	3.00
1 case Screws Assorted	1.00
1 lot Patterns for Cabinet Makers	.10
1 Copper Lamp and Glue Pot	1.00
2 Window Frames and Sashes	.50
	$573.57

SECOND STORY

LARGE FRONT ROOM

1	Carpet on Floor	7.50
1	Mahogany Press	10.00
1	Mahogany Press	5.00
2	Mahogany Foot Benches	.25
1	Mahogany Rocking Chair	3.00
4	Mahogany Chairs (French)	4.00
1	Mahogany Small Rocking Chair	1.00
2	Pier Tables	8.00
2	Pier Glasses	5.00
2	Cologne Bottles	.25
2	Mahogany Boxes	1.50
2	Rosewood Boxes	2.00
2	Mahogany Night Tables	3.00
1	lot Boxes	.00
1	Mahogany Candle Stand	1.00
1	Picture	.15
1	Rush Bottom Rocker	.25
1	Rosewood Portable Desk	2.00

SMALL FRONT ROOM

	Carpet on Floor	2.50
	Drugget on Floor	1.50
1	Field Bedstead and Net	3.00
1	Mahogany Bookstand	2.00
1	Mahogany Dressing Bureau	2.00
1	Mahogany Checker Stand	1.00
1	Gilt Mirror	1.00
6	Pictures	.25
		$648.17

4	Night Stand Chambers	.20
2	glass Basins for Basin Stand	.25
	Lot Sash Cord and 10^{d} Nails	.50
1	Screen, 1 Bellows and 1 Blind	.50
1	lot Oil Betty's, 2 Varnish pots and 1 lamp	.25
1	Tin Pan for Hat Stand	.25
1	Chopping Block	.20

BACK CELLAR

1	Oil Can and Bench	.50
1	set Stone Ware	.25
1	set Earthen Flower Pots	.50
1	set Old Barrels	.10
1	Small Table	.10
1	Bench and 1 Coal Sifter	.25
1	Rat Trap and 1 Parrot Cage	.25
1	Coffee Roaster	.10

STAIRS

1	Stair Carpet and Rods	1.50
	Drugget on do.	.50
1	Window Blind	.25

UPPER HALL

1	Painted Corner Table	.50
	Carpet on Floor	.50
	(Over)	$581.02

Amount brought down $648.17

3 Mahogany Chairs   1.50

SMALL BACK ROOM

1 Mahogany Work Table   1.50
1 Mahogany Bookshelf   .25
1 piece Oil Cloth   .10
1 Mahogany Chair   .50
1 Blind   .10

LARGE BACK ROOM

1 Mahogany Wardrobe   7.50
1 Mantle Glass   3.00
1 Mirror   2.00
5 Small Pictures   .10
2 Blinds   .10
Drugget on Floor   1.00
Garret Stair Carpet and Rods   .25

OPEN GARRET

1 piece Oil Cloth   .10
1 Mahogany High Post Bedstead   2.00
5 Pictures   1.00
1 Cot   .20
1 Mahogany Press   1.00
1 Painted Washstand   .25
1 Old Pier Table Rosewood and Gilt   .50
1 Mahogany Armchair   .25
1 Fancy Rush Seat Armchair   .10

        $671.47

(Over)

Amount brought over $671.47

1 Airtight Stove   1.00
1 Fire Screen   .20
1 Picture   1.00
1 lot Cabinet Makers Books & Drawings   .50
1 lot Chair Coverings
1 piece Red and green Silk de Laine for Chair
    Coverings   1.00

MIDDLE FRONT GARRET ROOM

1 Carpet   .50
2 Mahogany Chairs   1.00
1 gilt armchair   .20
1 Round Table (in 2 pieces)   .50
1 Mahogany Basin Stand enclosed top   .50
1 Maple Table   .50
1 Mahogany Night Stand   1.00

GARRET ROOM (Head of Stairs)

1 Mahogany Bureau   3.00
1 Mahogany Dressing Table   2.00
1 Field Post Bedstead and Tester   1.00
1 Armchair   1.00
1 Painted Basin Stand   .50
1 Mahogany Candle stand   .50

STORE ROOM

1 Mahogany Bedstead   1.00
1 Mahogany Butlers Tray and Stand   .25

        $688.62

Amount brought down — $688.62

1 lot Groceries	3.00
1 Pine Press	.50
1 Small Pine Table	.10
1 Astral Lamp	.10
1 Solar Lamp	.10
1 lot Tongs, Shovels and Stand	3.00
1 Tin Tea Caddy	.25
1 Wooden Box	.20
1 Painted Corner Stand	.10
1 Lemon Squeezer in case	.50
1 Plate Warmer	.20
1 Bench	.10
1 lot Glass Chimneys	.10
1 Tin Cake Box	.20
1 Gin Case and 5 Bottles	.50
1 Round Magnifying Glass	.75
1 lot Small Window Blinds	.10

WOMEN'S BEDROOM

1 Painted Table	.25
1 Dressing Glass	.20
1 Bedstead	.25
3 Chairs	.50
Carpet on Floor	.50

CLOSET IN REAR

3 Chairs }	
2 Pine Tables }	.50
1 Carpet }	

$700.62

(Over)

Amount brought over — $700.62

BATHROOM

1 Looking Glass }	
1 Painted Table }	1.25
1 Chair }	

MISCELLANEOUS

5 Feather Beds with their Bolsters and Pillows	30.00
3 Old Hair Mattresses	15.00
Bed Linen and other Bed Covering	50.00
Table Linen	10.00
1 case Knives and Forks	10.00
1 Silver Pitcher (Garret–Eoff)	100.00
1 Silver Castor and Bottles	65.00
1 Silver Tea Set (3 pieces)	70.00
1 Silver Coffee Pot	35.00
1 Silver Soup Ladle	7.00
3 Silver Butter Knives } 12 Silver Table Spoons } D R P	4.50
24 Silver tea spoons	18.00
12 pieces Cut Glass Ware	18.00
2 China Dinner Sets	25.00
2 China Tea Sets	30.00
1 China Breakfast Set	12.00
1 set Satin Damask Window Curtains (for 3 windows)	2.50
	100.00

$1303.87

Amount Brought Down	$1303.87
1 Gold Watch, Chain and Seal	75.00
1 Gold Pencil Case	6.00
1 Gold Pencil Case	5.00
Articles of Clothing Composing Late Personal Wardrobe of the Testator	30.00
	$1419.87

STOCKS, BONDS, NOTES AND CASH

United States 6 p.c. stock of 1867.
Interest payable January 1st and July.
Interest collected by the testator up to July 1st, 1854.   Viz

Certificate no. 1473 for $1000.00	
1474	1000.00
1475	1000.00
1476	1000.00
1477	1000.00
1478	1000.00
1479	1000.00
1480	1000.00
1481	1000.00
1482	1000.00
	$10,000.00

Present Value Appraised at 116 p.c.	11600.00
(Over)	$13,019.87

Amount brought over	$13,019.87

New York and Erie Rail Road Company 7 p.c.
Mortgage Bonds of 1859.
Interest payable 1st of September and March.
Interest collected by Testator up to March 1st, 1854.   Viz

Bond no. 1240 for $1,000.00	
2934	1,000.00
2975	1,000.00
2977	1,000.00
2978	1,000.00
3267	1,000.00
3503	1,000.00
3639	1,000.00
3849	1,000.00
3850	1,000.00
3851	1,000.00
3852	1,000.00
3853	1,000.00
3976	1,000.00
	$14,000.00

Present Value Appraised at 93 p.c.	$13,020.00

New York and Erie Rail Road Company 7 p.c.
Convertible Bonds of 1871.
Interest payable 1st of February and August.
Interest collected by Testator up to 1st of February 1854.   Viz
Bond 3282   for $1,000.00

Present Value Appraised at 70 p.c.	700.00
	26,739.87

Amount brought down $26,739.87

Bond of William Phyfe to the Testator dated May 2, 1853, conditioned to pay on demand the sum of   65,582.33

Bond of James D. Phyfe to the Testator dated May 2, 1853, conditioned to pay on demand the sum of   43,676.24

Bond of Edward D. Phyfe to the Testator dated May 2, 1853, conditioned to pay on demand the sum of   41,000.00

Bond of Mary Whitlock to the Testator dated May 2, 1853, conditioned to pay on demand the sum of   59,835.43

Bond of William Vail and Eliza his wife to the Testator dated May 2, 1853, conditioned to pay on demand the sum of   48,903.50

Promisory note of James D. Phyfe to the Testator dated New York August 14, 1854, payable on demand for the sum of   4,058.97

Promisory note of Mary Whitlock to the Testator dated August 14, 1854, payable on demand for the sum of   1,275.00

(Over) $290,071.34

Amount Brought over $290,071.34

Promisory note of John L. Brower to the Testator dated New York June 28, 1854, at 6 months with interest for the sum of   5,627.55

Amount unpaid with interest on same from June 28, 1854.   5,627.55

Promisory note of Stephen Burkhalter to the Testator dated New York August 3, 1854, at 3 months for the sum of   562.50

Cash collected by the Executors from Charles Henschel being amount principal and interest in full payment of his bond and mortgage to the Testator upon house and lot #71 Murray Street, New York   8,197.58

Balance deposited to the credit of the Testator in North River Bank, New York, as per his bank book   4,739.70

Cash on hand at the residence of the Testator at the time of his death found in box   473.00

    $309,671.67

New York September 14, 1854

John A. Livingston } appraisers
S. Burkhalter

[Minor changes have been made in reprinting this inventory. Ed.]

BIBLIOGRAPHY

ENGLISH REGENCY

ACKERMAN'S repository of arts. 1809–1828. (Contemporary accounts in monthly issues about the arts, literature, commerce, manufactures, fashions and politics of the day.)

ACKERMAN'S microcosm of London. 1811. 3 vols. (London in miniature. Architectural drawings by Pugin, figures by Rowlandson. Plates in color illustrating the life of the day at theaters, courts, fairs, public institutions, etc. Print and description of Carlton House in vol. I.)

ALISON, ARCHIBALD. Essays on taste. 1815. (A reflection of the times in establishing standards of taste.)

BIRNSTINGL, HARRY JOSEPH. Sir John Soane. (A study of the manner in which his work represents the development of the Classic Revival. Thirty-five fine illustrations of buildings designed by him.)

BISHOP, JOHN GEORGE. The Brighton Pavilion and its royal associations. 1875. (A full account of Brighton from 1783, the Pavilion, the history of the Regent. A guide to the Pavilion and chronological table of events associated with it.)

BRAYLEY, E. W. Illustrations of Her Majesty's Palace at Brighton. 1838. (Published with Nash's drawings of the Pavilion.)

CESCINSKY, HERBERT, and HUNTER, GEORGE LELAND. English and American furniture. (A comparison of Thomas Sheraton and Duncan Phyfe in the last chapter.)

CROLY, REV. GEORGE. Life and times of George IV. (Written in 1839. Anecdotes of distinguished persons of the past fifty years.)

DALE, ANTONY, B.A.B.LITT. James Wyatt, architect, 1746–1813. (Biographical sketch and account of his architectural work. Its relation to that of the Adam brothers.)

DANCE, GEORGE. Farrington diary. 1804. (Account of a visit to Thomas Hope and criticism of the new style of decoration.)

DE MONVEL, ROGER BOUTET. Beau Brummel and his time. (A spirited account of the personality and the adventures of the leader of fashion under the Regency.)

DENON, VIVANT. Antiquities of Egypt. 1804. (Account of the campaigns of General Bonaparte. An extensive study of Egyptian architecture among the descriptions of the battles and marches.)

DYER, WALTER ALDEN. Creators of decorative styles. (A survey of the decorative periods in England from 1600 to 1800.)

ELMES, JAMES, M.R.I.A. Metropolitan improvements, or London in the nineteenth century. 1827. (A fine series of engravings from drawings by Thomas H. Shepherd, showing the new bridges, streets, parks, gentlemen's mansions, etc., in London and its environs, in classic style.)

FITZGERALD, PERCY H. The life of George IV. 1881. 2 vols. (A detailed account of his letters and opinions. Review of the men, manners, and politics of his reign.)

GOLDSMITH, OLIVER. Life of Richard Nash. 1762. (A history of Beau Nash at Bath, the prototype of Beau Brummel.)

HOPE, THOMAS. Essay on architecture. London, 1835. 2 vols. (Study of classic and Egyptian architecture. The pointed style. Return to the classic and its adoption throughout Europe. Illustrated with drawings made in Germany and Italy.)

—— Household furniture and decoration, executed from designs by Thomas Hope. London, 1807. (A book of line drawings illustrating furniture and arrangement of the rooms destined to hold his vase collection. No text.)

JEWEL. Tourist's companion. 1819.

JOURDAIN, MARGARET. Regency furniture, 1795–1820. (Excellent collection of photographs of English Regency pieces; little text.)

LAING, DAVID, F.S.A. Plans, elevations and sections of buildings, public and private, executed in various parts of England, etc., including the New Customs House, London, with plans, details and descriptions engraved on fifty-nine plates by David Laing, F.S.A., architect and surveyor to the Board of Customs, etc. London, 1828. (Illustrating in the character of the buildings the result of the Classic Revival.)

MELVILLE, LEWIS. Bath under Beau Nash.

MOSES, HENRY. Modern costume, drawn and engraved by Henry Moses. 1823. 30 plates. (Examples of the effect of the Classic Revival on dress and decoration.)

NASH, JOHN. The Royal Pavilion at Brighton. 1824, 1825. (Including the alterations made by Nash while architect to the Regent. Exterior and interior views. Colored plates, plans, and drawings.)

NICHOLSON, ALEXANDER, LL.D. Memoirs of Adam Black. (Diary: an account of Adam Black's employment by Sheraton and personal reminiscences about the designer in London.)

POCOCK. Modern furnishings for rooms. 1813.

PYNE, W. H. The history of the royal residences of Windsor Castle, St. James Palace, Carlton House, Kensington Palace, Hampton Court, Buckingham House and Frogmore. 1819. (Many colored engravings of exteriors and interiors.)

RICHARDSON, G. The new Vitruvius Britannicus, 1802–1808. 72 plates. (Plans and elevations of contemporary buildings erected in Great Britain by celebrated architects illustrating the taste of the English nation at the close of the eighteenth century.)

ROBERTS, HENRY D., M.B.E. A history of the Royal Pavilion. (A new book. Charming prints of old Brighton. Account of the original furnishings and decoration of the Pavilion, and where they are to be found today.)

—— The Royal Pavilion, Brighton. (Official guidebook.)

—— The story of the Brighton Pavilion.

SCOTT, GEOFFREY. Architecture of humanism.

SHERATON, THOMAS. The cabinet-maker and upholsterer's drawing book in four parts. 1802. (Part I is largely concerned with geometry and its application, and the origin of the orders. Part II with perspective. Part III with furniture designs.)

342

—— The cabinet dictionary. 1802–1803. 88 copper plates. (Explanation of all terms used in the cabinet, chair, and upholstery branches, with directions for polishing and gilding.)

—— The cabinet-maker's and general artist's Encyclopedia. 1804–1807. (A series of plates of furniture, mostly in color.)

—— Designs for household furniture. 1812. 84 plates.

SITWELL, OSBERT, and BARTON, MARGARET. Brighton. (A delightful history of the place and its people from its beginnings, with special emphasis on the nineteenth century and the Regent's occupation of the Pavilion.)

SMITH, GEORGE. The cabinet-maker & upholsterer's guide. 1826. (A treatise on geometry and perspective and a series of colored designs for rooms and furniture with plans, profiles, and enlarged moldings, to assist the workman.)

—— A collection of designs for household furniture and interior decoration. 1804–1806. (A collection of 158 designs with descriptions by the "upholder extraordinary to H.R.H. the Prince of Wales.")

SMITH, H. CLIFFORD. Buckingham Palace, its furniture, decoration and history. (The treasures of Buckingham, Carlton House, and the Brighton Pavilion. Illustrations and detailed descriptions of furniture now in Buckingham.)

SMITH, JOHN THOMAS. Nollekens and his times, 1737–1822. (Life of the celebrated English sculptor and anecdotes of contemporary artists and others.)

STOREY, WALTER RENDELL. Period influences in interior decoration. (Chapter on "The Regency Fashion; the Last of the Great English Styles" is a good general survey of the period.)

SUMMERSON, JOHN. John Nash, architect to George IV. (A careful study of the life and work of this eminent architect with much valuable information about the buildings and other works undertaken by him during the Regency.)

THACKERAY, WILLIAM MAKEPEACE. The four Georges. (Strongly anti-George IV.)

AMERICAN

ADAMS, JAMES TRUSLOW. The epic of America. (A scholar's study of this country and its destiny. The background of 1800–1830 found in chapters IV, V, and VI. The Nation Finds Itself, America Secedes from the Old World, The Sun Rises in the West.)

AMERICAN STATE PAPERS. Vols. I and II, Commerce and navigation. Class IV, U.S. exports of household furniture, 1790–1822. (Alexander Hamilton's reports to the Treasury about the manufacture and exportation of furniture from 1790 to 1822.)

ASTOR, JOHN JACOB. The fortune of John Jacob Astor. *Journal of Political Economy,* vol. XVI. (How this eminent New Yorker amassed his great wealth through organizing the fur industry and making important investments in city property.)

AUDUBON, JOHN JAMES. Delineations of American scenery and character, 1808–1834.

(Sidelights on pioneer life in America, particularly in the Ohio and Mississippi Valleys. His ornithology. His home in Audubon Park, along the Hudson River. New York, Boston, Charleston, and Florida.)

BARRETT, WALTER. The old merchants of New York. (Gossipy accounts of many businessmen, including James and John Phyfe, Duncan's brother and nephew.)

BENJAMIN, ASHER. A reprint of five books in one volume: The country builder's assistant (1805); The new system of architecture (1806); The rudiments of architecture (1814); The practical house carpenter (1832); Practice of architecture (1833). (Plates and text selected and edited by Aymar Embury II.)

BERKLEY, DR. Register of Baltimore cabinet-makers, 1777–1820.

BIDDLE, NICHOLAS. *The Portfolio*. 1801–1825. (A weekly review of literature, drama, politics, and travel. Articles of general interest on poetry and the fine arts.)

BISHOP, J. LEANDER. A history of American manufactures. 1608–1860. 2 vols. (A year-by-year report of the development of different industries in various parts of the United States. Technical, not literary.)

BULFINCH, ELLEN S. The life and letters of Charles Bulfinch. (Edited by his granddaughter.)

CORNELIUS, CHARLES OVER. Furniture masterpieces of Duncan Phyfe. (Fifty illustrations of Phyfe's finest furniture and an essay on his methods and designs. Out of print.)

COUSINS, FRANK, and RILEY, PHIL M. The wood-carver of Salem. (A history of the life of Samuel and the other McIntires, with examples of their fine carving in private houses and public buildings, illustrating the refined taste of America in the early nineteenth century and McIntire's ability as an architect.)

DE CRÈVECOEUR, ST. JOHN. American letters. 1787. (Letters on American conditions and events in the late eighteenth century, written with insight and sympathy.)

DUNLAP, WILLIAM. A history of the rise and progress of the arts of design in the United States. (A chain of discursive biographical notices beginning with John Watson, including Benjamin West, Copley, Charles W. Peale, Gilbert Stuart, Fulton, l'Enfant, Trumbull, etc.)

DYER, WALTER. Early American craftsmen. (Among a series of sketches of the lives of important personalities in the early development of the industrial arts in America is a chapter on Duncan Phyfe, carefully done, well illustrated, with a good evaluation of Phyfe's work.)

HALSEY, R. T. HAINES, and TOWER, ELIZABETH. The homes of our ancestors. (A discussion of the rooms in the American Wing of the Metropolitan Museum, the development of the arts of interior architecture and house decoration, and the work of early American craftsmen, including Duncan Phyfe.)

HAMILTON, THOMAS. Men and manners in America. (A travel diary of 1833 with interesting glimpses of New York, Providence, Boston, Philadelphia, Baltimore, and Washington. The manners and customs of the different cities are depicted.)

Kimball, Fiske. Domestic architecture of the American colonies and of the early republic. (A group of lectures given in 1920 at the Metropolitan Museum of Art about the Classic Revival in America.)

Lannuier, Charles Honoré. Last will and testament in French with attested English translation signed by John Gruez and two other witnesses. (In New York Hall of Records.)

Lefever, Minard. Modern builder's guide. (On the order of Asher Benjamin's, but less complete.)

Longworth's American almanack, New York register and city directory. (The 1794 edition shows Phyfe's new spelling of his name. Succeeding years indicate growth and importance of the family.)

Mabie, Hamilton W. Writers of Knickerbocker New York. 1912. (A picture of New York in the early 1800's. Washington Irving, *Salamagundi,* Diedrich Knickerbocker's satire called "The History of New York." Paulding, Halleck, and Drake. James Fenimore Cooper, William Cullen Bryant, Edgar Allan Poe.)

Marryat, Capt. Frederick. A diary in America, with remarks on its institutions. 1839. (Critical account of observations during his travels on language, customs, etc., of Americans; not often complimentary.)

Miller, Edgar G., Jr. American antique furniture. (Illustrating periods and styles from 1600 to 1840. Copiously illustrated and annotated; full of valuable reference information.)

New York book for prices for manufacturing cabinet & chair work. Harper's, 1834.

New York revised prices for manufacturing cabinet & chair work. June, 1810.

Ormsbee, Thomas H. Early American furniture makers. (A chapter on Duncan Phyfe, the Great, and one on Phyfe's contemporaries among its contents.)

—— The story of American furniture. (Nine chapters on different sorts of furniture and cabinetmakers who produced them. References to Phyfe under each furniture classification.)

Place, Charles A. Charles Bulfinch, architect and citizen. His life, his work and his architectural designs, 1812–1817. (A scholarly and able work.)

Revised constitution and rules of order of the Society of Cabinet-Makers of the City of New York, adopted August, 1810. (Detailed accounts of prices to be charged for every kind of cabinetwork. In the library of the Museum of the City of New York.)

Scott, Geoffrey. The architecture of humanism. (An essay on taste, formulating the chief principles of classic design in architecture.)

Smith, F. Hopkinson. Fortunes of Oliver Horn. (A fictionized life of Samuel F. B. Morse.)

Smith, Matthew Hale. Sunshine and shadow in New York. 1869. (Chapters on Wall Street and John Jacob Astor.)

Stokes, I. N. Phelps. The iconography of New York City. (A great chronological compendium of useful information about the city.)

345

STONE, WILLIAM L. Narrative of the festivities in honor of the completion of the grand Erie Canal. 1825. (Account by an eyewitness.)

SVININ, PAUL. Picturesque United States of America. 1811–12–13. (Fifty-two reproductions of water colors from his own sketchbook. Views of New York, Albany, Philadelphia, Niagara, Washington's tomb at Mount Vernon, Natural Bridge, Virginia.)

TROLLOPE, MRS. FRANCES. Domestic manners of the Americans. 1831. (A not-too-kind criticism resulting from a trip through the States by the mother of Anthony Trollope.)

WATSON, JOHN F. Annals of New York. (Refer to interesting account of Fulton and the *Clermont*.)

MAGAZINE ARTICLES

CORNELIUS, CHARLES OVER. Article on Duncan Phyfe. *Antiques,* Nov., 1933.

HORNOR, W. M., JR. A new estimation of Duncan Phyfe. *Antiquarian,* March, 1930.

KIMBALL, FISKE. Furniture carvings by Samuel McIntire. *Antiques,* Sept., 1930.

—— William Hook. *Antiques,* April, 1934.

MARSHALL, JAMES C. Article on Duncan Phyfe. *Country Life,* 1915.

INDEX

INDEX

Numbers indicate pages unless otherwise stated.

351

352

plate 3; bronze chandelier, plate 4; furniture in Knoblock library, plate 40; center table and consoles, plate 55; Hope sale, xi

Hope, Thomas: portrait by Sir William Beechey, R.A., plate 2; *Household Furniture and Interior Decoration,* xv; protagonist of Regency, xviii; his family, xviii; grand tour, xix; settled in England 1796, xix; his two houses—Deepdene and London, xix, 16; collection of vases, xx; style, xxiii; bronzes, xxiii, xxiv; superb wood, xxiv; inlay of ebony, ivory, and silver, xxiv; bronzists, xxiv; ignores Gothic, xxviii; Regency, 3; criticism of furniture, 34; Phyfe reproduces, 172

Horseshoe seats, 169

House of History, xii, 85, 137, 143, 161, 176, 182, 183; flying staircase, plate 75; Phyfe dining-room, plate 96; Phyfe wardrobe, plate 141; Phyfe dressing table, plate 153; Phyfe cabinet desk, plate 167; New York console table, plate 194

Hove Museum (Sussex), Regency drawing-room, plate 60

Howell, Mrs. J. Bertram, xi, 122, 129; Duncan's spectacles and snuffbox, plate 105; Duncan's table silver, 129; Duncan's snuffbox, title page and 136

Howell, Miss Josephine: Hope chandelier, plate 4; Regency sideboard and torchères, plate 54

Howells, John Mead, Thomas House, plate 81

Hudson terminals replace Phyfe workshops, 135

Hunnewell, Mr. and Mrs. Hollis, 185, 295, 296, 298, 299; Phyfe furniture made for Miss Louisa Throop, plates 284–288

Hunting board, carved by McIntire, plate 203

Hurja, Emil, 129, 282, 283; Phyfe bill and order to pay, George P. MacCulloch, plates 268, 269

Index of American Design, 215; Zabriskie chair, plate 295

Indian Queen, New York tea house of 1794, 208

Inlay on furniture: ebony, ivory, silver, xxiv; brass or ebony, 30, 31, 166, 174, 215

Interior Design, magazine, 88

Irwin, Alice, portrait of William Akin, 248

Irwin, Anna Teller, Akin couch, 249

Izard, Mrs. Ralph, née Alice Delancey, 278

James, Edward F. W., Esq., Regency sideboard, plate 51

Jay, William: architect of Thomas House, plate 81; work in Savannah, Ga., 86

Jefferson, Thomas, leader in American styles, designer of Richmond Capitol, use of Temple form, Capitol at Washington, Monticello, University of Virginia, 79; monumental designs, 80

Jenkins, Mrs. Joseph E., Mrs. Izard's furniture, 278

Jersey, Lady, 8

Johnson, Benjamin Leonard, wedding gift, Allison table, plate 187

Johnson, Doctor, 6

Johnson, Edmund, Salem break-front secretary bookcase, plate 210

Johnson, Mr. and Mrs. Wayne, Phyfe writing table and sewing stand, plate 143

Johnson, Mrs. (Bowden Hall), armchair by Richard Smirke, plate 63

Katzenbach, Mrs. L. Emery, Foot furniture, 273

Keyes, Homer, xii, 154

Kimball, Fiske, xii

Kindig, Joe, Jr., bed attributed to Lannuier, plate 175

Kipper, Miss Katrina, 216, 217, 219; mahogany McIntire sofa, plate 202; hunting board, plate 203; McIntire secretary, plate 205

Knoblock, Edward, xi, 253; Foreword by, xv–xxix; Hope bookcase, plate 3; cabinet by George Smith, plate 5; Regency dining-room, plate 55; Regency library, plate 40; armchair by George Smith, plate 65

Labels, Phyfe, 159, 160; on Eliza's console, plate 112; on sewing table 1815, plate 117; on tambour sewing table 1800, plate 122; on Bowie secretary desk 1820, plate 234

358

DUNCAN PHYFE AND THE ENGLISH REGENCY, in an edition of 1350 copies, has been set up in fourteen point Baskerville type and printed by E. L. Hildreth & Co. on paper supplied by Herman Scott Chalfant, Inc. The binding has been executed by John M. Gettler. The halftones and line plates were made by the Chromatic Photo-engraving Co. The publishers wish to extend their sincere thanks to all the individuals and firms associated in the production of this book for their active interest and generous spirit of cooperation.

Nancy C. Mc Clelland